UNLIKELY SOLDIERS

Frank Pickersgill

Ken Macalister

UNLIKELY SOLDIERS

HOW TWO CANADIANS
FOUGHT THE SECRET WAR
AGAINST NAZI OCCUPATION

JONATHAN F. VANCE

HARPERCOLLINS PUBLISHERS
A PHYLLIS BRUCE BOOK

Unlikely Soldiers
© 2008 by Jonathan F. Vance. All rights reserved.

A Phyllis Bruce Book, published by
HarperCollins Publishers Ltd

First Edition

HarperCollins books may be purchased for
educational, business, or sales promotional use
through our Special Markets Department.

Page iv: Photograph of Frank Pickersgill courtesy
of the Pickersgill family. Photograph of Ken
Macalister courtesy of Guelph Museums.

HarperCollins Publishers Ltd
2 Bloor Street East, 20th Floor
Toronto, Ontario, Canada
M4W 1A8

www.harpercollins.ca

Library and Archives Canada Cataloguing
in Publication

Vance, Jonathan F. (Jonathan Franklin William),
1963–
Unlikely soldiers : how two Canadians fought
the secret war against Nazi occupation /
Jonathan Vance.

"A Phyllis Bruce book".
ISBN 978-0-00-200735-1

1. Pickersgill, Frank, 1915–1944. 2. Macalister,
Ken, 1914–1944. 3. World War, 1939–1945—Secret
service—Great Britain. 4. Spies—Canada—
Biography. I. Title.

D810.S7V25 2008   940.54'86710922
C2008-901852-4

RRD 9 8 7 6 5 4 3 2 1

Printed and bound in the United States
Text design by Sharon Kish

CONTENTS

MAJOR SOE CIRCUITS (F SECTION) IN FRANCE, 1942–44

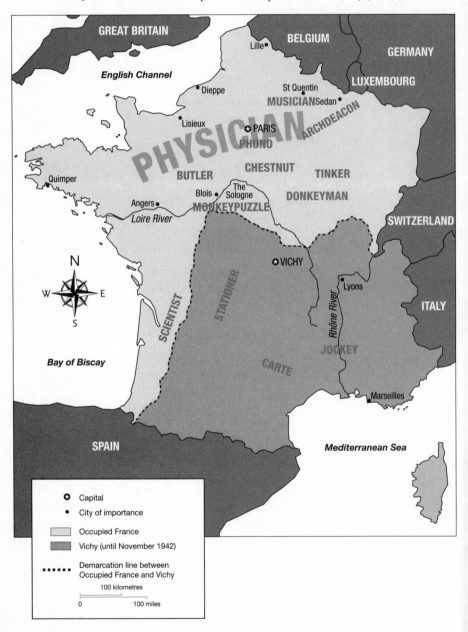

APRIL 1945

M ajor-General Georges Vanier peered out of the window of the airplane as it circled the city of Weimar, the capital of the short-lived German republic that had crumbled under the weight of post-1918 expectations. The previous afternoon, a staff car had collected him at the Canadian Embassy in Paris, and since then he had been on the move: a quick drive to Le Bourget airport for the flight to Croydon, in the south of England, overnight in London in a splendid hotel arranged by Canadian military authorities, and up early for the ride to a U.S. air base to catch another plane. Still, it had been a pleasant flight. The lunch was nothing to speak of—how much could one expect under the circumstances?—but the wine had certainly been drinkable. It would have been easy for Vanier to forget that the war was not yet over and that his mission, to investigate rumours of Canadians who had vanished into Nazi concentration camps, was hardly a pleasure trip.

Despite the noise in the cabin that made conversation difficult, his travelling companions were very congenial. They were all American senators and congressmen, four Democrats and four Republicans, most of them lawyers and a couple of them young enough to be his children. Henry Martin Jackson, known to friend and foe as Scoop, was a state prosecutor from Washington and had been in Congress for only five years; Missourian Marion Tinsley had been in Congress for only two. There were two lawyers from Alabama, Albert Rains and Carter Manasco, and Earl Wilson, a farmer's son and high-school principal from Lawrence County, Indiana, who seemed a bit out of place among all the attorneys. But Vanier got the most pleasure out of chatting with the three ex-soldiers in the group. Texan Eugene Worley had requested a leave of absence from Congress to enlist in the U.S. Navy, and Pennsylvanian Francis Walter had served in the U.S. Naval Air Service during the First World War. New Jersey lawyer Gordon Canfield was also a Great War veteran, an ex-signaller who had taken a break from his congressional duties to serve in another war, working the North Atlantic convoy route as an ordinary seaman in the merchant marine.

Although he shared a military background with Worley, Walter, and Canfield, Vanier was very much the elder statesman of the group. Tall and patrician, he had white hair and a moustache that made him look older than his fifty-seven years and lent him a distinct air of nobility. Descended from a family that had emigrated to New France in the eighteenth century, he was the product of a mixed marriage: his father was old-stock French Canadian, his mother the daughter of an Irish immigrant. Vanier had trained to be a lawyer, but the Great War intervened and instead he found himself steadily rising through the officers' ranks of the 22nd Battalion, Canadian Expeditionary Force, the legendary Van Doos. He won a Military Cross for gallantry in 1916, but in August 1918, while in command of the unit, he was wounded first by a bullet and then by a shell that exploded beside him and killed the stretcher-bearer who was dressing his wounds. His right leg shredded by shrapnel, Vanier was told that the limb couldn't be saved; when he returned to Canada after the war, it was with a prosthetic leg and a Distinguished Service Order, one of the British Empire's highest awards for gallantry.

After the war, Vanier gradually moved from military to diplomatic service. He became the military representative in Canada's delegation to the League of Nations in Geneva, and then secretary to the Canadian High Commission in London in 1931. Eight years later came his first diplomatic command: head of the Canadian Legation in Paris. That was on the eve of another war, and the Nazi occupation of France exiled Vanier from the

French capital until September 1944, just a few weeks after the Germans had surrendered the city. He was back at his desk as soon as the occupying forces gave him permission, and when the Paris legation was upgraded to an embassy two months later, Vanier became an ambassador. It was in that capacity that he found himself on the plane bound for Weimar on the twenty-second of April 1945. The war wasn't even over yet.

The aircraft touched down on a runway that was being hastily repaired by U.S. engineers (in a few days, the headquarters of the 9th Tactical Air Command would move in), and the small party of dignitaries piled into waiting limousines. While the cars sat idling beside what remained of a maintenance shed, a toothless old fellow wearing a suit that had once been quite posh shambled up and gave each of the visitors a pamphlet entitled *Führer Durch Weimar* (*Weimar Guidebook*). The last employee of the Weimar tourist office, Vanier thought wryly to himself.

As the cars drove through the city, heavily damaged in an Allied air raid in February 1945, Vanier glanced over the pamphlet. Ignoring the references to the Reich bureaus and Nazi Party offices in the city, he read about the cultural sites of Weimar: the home and museum of the great German poet Johann von Goethe, the house where the poet Friedrich Schiller had lived out his final years—both buildings had been badly damaged by Allied bombs—and the house where philosopher Friedrich Nietzsche died. The pianist and composer Franz Liszt had lived in Weimar intermittently. Johann Sebastian Bach played the organ there, Carl Maria von Weber composed music there, and architect Walter Gropius founded the Bauhaus there. In the Herderkirche was an altar painting by the great artist Lucas Cranach, on the Theaterplatz, an impressive statue of Goethe and Schiller. There was a monument to Liszt in the park; there was even one to William Shakespeare. "Where else can you find so many good things in one spot?" Goethe had written of Weimar.

Where else indeed, thought Vanier as the cars drove north from the city, along a beautiful road shaded by spreading pine and chestnut trees. If he had been a simple tourist he might have agreed with Goethe, but this was no tourist junket. As the cars climbed up the Ettersberg, the trees thinned to reveal a monstrous scar on the side of the mountain, an abominable contrast to the cultural gifts that Weimar had given to the world: the Buchenwald concentration camp.

In the summer of 1937, the Schutzstaffel, the ideological army of the Nazis known as the SS, had come to the Ettersberg with a group of political prisoners and others who were deemed "undesirable," and started to clear the trees to make room for an internment camp. The crew built a few modest huts, some administrative buildings, and a barbed-wire fence (later electrified) to surround everything. With a perverse sense of logic, the SS decided to save the Goethe Oak, a majestic tree that locals revered as the poet's favourite place to write. It was left standing, to remind camp inmates of the glories of German culture, in a place of honour in front of the camp laundry.

Eight years after the Nazis' slaves had built the camp, Buchenwald was a very different place, a huge complex of prisoners' barracks, factories, execution chambers, and crematoria. It was liberated by U.S. forces on 11 April 1945, and two days later Dwight D. Eisenhower, the supreme commander of the Allied forces in Europe, and American generals Omar Bradley and George Patton visited the site. Eisenhower immediately decided that there was considerable propaganda value in bringing small parties of visitors to Buchenwald, "where the evidence of bestiality and cruelty is so overpowering as to leave no doubt in their minds about the normal practices of the Germans in these camps."[1] Over the next few weeks, a succession of delegations made their way to Buchenwald: British parliamentarians, U.S. politicians, newspaper editors and publishers, labour leaders, churchmen, thirteen members of the United Nations War Crimes Commission, a special French mission. They kept coming until the ninth of May, when Bradley decided that enough was enough and put a stop to the visits.

But that was nearly three weeks after the eight congressmen and senators, personally invited by Eisenhower and with Georges Vanier tagging along, had come to the camp on that sunny Sunday in April. As they reached the main gate, which was graced by the inscription *Recht oder unrecht—mein*

Vaterland (My country, right or wrong), any pleasure from the drive and the glorious weather quickly drained away. For Buchenwald, although not on the scale of Auschwitz or Bergen-Belsen, was a death factory.

An indescribable aura of evil hung in the air as Vanier and the politicians were shown around by a conducting officer who was obviously not yet used to the task. The major-general had seen more than his fair share of gruesome sights in the trenches of the Western Front, but the studied and technical brutality of the camp appalled him. The cheaply built wooden barracks were lined with bunks, but they were little more than shelves on which the inmates awaited death by disease, starvation, or execution. The Nazis had built electric lifts to raise bodies from the killing chambers to the furnaces to be cremated; blackened human remains still lay in the ovens, and the fact that the crematoria couldn't keep up with the executioners was confirmed by the stacks of rotting corpses piled outside, a few handfuls of lime tossed on to keep down the stench. There was a noise-making machine to drown out the screams of the dying, a twisted concession to the feelings of the doomed (or perhaps so the shrieks didn't disturb the camp staff), and on the wall of the building a small plaque showing flames rising from a vase. The conducting officer translated the inscription: "Let not disgusting worms consume my body . . . Give me clean bright flame."

Vanier saw nothing around him that was clean or bright. There was a lampshade made from tattooed human skin and, in the camp hospital, row upon row of patients who appeared to be little more than masses of bones held together by thin layers of skin. Roaming the camp were hundreds of children, most of them Polish Jews who had been working as slave labourers in munitions factories and had long ago lost track of their families. They were among the 21,000 inmates found in Buchenwald, survivors of the Nazis' orgy of killing as they desperately tried to destroy the evidence of their crimes before the Allies arrived. Of the Goethe Oak there remained only the stump; burned in an Allied air raid, it had been cut down, although not before the poet's beloved tree had been pressed into service as a gallows.

When U.S. forces liberated the camp, prisoners were dying at a rate of a hundred a day. Decent rations and excellent medical care had brought that down to about thirty, but Vanier found little consolation in that. "One is forced to the conviction," the ambassador wrote after he had reflected on what he saw that day, "that those who did these horrible things saw nothing wrong in them; perhaps they were actually proud of their efficiency in producing death. These Germans are not as other humans, they are satanic. Though they have a veneer of Christianity, deep down they must still be barbarians—in saying this one is unfair to the barbarian because there is a scientific refinement about these horrors which barbarians, uncouth and wild, living in a primitive state, could not invent."[2]

But Vanier wasn't just on a public relations trip like his colleagues. In the fall of 1944, after receiving reports that a number of Canadians had been executed at Buchenwald, he began to investigate the rumours. When he caught wind of the American tour, the ambassador quickly made arrangements to join the group, to see what secrets the camp held. With a gaunt but dignified-looking German Communist (an inmate of Buchenwald since 1938) as his guide, Vanier left his travelling companions and went in search of the camp record office. There, thanks to the Nazis' passion for precise accounting, large ledgers recorded the disposition of various prisoners. After leafing through a few of the books, Vanier found a page from August 1944 that listed the recent arrival of thirty-seven prisoners. He ran his finger down the list, and it was only a moment before he found what he had hoped not to. Pulling a small notebook and a pencil from his pocket, he recorded what he had discovered:

9636 John Macalister 9–7-14 Guelph Avocat
8738 Guy Sabourin Montreal 1–1-23 Officer
9992 Pickersgill Frank 28–5-15 Winnipeg

Beside each of the names was a small black *x*.

There could be no more doubt that the reports were true—Ken (who was listed as John, as the British Army called him), Frank, and Guy had been executed. The ambassador knew little about Sabourin, but he certainly remembered the other two from the days before France fell to Nazi occupation. And now he would have to confirm their deaths to the Canadian government. Vanier, his mind far away, slowly put the notebook and pencil back in his pocket, looked down at the ledger book for a few moments, and walked from the building.

PART ONE

COMING OF AGE

ONE

TWO BOYS

Seventh Siding. Not exactly an inspiring name, thought Frank Pickersgill as he sat on the railway carriage clattering northwest from Winnipeg in 1910. Beside him, Bert Hyde scanned the scrub and bush that stretched out from the railway line as far as the eye could see. Frank and Bert had met in Cartwright, Manitoba, a few months earlier; both were transplanted Ontarians who had decided to head north and make their fortune. But when the train pulled into 7th Siding, 110 miles from Winnipeg, it didn't look like a place where fortunes could be made. Then again, Frank Pickersgill wasn't from the kind of stock to take the easy road.

In 1841, three generations of Pickersgills had left their native Yorkshire to homestead at Bookton, in Norfolk County, Canada West. Young Thomas, Frank's father, eventually moved to nearby Wyecombe, where he prospered both as a farmer and as a general merchant. With three hale and hearty sons (Frank was the youngest, born in 1879) and a substantial brick farmhouse, Thomas Pickersgill had much to be content with. But he was possessed by a restless spirit; having conquered Wyecombe, he craved a new challenge. Like thousands of other Ontarians in the late nineteenth century, Thomas was drawn by the lure of the West, then being aggressively promoted to potential settlers as a land of opportunity. In 1903, the family sold their store and headed west, to start all over again in Cartwright.

But Frank didn't go with them. Instead, he stayed behind on the farm, his father having decided early on that Frank's talents were better suited to raising crops than to gaining an education like his brothers. Besides, he had another reason for staying in Ontario. For some years, Wyecombe had been visited by a girl named Sara Smith, whose aunt had married a cousin of Thomas Pickersgill. This distant relationship by marriage was apparently all they had in common. Sara was reputed to be the best student ever to attend the high school in her hometown of Port Rowan, fourteen miles from Wyecombe, and after graduation she left for Simcoe to train as a teacher. But four years' teaching was merely a stepping stone that earned Sara enough money to enrol in the nursing school at the Toronto General Hospital. When she graduated in 1903, she took the highest standing once again. It was while Sara was at Toronto General that she renewed her acquaintance with Frank, who had bicycled to the city with a friend for a holiday. By all accounts, they were instantly smitten. A promised (and prestigious) job as superintendent of the hospital at Dawson City, Yukon, was declined, and instead Sara and Frank married in November 1903. They took up residence in the now-vacant farmhouse at Wyecombe; eighteen months later their first son, Jack, was born.

The young family wasn't destined to remain in Ontario, however. Frank was driven by the same restlessness that had sent his parents and brothers west, and Sara was wise enough to know that he wouldn't be content to work the family farm that someone else had built up. In 1907 they sold the old Pickersgill homestead and set out for Cartwright to join the rest of the family. The four years they lived there were both joyous and disappointing. Their second son, Tom, was born soon after they arrived, and the twins, Elizabeth and Walter, followed in 1909. But Frank's business ventures, a lumberyard and a stint as manager of a grain elevator, barely brought in enough money to keep the growing family afloat, and before long he was casting his eye around for other opportunities. Then he met Bert Hyde, and the two found that they shared a common ambition.

And so it was that the pair stepped off the construction train at 7th Siding in 1910. The train would continue north, slowly pushing the line toward Gypsumville, but Frank and Bert had decided to go no farther. The townsites were becoming sparser and less developed, and 7th Siding seemed as good a place as any to try their luck. Also known as Dodd's Siding (the townsite sat on the section belonging to George Dodd, a veteran of the South African War, his wife, and his brother Bert), there was nothing there beyond a few farmhouses, a bunk car serving as the railway station, and a couple of businesses, including a shed on stilts that operated under the name Hardisty's General Store. The Canadian Northern Railway had laid out five streets, mustering all of its corporate imagination to call them Railway Avenue, First Avenue, Main Street, First Street North, and First Street South. When it came time to give the town a proper name, the railway chose Ashern, in honour of A.S. Hern, a surveyor who had worked in the district.

The more they poked around, the more Frank and Bert could sense opportunity; they decided to take up adjoining quarter sections, buy the ramshackle shed from Bill Hardisty, and open a proper store. Bert got started first and put up a small log hut on his land; the Pickersgills followed in 1911, living in the Hyde cabin while Frank built a two-storey frame house for his family. It wasn't much—two rooms upstairs, two down; tarpaper and siding on the outside; bare studs on the inside; no electricity, telephone, running water, or indoor plumbing; nearby a granary and a log barn with a hayloft and a concrete shelter for chickens and pigs—but it would serve the family well. In town, Frank and Bert rebuilt Hardisty's shop at the corner of Main Street and Railway Avenue as an imposing, two-storey structure. Hyde and Pickersgill's General Store and the Ashern Post Office occupied the ground floor, and the upper rooms (except for one that served as the local court) were rented to Joe Safioles, a newcomer from Greece who ran a boarding house.

But Ashern was on the verge of a boom, or at least what passed for a boom in a village whose population wouldn't climb above a couple of hundred for another fifteen years. The rail connection with Gypsumville opened in July 1911, and Ashern soon grew into the biggest settlement between there and Winnipeg. New businesses sprang up—the Ashern

Trading Company, J.J. Wilson's Fish Shed and Store, Charlie Price's boarding house, Fluke and Whittaker's livery stable, William Kidd's blacksmith, and the Dominion Creamery. Joe Safioles moved out of Frank and Bert's store and opened the St. George Hotel; one of his tenants was Winnipeg-born Dr. Charles Bunn, who set up a medical practice in two rooms of the hotel. A new school was built in 1917 to replace the original log building that was now three miles from downtown Ashern. There was a new train station, a telephone exchange (with twelve telephones), and a Standard Bank of Canada branch. The Anglican parish was founded in 1911, holding services in a local boarding house until the church building was finished. Holy Cross Church held its first mass in 1915, and the Ashern Presbyterian Church was dedicated in 1919.

The Pickersgill family was at the centre of the boom. Frank worked the farm and operated the general store, but he also used his solid Conservative Party connections to collect a few patronage appointments, serving as postmaster, registering vital statistics, and compiling the voters lists for provincial elections. Sara put her training to use and provided free medical care to residents when there was no doctor available in town. One person she nursed was a lad named Genest, whose family had moved to Ashern from Montreal when a doctor told them that the climate might help the boy recover from a spinal injury. The Genests spoke little English, so young Jack Pickersgill helped Gideon Genest learn the language to get him through school while Sara tended his ailing brother. Even the Pickersgill homestead became a centre of village life, the family's meadow hosting the annual town picnic, usually held on Dominion Day. There was something for everyone—food booths, foot races, games, a potluck lunch, ice cream, even a horse race. But then Andrew McTavish, a local blacksmith, fell from a horse and died of his injuries. There would be no more horse races on the Pickersgill meadow.

By that time, there was an addition to the family. On 28 May 1915, Sara gave birth to a baby boy at Winnipeg's Grace Hospital. The Pickersgill children were given the honour of selecting a name, and they chose to name the baby after the most important man in their lives: Frank. By the time the little one was able to recognize him, that man was already in uniform.

When the First World War began in August 1914, Ashern, like much of the rest of Canada, was caught off guard. It was a holiday weekend, and people cared more about the coming harvest than the doings of some petty European monarchs no one had ever heard of. But soon the area was seized with patriotic fervour, and the men of the district, young and old, began to enlist for service. Bert Dodd was one of the first to go, in December 1914, with the whole town turning out to see him aboard the train for Winnipeg. Dr. Bunn joined the Canadian Army Medical Corps, as did the physician who replaced him, Dr. Jean Marc Prévost of Maskinonge County in Quebec; with their departure, Sara was left to minister to the needs of Ashern's residents.

Then in late 1915 came word that a new infantry unit, the 108th Battalion, would be recruiting in the Ashern area. No longer facing the prospect of a long train journey to enlist, the local men came forward eagerly, leaving their wives and children to manage the farms in their absence. Since the village was too small to have a justice of the peace or a magistrate, either Frank Pickersgill or Bert Hyde signed each attestation form as a commissioner of oaths, and those forms revealed how diverse a community Ashern had become. Some of the volunteers were natives of the Prairie provinces, but they were in the minority. Fred Turley, like Frank and Bert, was born in Ontario. Bjorn Gislason was an Icelander, like so many of the early settlers of the district. Angus Smith was a Scot, and Victor Gates was born in Brighton, England. Axel Carlson came from Sweden, Joe Marcon from France, Hans Nissen from Denmark, and Peter Nieuwstad from the Netherlands. Bob Thickins was born in the Punjab, in India, while Claude Coffman hailed from Minnesota. Reinhold Krinke and Edmund Klan were both born in Russia. Even Bill Hardisty, who was born in Fort Simpson before it was the North-West Territories, enlisted, despite the fact that he was over-age.

But Frank Pickersgill had more immediate problems than enlisting new recruits. When little Frank was just a few months old, the family was struck by scarlet fever. The elder Pickersgill escaped, but the others were infected and Frank decided to move into the St. George Hotel. He hired a nurse from Winnipeg to take care of the family, and came to the farm himself every morning and evening to do the chores. Young Frank, not even six months old, seemed to be the least affected, but when his fever subsided he took a terrible earache; for the rest of his life, he would be plagued by ear trouble and partial deafness.

Those were difficult days for the family. Frank wasn't the savviest of entrepreneurs at the best of times, but now he found himself having to do everything: run the farm, manage the store, attend to his duties as postmaster, and pay for the nurse. Soon the money started to run out and there was no sign of the sickness passing. Frank borrowed where he could, but ready cash is a scarce commodity in a small farming community in the winter. Before long, he had run out of favours. What happened next is a bit of a mystery. Some money went missing from the post office accounts and then there was a small fire in the Hyde and Pickersgill building, a fire that, coincidentally, struck only the corner of the office where the post office records were kept. There is nothing in Manitoba's newspapers to shed any light on the episode, and the pre-1926 records of the Ashern post office are unaccountably missing from the archives in Ottawa. But Pickersgill family lore says that Frank, desperate to feed his family, borrowed money from the post office receipts. He took only what he needed to tide him over until the family got better and had every intention of paying it back, but before he could, the boom fell: the Post Office Department in Ottawa notified him that someone had reported irregularities in Ashern's accounts, and an auditor would be dispatched to examine the books. Frank was devastated. He had no time to replace the money he had taken, so to cover his tracks, he set fire to the post office, trying to make it look like an accident. But in trying to avoid ruin on one side, he dropped straight into it on the other. He was arrested on suspicion of arson and sent to Winnipeg for trial.

By now it was early 1916, and the war had degenerated into a brutal slogging match in which successes were few and gains came to be measured in yards. As the bloody offensives on the Western Front consumed men at a frightening rate, the need for soldiers became ever more pressing. Soon, the Canadian Expeditionary Force would put almost anyone in uniform—young teenagers, senior citizens, men missing fingers and toes, the visually impaired, even convicted criminals. And so Frank Pickersgill was offered a kind of plea bargain: he could face trial and possibly go to jail, or he could join the army immediately. He didn't hesitate. He returned to Ashern and, on 26 February 1916, enlisted in the 108th Battalion.

The Ashern men started their training in the village so they could live at home and keep up with the farm work (and, not incidentally, save the government some money on their keep). Not long after, the recruits got word that the 108th would assemble at the province's largest training base, Camp Hughes, eighty miles west of Winnipeg. There, Frank was initiated into the routines of the army—inoculations, days spent on the firing range, drill, route marches, fatigue duties—as the unit prepared to move to England. In September, the lot of them boarded a train in Winnipeg for the long ride to Halifax. Then, it was on to the SS *Olympic*, the sister ship of the *Titanic*, for a something less than luxurious crossing of the Atlantic. Their eventual destination was an encampment in southeast England, near the town of Folkestone, where thousands of newly arrived Canadian troops lived and trained before being sent to the front.

Despite promises that the unit would serve together, the men of the 108th learned in England that they were to be parcelled off as reinforcements to different battalions. Frank ended up with the 16th Battalion (Canadian Scottish), a Vancouver unit commanded by Cyrus Peck, an incredibly brave man whose walrus moustache and substantial stomach made him look anything but soldierly. When Frank joined the battalion in March 1917, it was clustered around a small farm known locally as Le Pendu, but ten days later he took his first tour in the trenches, when the 16th moved up to Maison Blanche, just north of what had once been the tiny village of Écurie, for a quiet spell in the trenches. Things wouldn't be quiet for long.

Even before Frank arrived, the 16th had been practising for a big push. The officers pored over maps and aerial photographs, the infantrymen walked through taped lines that approximated their attack routes, the engineers dug trenches, and the railway troops built light railways to bring supplies up and casualties back. The objective was Vimy Ridge, a feature that dominated the Douai plain and was the key to holding the ground south of the coal-mining city of Lens. On the morning of the ninth of April, as a cold dawn broke, the Canadian Corps moved up the ridge and into history. For the 16th Battalion, it was a textbook operation. The men reached their first objective on time, waited for forty minutes to rest and rearm, and then advanced to capture their final objective right on schedule. With that, their fighting was over; they spent the rest of the day as spectators while other battalions pushed through them and up the ridge. It had been a costly day— over 330 all ranks killed, wounded, and missing from an attacking force of just over 600—but the unit had every reason to celebrate its achievement. It was the same across the front. Almost every battalion reached its objective on schedule, although at a cost of some 10,000 men over five days of fighting. Whether Frank Pickersgill appreciated it or not, he had been in on what would become a defining battle for the Canadian Corps.

For the next few months, the battalion was largely out of action as it rested, refitted, and absorbed the reinforcements who had been transferred in to replace the men lost taking Vimy Ridge. By August, they were being readied for another attack. The unit had taken up billets in the town of Mazingarbe, on the edge of the battlefield of Loos, where the British Expeditionary Force had been gutted in 1915, and once again there was a large clay model of the battlefield to be studied and a taped course, laid out on the western slope of the Bully Grenay ridge, that the men used to rehearse their attack. On the night of the fourteenth of August, the 16th moved into its attack positions, east of the village of Loos, and just before 4:30 a.m., they pushed the attack toward Hill 70, another nondescript mound that controlled the approaches to what remained of the city of Lens. Again, they found success: the first objective fell within twenty-five minutes, their final objective almost as quickly. With that, the Scottish hunkered down to see how the other battalions fared. They soon came under heavy counterattack and Frank was hit in the hand and left knee by rifle fire. The medical officer sent him to 18 General Hospital at Camiers; it would be nearly six weeks before he was back with the unit. Even then, Frank knew he wasn't right. He started to suffer from persistent headaches and pain and swelling in his lower legs. He fought it as long as he could, but in November 1917 he presented himself to the medical officer at the nearest field ambulance, who diagnosed nephritis. He didn't know it at the time, but his war was over.

The next five weeks were spent in bed on a milk diet, and then it was on to a series of different hospitals for treatment. A younger man might have been able to fight off the disease, but Frank was then thirty-nine years old and the rigours of life in the trenches had taken their toll. The army decided that he was of no further use in England, and in September 1918 he left Liverpool for Canada. The doctors who examined him in Winnipeg concluded that Frank was fit only for home service, and that his condition wasn't likely to improve within six months. Specifically, he was diagnosed with impaired kidney function and dyspnoea but his medical file simply noted that he had "general debility." With that, Frank Pickersgill was discharged from His Majesty's service. By then, the war was over. An armistice agreement had brought the fighting to a close on the eleventh of November, and the men of Ashern would soon be making their way home. But not all of them would return. Axel Carlson and Bob Thickins died at Vimy Ridge, Victor Gates at Passchendaele a year later. Joe Marcon made it through the fighting, only to succumb to influenza two months after the armistice. And many of those who did come back to Ashern would never be the same again. Like Frank Pickersgill.

He was a stranger to his youngest son when he returned to the village and the boy, then four years old, was genuinely puzzled by the kilt of the 16th Battalion that he wore. "Are you really my father?" he asked dubiously. When Sara replied that he was, young Frank paused thoughtfully, then said, "If you are my father, will you please wear pants?"[1]

The elder Pickersgill came back thin and drawn; once able to work in the fields for hours without a break, now he found that the lightest of chores tired him out. When it became clear that he could no longer work on the farm, he found a job managing a lumberyard in Ashern but even that proved beyond his failing strength. By the spring of 1920, he was spending more time sick at home than at the yard (his eldest son, Jack, filled in for him when he couldn't work). In June, doctors decided that an operation was necessary, and they discovered that Frank had cancer. He was dead within the month, leaving Sara a widow with five children to support.

But she was a woman of enormous inner strength, and it simply wasn't in her nature to let herself bemoan her fate; the success of her children became her life's project. Young Frank was now old enough to attend Ashern's new school, named after the great British naval hero of the war, Admiral Sir David Beatty; the others had all attended the village's old two-room school. Jack, who went from being the oldest sibling to a kind of father figure, felt it was important that they all learn French. He had studied with the Acadian housekeeper of Ashern's butter maker, a young girl who taught Jack in exchange for milk. Tom, Walter, and Bessie struggled away on their own, with Jack marking their lessons. It wasn't easy, but they all eventually passed the French examination that was required for admission to university. For that was Sara's dream—that the young Pickersgills would all get a university education and not have to scrape by on the farm as her husband had done.

Jack had been accepted to university in Winnipeg, so Sara decided to move the family there; he could live at home while studying, the other children could attend school there, and she could support them by working as a nurse. But in July 1922, her brother in Port Rowan died, leaving no one to care for their ailing mother. Sara had no choice but to put off her plans; she and Frank went to Ontario to bring back her mother to live with the family in Ashern. Jack went away to Winnipeg on his own, and the rest of the Pickersgills stayed on the farm while Sara nursed her mother.

In early 1925, Sara had a new patient. Young Frank's ears started to bother him again, and he rapidly developed a high fever. Realizing that his illness was beyond her capacity to treat, Sara took him to Winnipeg, where a specialist diagnosed badly infected mastoids. The prognosis was not good—the specialist said that only a delicate operation, offering just a slim chance of success, could save his life. Sara didn't deliberate for long, and Frank went under the knife. The operation on one ear was a success, and three weeks later the surgeon tackled the other ear. Frank surprised everyone but Sara by making a remarkable recovery; he was soon back home in Ashern, and at the end of May the Winnipeg specialist gave him a clean bill of health. He celebrated by spending the summer months with Jack, who was teaching at a rural school north of Winnipeg. There was fishing, swimming, and hiking, but there were also French lessons, thanks to Jack's determination that all of his siblings learn the language. Fortunately, Frank was a keen student and picked it up easily; by the end of the summer, though he was still just ten years old, he had finished Grade II French.

A few months later, Sara's mother died, and Sara and Frank took the body back to Port Rowan to be buried. It was one more loss for the family to mourn, but it meant that Sara was now free to move everyone to Winnipeg as she had planned years earlier. After spending the summer with Jack, who was now teaching at Happy Lake near Roblin—another fascinatingly heterogenous community with Métis, Mennonites, poor migrants from Ontario, and even some hillbillies from the Cumberland Gap between Virginia and Kentucky who, according to rumour, had come north because one of them had killed a neighbour in a feud—Sara and Frank went back to Ashern in August 1926 to close that chapter in the family's life. The farm was sold, and the Pickersgills were on their way to Winnipeg. It would be Frank's first experience living in a big city.

•

City life was nothing new to Ken Macalister. Granted, Guelph, Ontario, wasn't exactly Winnipeg, but it was everything Ashern wasn't. Founded in the 1820s and named in honour of the Hanoverian dynasty then occupying the British throne, by the early twentieth century it was a booming city of over fifteen thousand people. It had originally been established as an agricultural centre, but industries had grown up and now its wares—musical instruments from the Bell Piano and Organ Company, chemicals from the Standard White Lime Company, beer from Sleeman's Silver Creek Brewery, sewing machines from the White Sewing Machine Company—spread through Canada on the Grand Trunk and Canadian Pacific railways, which crossed in the city centre. Despite its German name, Guelph was solidly British. Three-quarters of the Royal City's population traced its roots back to the British Isles, and the city was divided into wards named after the patron saints of the United Kingdom and Ireland: St. Andrew's Ward, covering much of the downtown core; St. Patrick's Ward, where Guelph's workers lived among rail lines and intractable sewage problems; and St. George's Ward, the "city on the hill" where large and well appointed villas housed the families that mattered.

Ken Macalister came from one of those families. His grandfather was a newspaperman, the business manager of the *Guelph Mercury* no less. The *Mercury* had been founded in the 1850s, in the days when papers were resolutely partisan. After the directors of the Galt and Guelph Railway learned that both of the city's dailies, the *Herald* and the *Advertiser*, believed them to be either bunglers or confidence men out to hoodwink local ratepayers, they decided to take matters into their own hands. With a vote on municipal support for the railway's expansion looming, the directors decided to establish their own newspaper. And so was born the *Mercury*. Over the years, the newspaper would be a tireless champion of the city's business interests, and few proposals—from the Guelph Gas Company to the Agricultural Implement Company to the Guelph Junction Railway Company—failed to elicit the enthusiastic support of successive editors. In 1862, the *Mercury* was bought by James Innes, a Scot who came to Canada as a young man and eventually worked his way from junior reporter to newspaper owner. After more than forty years at the helm, during which time the *Mercury* was transformed from a small-circulation weekly into one of Ontario's most respected dailies, he sold it to his nephew, James Innes McIntosh, in 1905. A few years later, McIntosh brought another relative into the business when he lured his brother-in-law, William Macalister, to Guelph to run the paper's day-to-day operations.

Macalister also traced his roots back to Scotland, but more recently to Kingston, Ontario, where his father, Alexander William, was an accountant. William had married Marion McIntosh, and the couple had three children: daughters Menotah and Marion, and their eldest, Alexander Masson Macalister, born in 1877. When they moved to Guelph, they took up residence in St. George's Ward, in a fine, cut-stone house at 14 Mitchell Street. But Alexander was destined to be just a part-time resident. As soon as he finished high school, he set out for northern Ontario, working on a railway survey crew managed by a Guelph city engineer. He spent the summer months helping to tame the wilderness, returning home each fall when the surveying season ended. He busied himself working as a reporter for the *Mercury*, and also availed himself of something that the survey crews had to do without: female company. During one of his winters in Guelph, Alexander met a young woman named Celestine Doran, whose family lived on Glasgow Street, not far from the *Mercury* office. The Dorans were devout Roman Catholics, and Matthew and Sarah Doran probably imagined their youngest daughter marrying in a full mass service at the Church of Our Lady of the Immaculate Conception. Instead, on 23 February 1914, Alexander and Celestine were wed in a quiet ceremony in the rectory, the usual practice when the marriage involved a non-Catholic. Given the circumstances, the Dorans probably didn't want anything more elaborate. That Celestine was marrying outside the faith was bad enough—more than a few parents disowned their children for less—but even more embarrassing was the fact that Celestine was pregnant. For pillars of the Catholic community like the Doran family, the shame could hardly have been more intense, and it put a heavy burden on the young couple starting out their life together. They moved into a humble brick side-by-side at 22 Robinson

Street, in St. Andrew's Ward, and on 9 July 1914, their only child, John Kenneth Macalister, was born. Within a month, Canada was at war.

Guelph responded the way the Royal City should: with enthusiastic and unconditional displays of patriotism. Crowds spilled out into the streets, first to celebrate the coming of war and then to bid farewell to local men as they left for training camps and, eventually, overseas. The Macalisters' neighbours started joining up—Gilbert Walsh was the first to go, in September 1914 (he would survive the war, only to fall victim to the Spanish flu in 1919), then George Leadlay, from whom Alexander had rented the Robinson Street house, and Joe Heeg, whose son would later attend high school with Ken Macalister. And before long, Alexander followed suit; on 14 October 1915, he enlisted in the 2nd Canadian Pioneer Battalion. Exactly two months later, he was in England.

Alexander reached the front in early March 1916, just in time to experience the Battle of the St. Eloi Craters. On the twenty-seventh, Allied engineers detonated a series of enormous mines under the German lines near what had once been the village of St. Eloi. The 6th Infantry Brigade was given the task of defending these newly won positions; it fell to the 2nd Pioneer Battalion to make them defensible. Alexander's baptism of fire was a harsh one. He and his fellow Pioneers had to turn what remained of the German trenches into strongpoints, pump the water out of them, dig support trenches to link up the craters, and complete that most unpleasant of tasks, collecting the dead from the battlefield. And all the while, the Germans launched fierce counterattacks to push the Canadians back.

April was a bad month for the 2nd Pioneers—they took casualties almost every day from the heavy bombardments—but soon the battalion settled into a routine. Its four companies rotated between the front lines and the support trenches, and the men tried to go about their business repairing, draining, and revetting trenches, laying telephone cable, reinforcing barbed wire, and strengthening dugouts. The Pioneers never had to go over the top like their comrades in the infantry but they faced all the other hazards of the front, including artillery. It was the bane of the soldier, for it killed randomly and from afar. Shellfire could erupt along the front at any time—one minute a group of soldiers might be playing cards or preparing a meal, the next minute there might be no trace of them except a smoking crater and some mangled body parts. With his rifle and grenades, the infantryman at least had the chance to give the enemy some of his own back. But the Pioneer carried only a shovel, a roll of barbed wire, or a bundle of trench matting. The shelling took a toll on their numbers, but their impotence took a toll on their minds; through the spring and summer of 1916, a steady trickle of Pioneers, damaged in body or mind, headed for the rear-area hospitals.

On the twenty-fourth of August, Alexander Macalister was one of them; the regimental medical officer said he was suffering from shell shock and sent him out of the trenches. A week later, he was a patient at the Canadian Convalescent Hospital at Woodcote Park, a sprawling collection of army huts near the famous horse-racing town of Epsom, in the south of England. He was treated for seven months, but showed so little improvement that, in July 1917, he was sent to the discharge depot at Buxton to wait for a ship to Canada. He sailed a month later and in September, military doctors in Quebec City concluded that he was suffering from "traumatic neurasthenia received on duty." Of no further use to the army, Alexander was discharged in London, Ontario, on 30 November 1917.

Like a generation of soldiers, he returned to a family that didn't know him. Ken was now four years old and in a year or two would be starting at St. Stanislaus School, on the grounds of the Church of Our Lady of the Immaculate Conception, but he had no memory of his father. For Celestine, the haggard and haunted man who came back to her bore little resemblance to the hardy woodsman who had wooed her just a few years earlier. Still, Alexander seemed to improve much more quickly than anyone expected and before too many months had passed, he was his old outgoing self again. His health being what it was, a return to the railway survey crews was out of the question, so instead he joined the staff of the *Daily Mercury* on a full-time basis. William Macalister had decided to leave the newspaper business and go into the sand and gravel trade, and Alexander quickly moved up in the business; by 1931, he had become the paper's editor-in-chief.

Ken was drawn to his father's workplace, and spent many hours haunting the hallways of the *Mercury* offices. He didn't say much—staffers of the time recall him as a painfully shy lad who peeked around corners and into offices to see what was happening—but he soaked up everything he saw and heard. When Ken was ten years old, he started his own small newspaper that, as he later put it, "was imposed on relatives at three cents a copy."[2] When he was older, he took on more responsibility at the paper. During the summers, he did odd jobs around the office and even wrote the occasional editorial on current affairs, something that consumed more of his time as he got older and grew more interested in world politics. As one of his friends later wrote, Ken "does reporting on the sideline, and helps run the *Evening Mercury*. It is rumoured that he is considering taking school as a sideline instead."[3] There was more than a little truth in the comment, for it seems that Ken spent time writing newspaper editorials when he should have been writing school essays.

When Ken started at Guelph Collegiate–Vocational Institute (GCVI) in September 1928, it was only five years old, a fireproof state-of-the-art school built from one million bricks and boasting three huge ten-ton boilers, space for 1,240 students, and one of the first high-school swimming pools in the province. The latter was not a great success—while Ken was a student, the pool was drained because of a phantom leak that defied all repair efforts, and the space became a rifle range for the cadet corps—but in all other respects GCVI was a happy institution, and Ken loved his time there. He was troubled by nearsightedness, and was a peril in the hallways because he frequently couldn't see where he was going (that is, if he didn't have his head crammed in a book), but that didn't stop him from taking up any sport that came along—hockey, skiing, and snowboarding in the winter, baseball, tennis, golf, and running the rest of the year. His favourite, however, was football. He played for the city team and spent four years on the wing line of GCVI's senior team (coach Jack Achtzener, who had won the

Dominion championship as a player with the Regina Pats, steered him to that position because perfect vision wasn't a requirement), later becoming the team's chronicler for *Acta Nostra*, the school's yearbook. The team wasn't very good—as Ken wrote in the 1931 yearbook, "we are proud of those men who played on our teams of the last four years; this in spite of the fact that, between them, they have succeeded in winning but one encounter—a never-to-be-forgotten epic with Brantford in 1930"—but Ken loved every mud-spattered, bruising, exhausting minute of it.[4]

Off the field, Ken had plenty of other interests. He was a keen debater in the Guelph Hi-Y Club, and played an active role in the Literary Society; both gave him an outlet for the strong opinions that he fostered while helping out at the *Mercury*. He had enormous strength of conviction, and refused to accept the views of anyone (even his teachers) unless he had satisfied himself of their validity. But he was never a stuffy intellectual. He loved a practical joke, even when it got him in trouble (he would often tear pages from his notebook and write jokes on them to pass around the classroom—caught in the act once, Ken played his poor eyesight for all it was worth and claimed he couldn't read what he had written), and when he was amused or teasing a friend, his soft voice would slide into a falsetto "Ahhhhh!" with such perfect timing that it rarely failed to send his friends into gales of laughter.

But despite Ken's usually cheerful demeanour, friends wondered if all was right at home. Alexander and Celestine—a garrulous, jolly Scots Presbyterian and a stern, devout Irish Catholic—were an unlikely couple. Some people thought they were just shy, but others sensed an ever-present tension around them. They could often be seen walking through downtown Guelph together, but would never speak to anyone unless they were spoken to first. Few people were invited to visit the Macalister home, which suited Ken's friends just fine because Celestine made them distinctly uncomfortable; in whispers, they debated whether she was an alcoholic or just odd. She doted on her only son, and Ken alternated between trying to find his own identity (the fact that he took after his father and had little interest in attending mass rankled her) and being overly sensitive to Celestine's opinions. One friend recalled that Ken "went to Mars to please his mother," and she seems to have fostered in her son an intense sense of guilt that she was quite willing to use to manipulate him. Years later, another friend remembered an impression that Celestine would be "the downfall of both of them."[5] Was this why Ken spent so much of his free time not at the family home on Metcalfe Street but under a tree in St. George's Park across the street, either surrounded by piles of books or canoodling with one of his girlfriends?

But Ken would soon be leaving his parents, and Guelph, and the security of GCVI. Despite glowing praise from his teachers (who included Olive Freeman, the future wife of prime minister John Diefenbaker), his high-school grades had been good but not outstanding—he had more second-class standings than firsts, and even took a poor third in geometry. Friends later wondered if his teachers had let him coast in school, rather than reprimand him for his laxity and risk the wrath of the formidable Celestine. Nevertheless, Ken had been accepted at the University of Toronto; like Frank Pickersgill, he was bound for the big city.

Two

UNIVERSITY

When the historian Arthur Lower arrived in Winnipeg to take up a teaching position at Wesley College, he declared himself unimpressed. His first glimpse of the city was of the slums around the Canadian Pacific Railway station ("the sunk rather than the swimmers"), and nothing he saw later gave him any reason to alter his initial opinion. "Winnipeg, topographically and climatically, is not attractive," he wrote. "Natural beauty; there was none . . . You could burn the whole physical city tomorrow . . . and there would be little aesthetic or sentimental loss . . . There is nowhere to walk, nothing to look at, no hills to ski on, no water of consequence." His new institution wasn't much better; Wesley College was "dingy and full of dust just one degree removed from dirt"; if not for the students, it would have been "stale, flat, and unprofitable."[1]

But for young Frank Pickersgill, the city was a joy. Its free and easy atmosphere appealed to his youthful exuberance, and he loved the ethnic diversity that reminded him of Ashern, if on a much larger scale. It was the most culturally diverse city in Canada, and was animated by every manner of tension and rivalry. In 1931, the Manitoba capital had a population approaching 200,000 and boasted more foreign-language newspapers than New York City. It was home to the Manitoba Music Festival, the largest in the British Empire, and the *Manitoba Free Press,* perhaps the most influential newspaper in the country. For sheer liveliness and an invigorating mix of eastern high society and the rough-and-tumble west, it was hard to beat Winnipeg.

Jack Pickersgill, more and more taking on the role of father, had found a home for the family in the Rozel Apartments on Clarke Street, which he chose because it would allow Frank to attend one of the best schools in the city, Earl Grey Junior High School. The board of education wanted Frank to do Grade 6 at Fort Rouge School, but Jack thought it was beneath him; he convinced the principal of Earl Grey to admit Frank on a two-week trial. He started in the fall of 1926, and soon showed the teachers that he belonged there; he finished top of his class that year, and in Grade 8 emerged as the top male student in the school.

Frank and Jack celebrated the success by taking a motorcycle trip to Toronto—Jack had won a scholarship to study at Oxford, leaving Frank to take the train back to Winnipeg on his own. When he got back, he was just in time to help the family move into the Waldorf Apartments on Broadway, closer to where Sara and Walter Pickersgill worked and near Kelvin Technical High School, where Frank started in September 1929. He continued to impress his teachers, taking top spot in almost every subject he studied, and when he finished Grade 11, he had a decision to make. Jack had a bequest from his grandmother to pay for his university education but Frank didn't, so his brother advised him to do Grade 12 and try to win a scholarship. It was a good idea; once again, he finished at the top of almost every subject with grades into the mid-nineties and won scholarships to cover his tuition and living expenses. He would follow in Jack's footsteps by going to the University of Manitoba, to study classics and modern languages.

Frank had enrolled in an institution that, according to the Dominion Bureau of Statistics, had the second-largest student body in Canada. Created by provincial statute in 1877 through the amalgamation of St. John's (Anglican), Manitoba (Presbyterian), and St. Boniface (Roman Catholic) Colleges to become the first degree-granting university west of Ontario, it grew by joining up with other schools in the city; the Methodist Wesley

College affiliated in 1888, a private medical school in 1883, the Manitoba Agricultural College in 1907, the Manitoba Law School in 1914, and a private pharmacy school in 1914. Eventually, all of these institutions became teaching faculties when they turned over their management to the university, which ran the operation and granted the degrees.

Through the 1920s, the university that Frank Pickersgill would know started to take shape. In 1914, Manitoba and Wesley agreed to amalgamate as United Colleges; Manitoba would teach theology, while Wesley would teach arts and religious knowledge. The teaching units struggled with space issues; despite the construction of a new science building and a series of lecture theatres known as the Cowsheds, classroom space designed for 900 students had to accommodate nearly twice that number. There was no room to work in the library and, although there was residence space for 430 women, there were only seven women's toilets available. A government-appointed committee looked at a number of possible remedies, including expanding the Broadway campus or moving to the grounds occupied by the Manitoba Agricultural College, but eventually decided to acquire a large parcel of land at Fort Garry, in the town of St. Vital. Senior students would be taught in new buildings to be erected at the Fort Garry campus, while the junior students (the first year of university was the equivalent of Grade 12 because most provincial high schools went only to Grade 11) would remain downtown.

The move had its drawbacks. Junior students were stuck at the Broadway campus with decrepit facilities, a poor library, no recreational facilities, and little interaction with the positive influence of older students and senior faculty. The new buildings were modern and well equipped but Fort Garry became a commuter campus, with the students and staff fleeing back to Winnipeg as soon as classes were done for the day. One detractor had envisioned students driving to Fort Garry every morning with Thermoses filled with liquor, but in reality most relied on the slow and infrequent 97 trolley to take them back and forth to Fort Garry. Frank, however, was given the use of the family car once his classes moved to the Fort Garry campus, on the condition that he find some friends to share the cost of gas. Unfortunately, he didn't get on well with motor vehicles. One morning while cranking the car, he forgot to check that it was in neutral and when the engine caught, the car lurched backwards with Frank grimly hanging on to the front bumper until a fence got in the way. Luckily Jack, who was teaching at the university, was around to take care of the repairs ... and the occasional speeding ticket as well.

The university's other great challenge was a scandal that threatened to bring down the institution. John Machray was a pillar of Winnipeg's financial community—a nephew of the Anglican archbishop, the university's honorary bursar, and chair of the Board of Governors—and in 1903 his prestigious law firm took over the investment of the university's endowments and land grants. Because of the high esteem in which he was held, he turned away all attempts to have the books inspected but, in 1932, when Machray fell gravely ill, the audit could be put off no longer. It revealed that the university's $869,000 endowment and the revenue from its land grant had vanished, piddled away by Machray in bad investments, shady real estate deals, and his own use. It was nothing personal—Machray also defrauded the Anglican Diocese of Rupert's Land—but of the total loss of about $1.9 million, only a little over $40,000 was recovered, from Machray's insurance policies after he died in Stony Mountain Penitentiary in 1933. For the students, the scandal meant they were attending a university that was suddenly poor; many improvements had to be put off, repairs were deferred, and plans that were in the works (such as uniting the parts of the university at the Fort Garry campus) were shelved. The fact that the Depression was now in full swing and the Prairie provinces were sliding toward financial ruin just made things more difficult.

But the students were a resilient lot (the grouchy Arthur Lower, who would go on to become one of Canada's most influential historians, admitted that the only good thing about his new employer was the enthusiasm and dynamism of the student body) and they made the most of the university, and then some. It was a stellar group of undergraduates enrolled at the University of Manitoba during Frank's time there: Marshall McLuhan, who had also gone through Earl Grey and Kelvin High School; the novelist W.O. Mitchell; historian W.L. Morton; politicians Stanley Knowles and Mitchell Sharp; physicist Harry Duckworth; university president David Carleton Williams; physicist Louis Slotin, who was to die after a nuclear accident at Los Alamos; actor Tommy Tweed; and legal scholar Maxwell Cohen. The university's vibrant atmosphere brought out the best in them. There was a distinguished English Club that attracted such speakers as the novelist Frederick Philip Grove, the celebrity and Indian impersonator Long Lance, poets Wilson MacDonald and Bliss Carman, publisher Lorne Pierce, and *Manitoba Free Press* editor J.W. Dafoe. The History Club met one Wednesday a month, and the International Affairs Group and the Cercle français (the French students' club) had large and enthusiastic memberships. For those whose interests lay in the dramatic, each college or faculty held a skit night, and the winners of each night would then perform at Varsity Night, later known as the Varsity Varieties. If you couldn't find something on campus to take your interest, you weren't trying very hard.

By the time he joined the freshman class at Manitoba, Frank had grown into a gangly young man, over six feet tall with a thin, powerful build. He had a longish face, with a dimple just threatening to form on his chin and thin brown hair that was retreating up his forehead rather earlier than it should. But like most adolescents who grow quickly, he was still getting used to his long limbs. This awkwardness, combined with the unsteadiness that was a legacy of his childhood ear problems, meant that he was constantly bumping into furniture and knocking things off tables. Frank always laughed off such things, although his closest friends knew that he was terribly self-conscious about his clumsiness. Even so, his bright eyes and the smile that was never far from his lips betrayed a playful sense of humour. He made simple that most difficult of balancing acts, retaining a childlike sense of fun and delighting in being downright goofy but showing a maturity far beyond his years. "Frank was the same age as I am," recalled his university friend George Ford, "but it always seemed to me that he was older . . . His mind seemed developed far beyond mine, and I was always racing to keep pace with his omnivorous reading and constant stream of fresh ideas."[2]

It was Frank's childlike (and occasionally childish) sense of fun that drew people to him, to revel in the friendly chaos that surrounded him. He was a social animal, although he was never a joiner. He was unapologetically informal—organized groups and activities, for the most part, bored him. He stayed away from most student clubs (the one exception was the University Society for Social Reconstruction, which he loved not only because its acronym was USSR but also because its tiny membership meant that nothing had to be taken very seriously) and, aside from a supporting role in a production of Molière's *Le malade imaginaire* (*The Imaginary Invalid*), showed little interest in university theatricals. Athletics held no appeal for him—sports had too many rules for his liking—and he never aspired to any leadership role on campus (except for a year spent on the Arts Student Council). He was much happier being the uncrowned king of his rather anarchic group of friends. They were pranksters and practical jokers, and Frank was often the ringleader. When he and fellow student Brock King saw a couple of chamber pots at an auction, they just had to buy them—so they could bang them noisily as they walked along Donald Street and then sneak them onto the roof of a passing car. For Frank, life was to be lived on the spur of the moment, even if his lunatic stunts made the good citizens of Winnipeg shake their heads, and sometimes their fists. He and his friends probably drank too much, caroused too much, and disturbed the peace of Winnipeg, but it was never out of a lack of regard for others. They were just a bunch of young people enjoying each other's company the best way they knew how.

But it would be a mistake to see Frank as a shallow hedonist. If he loved having a good time, he was even more passionate about ideas. One thing that held his interest was journalism, and he eagerly took up his pen to contribute to the student newspaper *'toba*, first as a writer and later as managing editor. His early attempts at writing reveal that he was, at heart, a philosopher—of politics, of culture, of society. "We are only on this earth for a very short time," Frank once wrote in *'toba*, "and our main business here is leading a life which is valuable and happy, and this cannot be done very satisfactorily merely by sticking grimly to one's task and never taking one's eyes off the road which leads onward and upward to financial success. Those who cannot pause and look around them in their struggling, when asked what their aim is, can only say *'to get There.'* And when asked where *'There'* is they are at a loss for an answer." In his eyes, "There" meant having fun with close friends, but it also meant using one's talents to help make the world a better place. Financial success was less important than the moral success of exercising a positive influence on humanity. To do so required the mobilization not only of strong backs but of creative minds. "I never knew anyone who placed so much value on ideas," recalled George Ford.[3] Frank was happiest when he was sequestered with a group of friends in the Pickersgill home, debating anything and everything under the sun. There were always breaks for party games and stacks of sandwiches, washed down with coffee from Sara's apparently bottomless pot, but sooner or later they got back to discussion, trying to solve the problems of the university, the country, and the world, all in one night. And although he was the product of a traditional, rather conservative upbringing, Frank was developing into a free thinker. He had no partisan political affiliations (or interests), and was quite happy to take solutions from wherever he could find them on the political spectrum. He had "the rare courage of an individualist," recalled fellow Arts student Jim Duncan, "who didn't care to go with the swim but thought things out for himself and acted with the courage of his conclusions." He was, by all accounts, a remarkable person to know, for "his incandescent enthusiasm and sturdy point of view on any and all topics and his unlimited zest and brilliant common sense," as his friend Elsa Lehman put it. Those who knew him well were devoted to him, and those who knew him slightly wished they had known him better. Years later, W.O. Mitchell would regret that he hadn't been closer to Frank, for only in hindsight could he truly appreciate Frank's independence of thought, intellectual courage, and his "greatness in giving so magnificently to all of us."[4]

Perhaps because he gave so much to others, Frank tended to shortchange himself and when he graduated in 1936, his grades were a disappointment. He did well enough, but he wouldn't be following Jack to Oxford, something that he had plenty of time to ponder as he left Winnipeg for the summer holidays, as he did every year. Sometimes he went with Brock King to Matlock, on the southern end of Lake Winnipeg, where the King family had a cottage. Each of the boys would drag a suitcase full of books up north and, when the books were all read, spend their days playing badminton or building sand and rock canals beside the lake. For a time, Frank and Brock would drink only milk, and lots of it; when they were up to four or five quarts a day, Mrs. King told them in no uncertain terms that they would have to start drinking something that was easier to come by in the north.

More often, Frank went with the family to Clearwater Bay, on Lake of the Woods in northwestern Ontario, where Jack had bought some waterfront property soon after the highway between Winnipeg and Kenora opened. But waterfront didn't mean lakefront—the cottage they built, christened Highbrow House, stood some eighty feet above the shore on a hill, and a mile's walk from the main road. What it lacked in convenience, however, it more than made up for in view, and the long living room on the front of the cottage had a glorious view out over the lake. Most of the construction was done by Frank and Jack's uncle Walter Pickersgill, with various friends from the university pressed into service whenever they were available. Frank loved the months spent at Highbrow, partly because some of his best friends from Winnipeg were near at hand. Lloyd Wheeler, a young instructor in the Department of English to whom Frank became very close, had a cottage on the same piece of shoreline, and Celine Ballu, Frank's favourite lecturer in the Department of French, vacationed not far away. The other source of joy was work. He had a seemingly endless capacity for chopping wood, which he did with the assurance of a seasoned lumberjack. But no matter how hard he worked clearing brush, Frank never seemed to run out of energy. He could chop wood all day, spend the evening discussing French literature with Celine Ballu, and still he tossed and turned all night, mumbling and grunting as he fought for sleep. It was almost as if, with so much to fit into a day, he begrudged having to give a few hours to sleep.

Just before leaving Winnipeg for the summer of 1936, Frank got the good news that he had won a scholarship to do his master's degree at the University of Toronto. He had been to the city before, but as a visitor rather than a resident; after installing himself in a house at 602 Spadina Avenue (now Fenwick House, a co-op residence of the university) and with memories of a glorious summer spent at Highbrow House fresh in his mind, he decided that Toronto wasn't as he remembered it. Frank's initial reaction was very similar to Arthur Lower's response to Winnipeg. "Toronto is certainly a very ugly city except for the trees, a couple of ravines, Hart House and Knox College," he wrote to George Ford. "I'm constantly astonished by its ugliness. And Americanised—it's far more uncivilised than Winnipeg." He hated the newspapers (the *Mail and Empire* was "proto-fascist" and the *Toronto Star* was "clear proof that a million people *can* be wrong"), and thought the undergraduates were a "collection of shoddy stick-in-the-muds" and the city's upper crust was "an aristocracy which accepts the cheapest aspects of English upper class life and combines it with all the cheapness of American life."[5]

Academically, however, Toronto was excellent. Frank planned to write his master's thesis on St. Augustine of Hippo and would be working with Charles Cochrane, one of the country's leading classicists. He was connected to the Institute for Mediaeval Studies at St. Michael's College, which had been founded in 1929 and was famous for bringing in French academics Étienne Gilson, who spent a term in Toronto every year from 1929 to 1939, and Jacques Maritain. To earn a little pocket money (especially to pay for cigarettes, which he was starting to smoke almost constantly), Frank also found a part-time job with historian Donald McDougall, who had lost his sight at the Battle of Courcelette in 1916. Sometimes Frank would read to him, but when McDougall was working on a book Frank would be on call—he sat in McDougall's office doing what he pleased, and every half-hour or so the professor would ask him to look something up. The money was welcome but the experience was even better, for Frank found himself reading (and enjoying) things that he wouldn't have otherwise picked up. He became a fixture at the university library, and later recalled how spoiled he was at the University of Toronto, with centuries worth of great writing just a short walk from his apartment.

Frank's letters from Toronto show how much he was changing as he studied—he even chastised his friends for their supposed intolerance of the man he had become. He was still driven by ideas but had realized that, before he could solve the world's problems, he had to understand himself better. He grappled with religion, finally coming down on the side of Anglo-Catholicism (the doctrine of papal infallibility turned him off Roman Catholicism), and wrestled with his volatile political views. In one letter, he professed himself to be a conservative at heart; weeks later, he was a committed socialist—almost any political doctrine was worth consider-ing at a time when the Western democracies seemed poised on the brink of financial ruin. Frank was, like so many young people, trying to come up with his own personal philosophy, embracing ideas wherever he could find them. But his letters weren't all about high ideals. He was preoccupied with his health, and repeated references to stomach problems point to either a stress-related condition or a tendency to hypochondria. Much to his dismay, he also suffered from bad teeth, and once reported that he was having to save money to pay for the eleven fillings and one extraction that he needed. Frank was very conscious of his financial well-being, typical of someone who relied on others (in this case his brother Jack) for support. He would buy things on impulse and then spend days regretting it. After a grand day at the Eaton's book sale, buying Aristotle, Cicero, Dryden, Goethe, Santayana, Chesterton, and a pile of others, he pleaded with George Ford, "Don't tell Jack that I spent $15.20 [more than $200 in current values] at one fell swoop or he'd probably burst a blood-vessel."[6] On another occasion, he borrowed forty dollars to buy a new suit to impress a university president who was coming to interview him—it seemed like a good idea at the time, but he hated himself for his rashness later. Eventually, he would outgrow his impulsiveness, but never his intensity of feeling.

•

When Frank arrived in Toronto in September 1936, Ken Macalister was starting his final year at the university. He had come from Guelph as something of an unknown commodity, a young man of many gifts who nevertheless showed a maddening reluctance to apply himself. He could excel when an assignment took his interest, but he also tended to coast when he wasn't being challenged. Perhaps, hoped Alexander and Celestine, a new environment would offer Ken the intellectual stimulus that his agile mind craved. For the next four years, he wouldn't get back to Guelph very often. He came home for the first couple of summers, but then took a job as secretary to Celestine's brother-in-law, Harry Gadsby, who worked for the *Toronto Star*. And in any case, Celestine didn't care for Ken's new girlfriend. It was bad enough when he dated a Guelph classmate who attended the United Church, but now he had taken up with a Christian Scientist. Ken was slipping away from her and every time Celestine thought of it she was gripped by a mix of panic and irritation.

Celestine might have been happier had Ken chosen to study at the Catholic St. Michael's College, or perhaps even the Presbyterian Knox. But he had picked University College, the only religiously unaffiliated college at the University of Toronto, to study law. One of the most venerable institutions in the British Empire, it was founded in 1853 as the provincial arts and science college. The original building, an unrestrained jumble of architectural styles, was gutted by fire on Valentine's Day 1890, but a new college had risen from the rubble, although it wasn't new in the kind of students it attracted. Even with a leavening of middle-class children whose brilliance had won them scholarships, in the 1930s the university was still an institution for the elite—less than 5 per cent of Canadians went on to higher education. The University of Toronto's goal was to prepare young men and women for lives of achievement, to train the next generation of leaders. And just like Manitoba, it graduated some famous names—William Lyon Mackenzie King, Arthur Meighen, and Vincent Massey, to name just three—and among Ken's contemporaries at Toronto were future university president Claude Bissell, diplomats Saul Rae and Arnold Smith, literary scholar Northrop Frye, and poet Douglas LePan.

The atmosphere of the place may have had something to do with it. There was a strong undercurrent of veneration for the achievements of previous generations of undergraduates, and everything about the university encouraged each class to try to live up to the example of those who came before. In all of Ken's favourite places, the ghosts of the past were alive—in the Junior Common Room, which had been the dining hall before the great Valentine's Day fire, where generations of students had gathered around the massive stone fireplace or the old upright piano; in the East Hall, which bordered on University College's stately quadrangle, where the sun shone through an intricate stained-glass window dedicated to three undergraduates who had lost their lives fighting the Fenian raiders from south of the border in 1866; in the Gothic triumph that was Soldiers' Tower, east of the college and next to Hart House, where the members of the university who had sacrificed their lives in the Great War had been commemorated. It was a powerful legacy.

After delighting his high-school teachers with his accomplishments, and frustrating them with his occasional laziness, Ken came into his own at the University of Toronto. But he remained a study in contrasts, perhaps a reflection of his parents' very different personalities. The private Ken was still like the little boy who had haunted the *Daily Mercury* office, saying nothing and trying to keep out of sight but watching everything with intense fascination. He had had lots of friends at GCVI, but remained something of a loner who was quite happy to spend hours or days on his own, reading or studying. He didn't crave human contact because he was still very shy. It wasn't so much that large groups of people made him nervous; it was more that he never considered himself to have the kind of personality that attracted attention. That was one of the great mysteries of his high-school years: for the life of him, Ken couldn't understand why he had so many friends.

The people around him now saw a different Ken, an urbane and worldly young man with an easy formality that was very appealing. It may have been a facade, but it was a very convincing one. He had all the social graces and carried himself with an air of nobility that was softened by his warm brown eyes and the thick black hair that he wore slicked back. He even had a tuxedo that he was quite willing to lend to his housemates if the occasion demanded. However diffident and unprepossessing he felt on the inside, to others he was confident and outgoing, one of the busiest students in University College. Member of the Historical Club and the French Club ("although my French does it no credit," he observed drily); keen participant in the Hart House Debates and the Robinette Trophy Debates; participant in the Parliamentary Club; member of the University of Toronto's Moot Court; secretary of the Literary and Athletic Society; treasurer of the University College men's residence; middle wing for the college's entry to the Mulock Cup, the inter-faculty football tournament; president-elect of his graduating class—he squeezed in every possible extra-curricular activity.[7]

Ken was one of the most well-known people on campus during his senior year. Coincidentally, that was the one year, the 1936–37 academic term, when he and Frank Pickersgill were together at the University of Toronto. Did they ever meet? There were, after all, some eight thousand students enrolled in the mid-1930s, and the fact that Ken was an undergraduate and Frank a graduate student would have been a barrier. But they were both at University College (which Frank had described as being "made up of what are politically hidebound Conservatives—and in every other way completely rootless and traditionless"[8]) and the dean of Ken's residence and his professor of Greek and Roman history, Charles Cochrane, was Frank's MA thesis supervisor. More important, they had similar world views, even though Frank was probably a little to the left of Ken. The Nazi seizure of power in Germany might not have seemed especially alarming when it happened in 1933, but the increasing violence of fascism in Europe certainly did. As Italy completed its annexation of Abyssinia in the spring of 1936 and Spain descended into civil war a few months later, the prospect for a lasting peace grew dimmer. University students, who had been among the most active members of the pacifist movement in Canada in the early 1930s, found themselves having to make a tough choice: should they campaign for peace at any price, or resign themselves to war as the only way to defeat tyranny? Slowly and by the pressure of events, Ken and Frank were probably both pushed toward the belief that war was a lesser evil than peace at any cost, and that sooner or later they would have to make a stand against fascism. This shared belief would have given them a basis for mutual respect. Even if Frank hated the newspaper for which Ken had worked, he certainly wouldn't have dismissed him as a "shoddy stick-in-the-mud." On the contrary, one can easily imagine Frank being impressed by the soft-spoken and articulate young man holding forth from the debating platform, or the two being introduced by Professor Cochrane after a chance meeting in his office. In fact, it is difficult to believe that they didn't meet in Toronto. But without direct evidence, it remains a matter of conjecture.

The intellectual atmosphere of the university was perfect for Ken. Australian jurist Julius Stone later wrote that Toronto offered the best legal education in the British Commonwealth; it was humane, ranged over everything from Roman law to labour law, and encouraged students to become interested in public policy. It was enough to ignite Ken intellectually and motivate him to work to his full potential. After four years, he emerged as one of the finest students the University of Toronto had seen in recent memory. Every year, he took a first-class standing in every subject and along the way had won every prize for which he was eligible: the Carswell Prize in English Constitutional Law; the Dent McCrea Scholarship in Law; the Angus MacMurchy Gold Medal for the highest cumulative average in law; the Gordon Southam War Memorial Scholarship (twice); the Carswell

Prize in Federal Constitutional Law; the Maurice Cody Scholarship in Modern History, which he shared with his friend George Ignatieff, and half a dozen others. The principal of University College called him "one of the ablest men in the college," and it was a foregone conclusion that he would be put forward for the Rhodes Scholarship.[9] Funded through a bequest from the South African mining magnate Cecil Rhodes in 1904, the scholarships were intended to bring exemplary male students from the British Empire, the United States, and Germany to study at Oxford. Rhodes made it clear that academic achievement wasn't enough; the winners should excel in "manly outdoor sports" and show "qualities of manhood, truth, courage, devotion to duty, sympathy for, and protection of, the weak, kindliness, unselfishness and fellowship . . . moral force of character and instincts." In short, they should be "the best men for the world's fight." The stipend of four hundred pounds a year for three years would cover tuition, room and board, and living expenses, and still leave enough money for some educational travel around the continent.[10]

The men who wrote letters in support of Ken's application could barely find superlatives sufficient to describe his achievement. "His academic career has been one of the most remarkable in the history of our honour schools," wrote Professor W.P.M. Kennedy, a literary scholar, historian, and later dean of the law school. "This is an academic record which is unequalled . . . He has the finest mind which I have met with for many years." Professor N.A. Mackenzie, who taught international law and later sat on the Massey Commission that examined the state of Canadian culture after the Second World War, thought that Ken was "probably the best student that has taken work with me, during my association with the University of Toronto." He possessed a powerful intellect marked by "insight, judgement, and critical faculties remarkable in a man of his years," as Kennedy put it. What passed for shyness was as much a manifestation of his determination to think carefully before he spoke, "to arrive at his conclusions for himself, to see a problem in its varieties of points of view, to suspend decision, to weigh evidence." He wasn't cynical or dismissive of the opinions of others;

he just had his own standards of proof. "He is a very independent thinker," wrote Harry Gadsby. "He has a great respect for authority but takes no man's word as final until he can agree with it himself." He was also a passionate defender of social justice. He had a legalistic mind, but one that was tempered by an interest in broader historical and philosophical matters. "He exhibits a remarkable moral force of character," wrote E.C. Young, president of the Guelph *Daily Mercury,* "and has a mature understanding of humanitarianism which I can vouch for." It all added up to a young man with enormous potential, said Kennedy: "He will become, if all goes well, an outstanding Canadian."[11]

Ken's University of Toronto transcript reveals his academic excellence, but his application to the Rhodes Committee for Ontario shows what kind of person he had become. Candidates had to submit two essays, one autobiographical and one on a subject of general importance (Ken wrote on the evolution of Canadian external relations)—together they offer a glimpse at how Ken saw the world and his place in it. His childhood enthusiasm for journalism had given way to an interest in economic and political reform. Writing in the newspaper about problems wasn't enough; he wanted to work on solving them. And he had certainly given some thought to the practical problems facing Canada. He had studied Quebec marriage law and come to the conclusion that the French and English parts of the country hadn't made enough of an effort to understand each other. Research into the economies of the Maritime provinces persuaded him that the gap between the have and the have-not regions was one of the greatest challenges facing Canada. He believed that standards in the civil service and the judiciary were too low, that the British North America Act needed modernizing, and that Canada would benefit from a non-partisan press— an odd notion coming from the son of a man whose newspaper was still resolutely partisan.

His great love, however, was law, not in the sense of representing a defendant in court or concluding real estate transactions, but as a force to improve the human condition. "The practising barrister," he wrote, "who refuses to allow himself to become narrowed to the shallow technicalities of his craft, who maintains broad human sympathies, who attempts to feed his legal principles with the vivifying food of the dynamic social sciences, who makes his voice felt within his profession and without on the side of needed reform, modern, and orderly and dispassionate consideration of public questions on their own merits, has a great and a demanding role to play in the salvation of his country." For Ken, that engagement in public life was critical; the lawyer's most important quality was a willingness to act for the betterment of society. The slide toward extremism in Europe moved him to support the aims of the League Against War and Fascism, an American organization established in 1933 to campaign for a social-ist alternative to right-wing politics, but he found its methods inadequate because they seemed more interested in talking about problems than work-ing to solve them. By the same token, he appreciated the thinking behind the League of Nations, which had emerged from the ashes of the First World War as a forum for resolving international conflict peacefully, but believed it had been fatally weakened from within; after years of regarding the League as "a convenient place for round table discussion but not for the dictation of strong coordinated action," world leaders had succeeded in making a mockery of the principle of collective security. If the drafters of the League of Nations covenant weren't going to act on their obligation to give the League some teeth and allow it to act, with force if necessary, to secure the rule of law, then it was up to the individual to take up the chal-lenge and do the job. He hoped that his own generation was willing to do its part; he was certainly ready to get involved in defending the values that he had come to love and respect, and declared that he was "keenly alive to the necessity of decisive action."[12]

Ken's application reveals that he had become just the kind of well-rounded person the Rhodes Scholarship was intended to assist. He was, to use Rhodes's words, one of "the best men for the world's fight." The Ontario Rhodes committee agreed; Ken would be one of the province's two representatives at Oxford.

THREE

SEARCHING FOR A PATH

On the morning of Thursday, 7 October 1937, with his hair neatly greased down and wearing his best grey suit, twenty-three-year-old Ken Macalister presented himself at the porter's lodge of New College, Oxford. He felt a bit dazed, for the last few months had been a whirl of packing and unpacking, shopping lists, telegrams, phone calls, and farewell parties. There had been so much to do before leaving Canada—moving out of his residence in Toronto, buying what he needed to survive in the damp English climate, arranging for steamer passage, making sure he had a place to live in Oxford. He even had to secure a medical certificate saying he was physically fit (there was no mention of his poor eyesight, something that would undoubtedly get worse with the volume of reading that would be expected of him) and free from disease. He also wanted to enrol in one of the Inns of Court, to which all practising lawyers in England must belong, to get a foot in the door of the legal profession, and the Rhodes people convinced the authorities in London to waive the customary one-hundred-pound deposit as long as Ken paid a twelve-pound fee in lieu of membership dues. But that was all in the past now; as he waited for the scout, the college employee who would take care of his day-to-day needs while he was in residence, Ken wondered what Oxford would hold for him.

Established by William Wykeham (who created the English public school) in 1370, New College was one of Oxford's most revered foundations. Architecturally and administratively, it served as a model for many of the institutions that followed, although few of them could match its breathtaking chapel and the cloisters that ringed its quadrangle. New College was nestled against the last crumbling pieces of the ancient walls of Oxford—when its first buildings were erected, it had been on the edge of town; by 1937, it was in the heart of the city. A short walk to the east, along the narrow sidewalks of Holywell Street, took you to Magdalen Grove and the Deer Park. To the south were Queen's and All Souls College and to the west, Hertford. In the midst of these bastions of the establishment stood Manchester College, the first institution to accept women to study for the non-conformist ministry. Nothing was very far from New College—not Manchester College to the north of it, not the Sheldonian Theatre with its graceful cupola, not the Science Museum guarded by a row of stone heads gazing at passersby, not that most famous of bookshops, Basil Blackwell's. There was a timelessness about Oxford that was impossible to miss. An economic blizzard had settled over much of the Western world, but this was one of Oxford's golden ages. With the soft click of croquet balls on college lawns, senior fellows gazing indulgently out from High Table at dining halls full of undergraduates, black-robed tutors sheltering from the rain under the Bridge of Sighs that vaulted over New College Lane—the troubles of the wider world seemed far away.

Soon after arriving in Oxford, Ken met the men who would guide his education. His tutor at New College would be David Boult, a very popular scholar who had been elected to a fellowship in law shortly after finishing his degree. Plagued by a weak heart that would kill him within a few years, at the age of thirty-four, Boult nevertheless gave everything he could to his college. He was wise beyond his years but close enough to his undergraduate days to remember what his students were going through, and they worshipped him for that. Ken's other contact in Oxford was a man who would have an enormous influence on his life, and who would become almost a surrogate father: Carleton Kemp Allen, known to his friends as "C.K." Formerly professor of jurisprudence, Allen was born in Australia and had himself come to Oxford on a travelling scholarship before the First World

War; so he was sensitive to the challenges that a student from the colonies faced upon arrival in the institution's hallowed halls. He was also a military man; he had enlisted in January 1915 with the 13th Battalion, Middlesex Regiment, and had been badly wounded at Loos in 1915 and on the Somme in 1916, before winning a Military Cross in September 1918. Short and stocky with a neatly clipped moustache and a head of snow-white hair, he looked the part of the stern taskmaster. But Allen was more than he seemed. What his biographer called "a shrewdly dispassionate common sense" was matched by a deep empathy for the students. He had very strong likes and dislikes (he later refused, on principle, to use the National Health Service), but was scrupulously fair in everything he did.

As well as being one of the university's most respected legal scholars, Allen was the Oxford secretary to the Rhodes Trustees and warden of Rhodes House, where he lived with his wife, Dorothy, and their two children. Rhodes House, a luxurious thirty-room mansion on the north edge of Wadham College's old garden, had been built a decade earlier as the Oxford headquarters of the Rhodes Trust. It was a meeting place for visiting scholars and dignitaries, the site of almost daily cocktail parties and socials, and a safe haven for the nearly two hundred Rhodes Scholars in Oxford, for whose welfare the Allens were constantly looking out. Rhodes House was a place of comfort and warmth for the young men thousands of miles from home—with seven bathrooms, eight servants, central heating, and glorious views of the sturdy stone tower of New College and the stately copper beech trees that graced Wadham College garden, it was sometimes difficult to get the scholars to return to their lodgings.

As Ken surveyed his spartan room in New College, he couldn't help but wish that he was back on one of the overstuffed couches in the Allens' parlour. It may have been historic, but New College was cold, and he had been told that there wasn't much chance of convincing the scout to turn on the room's heat. The response to any such request was invariably that there would be no heat without a doctor's certificate. And the doctor, when approached by a student complaining of bronchitis or chilblains, inevitably declared that what the student needed wasn't heated rooms but some fresh air and exercise—perhaps on one of the university's rowing crews. But Ken wouldn't spend much time in his room. The Bodleian, perhaps the greatest library in the world, was just a few steps away and Ken would spend countless hours there—once he had signed the centuries-old declaration pledging, among other things, that he wouldn't set fire to any of the books. In the winter, when the frost whitened the grass on the quadrangle, there was always a fire and a cup of tea in the Junior Common Room. On a warm spring day, he would lounge under a tree in Christ Church Meadow, often for an entire afternoon, until either the tolling of the bell in Tom Tower or the gathering darkness told him that he had long ago missed dinner.

Ken loved the atmosphere of Oxford, but was disappointed by the academic side of life. It was a very flexible system, which appealed to a self-starter like Ken—there were no set textbooks to get through, no appointed class times, and only the occasional lecture by a faculty member (this was one of the few opportunities for an undergraduate to hear from the senior faculty), and even those were optional. Everything revolved around individual work with the tutor. Every week, Ken would head over to David Boult's lodgings, take a chair before the fire, and read the paper that he had researched and written since their last meeting. The tutor's job was to question the student to ensure a grasp of the material—"Doubtful statements are challenged and proof demanded. Careless analysis of cases is corrected. Cases omitted or neglected are called to mind," recalled one former student[1]—and Boult was a sympathetic yet firm teacher, and a very pleasant chap besides. But Ken had a degree in his pocket, and had already been through Roman law, jurisprudence, English law, and international law. Now he found himself studying the basics with people who were three or four years younger. Soon, he started to get a little bored.

Part of the Rhodes stipend was intended to pay for travel, of the kind that would broaden the scholar's outlook and experience, so Ken decided to cross the Channel and see what the Continent was like. And, if he was going to master the two legal traditions of Canada, the English common and the French civil, he had better learn the language of France. He had studied French through high school and university but that was no substitute for being immersed in it. To get that kind of experience, he would see about living with a French family, preferably one that didn't speak too much English. No account of his travels has survived so it's impossible to say where he started, but we know where he finished: at Lisieux, in the Calvados region of Normandy. Perhaps with the help of someone at New College, Ken made contact with Jacques Lucas, who had recently retired from a professorship at l'Université de Paris. Lucas said he would be delighted to have the young Canadian as a guest in his home, to introduce him to French customs and show him what life was like in a fairly typical modest French home. The Lucases were wonderful hosts, and excellent teachers. Professor Lucas could speak English, but he didn't resort to it unless Ken was really stuck. As the weeks of the summer holiday (or the Long Vacation, as it was known in Oxford) passed, Ken's French gradually improved; by the time he returned to Oxford in late August, he was completely fluent, although with a strong Canadian accent.

In the spring of 1939, Ken approached the Rhodes Trustees with an unusual request. As his second year of Oxford passed, he had found it increasingly difficult to focus on his work. He still enjoyed the meetings with David Boult, but was happiest when their conversation strayed from that week's paper. Every week, it got harder to keep his mind on the material, and easier to find an excuse to put it aside. But when Ken was in France, everything was different. He could listen for hours as Professor Lucas talked about the French legal tradition, and was fascinated by the contrasts with the British system of law that he knew so well; the fact that he was doing it all in another language simply made it more challenging, and therefore more appealing. Once again, he planned to spend the summer with the Lucases at Lisieux, but now he asked for the trustees' permission to remain there for his third year of study, to take courses at a French university. They didn't look favourably on the request, which was quite out of the ordinary, and provided an interesting assessment of Ken's achievements and potential. "This man is rather a puzzle to me," wrote one: "He came with a great reputation from Toronto, but his tutor, Mr. Boult of New College, has never been convinced that he was a first-class man, and I confess that that has been my own impression . . . I shall be rather surprised if he gets a First . . . He has been discontented at Oxford and complains that he is merely repeating what he already knows. I don't think he will get much out of a third year at Oxford, but, on the other hand, I do not believe that he will derive very much from a year at a French University. I have a suspicion that this is merely an escape, as he does not want to do the B.C.L. [Bachelor in Civil Law] at Oxford, and his tutor thinks that he will be very stale and spiritless if he does." Ken had made the application on the basis of a desire to obtain a better grounding in Quebec law before returning to Toronto to practise, but the trustees thought his time would be better spent in Quebec than in France. On the whole, they concluded that, in the third year of his studies, Ken should take up another subject that would give him insight into the civil law of France and Quebec, rather than studying in France. As a result, concluded the report, "I am not disposed to recommend his application."[2]

Of course, Ken knew nothing about the trustees' deliberations but he may well have expected them to want some evidence of his good intentions. So he put his mind into his work and surprised everyone—himself as well as his tutor—by winning a first in jurisprudence. This fine result changed the minds of the Rhodes Trustees. They decided that, given his outstanding academic performance, Ken would be allowed to spend his third year at l'Université de Paris, and could collect his scholarship stipend while he was enrolled there. Their only caveat was that, should the European situation deteriorate, he was to get in touch with Rhodes House as soon as possible and arrange to return to Oxford. As he packed his bags for France at the end of Whitsun (spring) term, Ken pondered the advice. He didn't like the idea of running back to England in the event of war, because it went against everything he believed about the individual taking personal action. If something did happen on the Continent, he wanted to see it close up.

•

In July 1938, with only a knapsack of clothes and toiletries, a few books, and his typewriter, Frank Pickersgill arrived in Paris. Jack had arranged (and paid) for him to spend a year in Europe, studying, improving his French, and maybe even taming the restless spirit that he had inherited from his father. If everything went according to plan, Frank would come back to Canada in the summer of 1939, ready to settle down and find a permanent job, perhaps with the federal government or a university.

It wasn't his first trip to Europe. In 1934, while he was still an undergraduate, Frank had ridden a succession of cabooses to Montreal (an experience that was remarkable, he wrote, chiefly for the railwaymen's astonishing vocabulary of profanities) to board a cattle boat, the *Manchester Producer*. The name makes it sound like the flagship of a prosperous Midlands shipping company, but it was small and dirty, and rolled so much that the passengers were in a near-constant state of seasickness. Over the ten-day crossing, Frank could keep down only a dozen apples, a dozen oranges, some cookies, a few potatoes, and dill pickles. On this diet, and with stomach churning, he had to water and feed the cattle, a task made bearable only by the companionship of his fellow sufferers, many of whom were, like Frank, of northern English stock.

Arriving in England, Frank had met up with his Winnipeg friend Brock King and the two set out on a typical undergraduate grand tour, of the kind that young North Americans have been doing for decades. With second-hand bicycles, a pup tent, backpacks, and only enough money to get them to the next poste restante (and the next cheque from Jack Pickersgill), Frank and Brock hit as many of the highlights as they could in six weeks—Stratford-upon-Avon ("jam factories, souvenir-vendors and Anne Hathaway's beastly cottage"); Oxford (where they looked up former University of Manitoba classmate W.L. Morton, who was there on a Rhodes Scholarship); London; Windsor Castle; the Tuileries ("appalling statuary, and ghastly ornate architecture") and Notre Dame in Paris; the Black Forest; and the Hofbrauhaus in Munich.

Frank's letters home were just what one would expect from a university-educated teenager on his first great adventure. There's a little bit of New World superiority, some wide-eyed awe, the blithe egotism that only a nineteen-year-old tourist in Europe can exhibit, and a turn of phrase that owed a lot to P.G. Wodehouse. Things were "really too quaint" or "rather a bore," and people might be "faintly amusing" or "frightfully kind." He had little good to say about France; the people "look as though they'd murder their mother for tuppence" and Paris was "a definite bore" that he "rather abominated" because no one would do anything without a tip. He was annoyed, for example, when a Parisienne gave him a few centimes to stand in line and buy a train ticket for her. Germany, on the other hand, was a revelation. The Nazis had been in power for a little more than eighteen months and the horrific excesses of the regime were in the future. In the summer of 1934, they were most concerned with proving their respectability to the world. As one journalist put it, they aimed to cover Germany in a coat of cheap whitewash so that no one saw the rot within—and most people were completely fooled. Frank certainly was. In his eyes, the beer was tasty, the people were friendly, Nazi drinking songs were terribly good fun—all in all, he confided to his University of Manitoba friend Helen Magill, the more he saw of Germany, "the more I come to admire Hitler and Co."[3]

When he returned to Europe in the summer of 1938 at the age of twenty-three, Frank was a very different man. Gone was his gee-whiz enthusiasm, replaced by a serious cast of mind and, it must be said, a fragile self-confidence. Not long before he had left Canada, he spent an afternoon in Toronto with Brock King. They drank far too much at an impromptu going-away party for a friend near Union Station, then headed north, stopping at the Belvedere at Bay and Dundas Streets. Over steaming bowls of chili, they talked about what lay ahead. Brock was starting to make his way in the advertising business, but Frank was at loose ends. "I know that Frank was uncertain about many things," Brock later wrote. "Frank was searching for something . . . He wasn't interested in and didn't know about the kind of experience I was trying to hack out for myself." Despite the hilarity of their impromptu party, Brock recalled that they parted on a sombre note: "There was a general sadness about Frank which I often wished I could help."[4] Brock wasn't the only person to recognize a change. Other friends noticed that Frank tended to brood more—he wasn't exactly depressed, just dissatisfied. He had loved nothing more than being the class clown at the University of Manitoba, but that didn't hold his interest anymore (in early 1939, he wrote to his university friend George Ford that anyone who didn't die of shame when pondering their undergraduate years deserved harsh punishment). Now, it was time to move on to something else. The trouble was that he didn't know what else to move on to. He had thought that his future might lie in university teaching, but now he wasn't so sure. St. Augustine fascinated him personally, but the subject never really took firm hold of his imagination as the basis for a career choice. Writing a thesis was a bit of a chore, but he could easily write long letters to his friends about religion, politics, economics, international affairs. He couldn't imagine himself in a normal job, even one that offered the relative freedom of a faculty position—was it because of the distractions of student life, or his own lack of motivation? He really didn't know, but perhaps he would find the answer in Europe.

Frank had lots of contacts in Paris, and planned to look up the medievalists he had studied with at the University of Toronto, Étienne Gilson and Jacques Maritain. He also had a friend there: Kathleen (Kay) Moore, who had won a scholarship from the University of Manitoba that enabled her to study at the Sorbonne. She had been in Paris since 1936, and would eventually take a position with the British Embassy. She was Frank's first call when he reached France, and Kay introduced Frank to some of her friends in Paris, including Madeleine Probert, who worked at the British Embassy, and a young Scottish woman named Mary Mundle. In Mary, Frank found a formidable opponent; she was strong-willed and intelligent, and her soft Lowland brogue camouflaged the steadfastness with which she expressed herself. She and Frank soon developed a hearty dislike for each other, forcing Kay to act as peacemaker between them whenever

Frank visited. Many an evening passed in the Hotel Lenox with Mary and Frank locked in a heated argument, and Kay desperately trying to calm them both down.

Although Frank was a frequent visitor to the Hotel Lenox, he had found himself a room at the Maison Canadienne, a residence of l'Université de Paris on the boulevard Jourdan; Jack had recommended it, having stayed there on his first trip to Europe in 1928. It housed a couple of dozen Canadian students who were studying in Paris (most of them from Quebec), an equal number of French students, and a rotating cast of others who stopped in for varying periods while they were on vacation. It was cheap and comfortable, and would do until Frank arranged his academic standing, but he didn't intend on staying there—with so many Canadians in residence, Frank feared he would get into the habit of speaking too much English.

He needn't have worried. Soon after settling at the Maison Canadienne, Frank fell in with a group of French students—Jean Pouillon, Robert Lapassade, Marc Maurette, Jean Varille, Henri Robillot—who were enrolled at the university. Frank felt "instinctively and almost immediately at home" with them, and marvelled that he had "never been anywhere before where I felt at ease with people so quickly."[5] Soon they were spending all their free time together, either at the Maison or at one of the dozens of cafés along the River Seine. A favourite haunt was the Café de Flore, where a jolly waiter named Jean Jezequellon adopted them and made sure that they were never without a round of coffee. They made for a boisterous table, and passersby would never have known that the tall, balding young man puffing furiously on the Gauloises bleues to which he had become addicted ("the habit costs 3c a day here & is not worth breaking for that,"[6] he wrote to Jack) wasn't a local. Frank's French, which had been very good at university ("Why can't you all speak French like Frank Pickersgill?" one of his professors was fond of asking his classes), quickly got even better, as did his knowledge of the country. He was desperate to learn everything about France and soaked up as much as he could. His new friends marvelled at how well he grasped the essence of the country. "Il avait pour la première fois de sa vie pris contact avec l'esprit

55

français universaliste, rationnaliste et une certaine bonne humeur générale de vie qu'il avait infiniment appréciée," Jean Varille later recalled. ("For the first time in his life he was in touch with the French spirit—universalist, rationalist, and with a general good humour toward life that he truly appreciated.") Frank basked in the atmosphere of the famous Left Bank of the River Seine, which had been the meeting place of expatriate writers and artists from around the world since the nineteenth century. Painters Pablo Picasso and Henri Matisse and philosopher Jean-Paul Sartre had been fixtures in its restaurants and cafés; the enigmatic Irish novelist James Joyce had frequented the Hotel Lenox; and the American writers Alice B. Toklas and Gertrude Stein had for decades offered an entree into the Paris intelligentsia. Frank, who had savaged all things French on his earlier trip, fell in love with the country, so much so that he sensed himself drifting away from Canada. In one letter, he mused that he had acclimatized himself so well to living in France that he was afraid of returning home. "The only thing that worries me now," he wrote to Jack, "is that I'm beginning to get a queer feeling about Canada, which makes me wonder if I'm losing my moorings."[7]

Before long he had his studies arranged. He had originally enrolled in the Alliance Française, the famous language school on the boulevard Raspail, but found the courses too basic to be of any use. So he applied to the Faculty of Letters at l'Université de Paris to do his doctorate on later Scholasticism, a method of learning taught in medieval universities that emphasized the importance of reason. He was very interested in the relationship between faith and reason, and eventually decided to study the life and thought of Gregory of Rimini, an Augustinian hermit who became master of theology in Paris in 1345. He never did track down Étienne Gilson, but Jacques Maritain suggested that Frank spend a few weeks at a monastery in Belgium, reading under the direction of a noted medievalist. Rather to his surprise, he found the asceticism of the monks refreshing; far from the distractions of the Left Bank, he had no trouble working for twelve or fourteen hours a day. He followed that with a trip to Germany to brush up on his language skills, and he spent the Christmas 1938 holidays in Rome with Madeleine Probert.

By the time he returned to Paris in January 1939, Frank's plans had changed. The visit to Germany had merely confirmed his love of France—"Gosh I like this country," he wrote to his family. "I think it was a great mistake to come here in 1934—I was too adolescent to appreciate any of it. The idea of preferring Germany to France rather appals me now."[8] But it had also convinced him that all was not right in central Europe. It was a very different place from the one that the starry-eyed young man had visited in 1934. The Nazis had lost interest in putting on a good show for visitors, and the evidence of the drift to extremism was all too clear. In March 1936, German troops returned to the Rhineland, a clear violation of the Treaty of Versailles that had ended the First World War. In September 1938, six months after Austria had been taken over by the Nazis in a "friendly" annexation known as the Anschluss, the great powers of Europe bent to Adolf Hitler's demands and made him a present of Czechoslovakia. The war against the Jews had reached a new level of intensity with Kristallnacht in November 1938, when thousands of Jewish-owned businesses were ransacked and their owners imprisoned. The true nature of the regime was now obvious. Nazi Germany wasn't just barbaric, Frank wrote to Helen Magill in Canada; it was possessed by some "alien spiritual force" that had taken hold of good, decent Germans and turned them into monsters.[9] He characterized Nazism as a kind of viral religion that had infected the country. Nothing was safe from it: the art of the Third Reich "reeks of sadism"; the school system had been perverted to the point that it produced National Socialist Spartans; the family was being destroyed as the Hitler Youth undermined parental authority and replaced it with party loyalty; and the long tradition of German diplomacy was just a vague memory in a society that regarded other peoples as bestial and subhuman.

As he and his French friends debated the consequences of the new faith for the world, Frank wondered why he would start a career studying the fourteenth century when the twentieth was so much more exciting.

Gregory of Rimini seemed like very dull stuff, and pointless too: "As a solution to world problems or even as a valid approach to them," he wrote to a friend, "the relevance of medieval philosophy seems to me to be virtually null . . . I want less and less to be an academic, and more and more to get my teeth into something." He began to think about a career in the civil service, although when Jack suggested he write the civil service exam, Frank wondered if he was up to the task: "I have less confidence in myself than ever," he confided to Jack.[10] Much more appealing was journalism. When he thought about interviewing labour leaders, politicians, or novelists for the newspaper or making radio broadcasts explaining the subtleties of European politics, Frank felt more enthusiasm than Gregory of Rimini had ever made him feel. More and more, Scholasticism took a back seat to fascism, communism, anarchism, and a dozen other ideologies that were percolating through Europe (after due consideration, Frank pronounced himself a syndicalist who thought that labour union federations should run government and industry).

In the spring of 1939, Jean Pouillon introduced Frank to a good friend named Jean-Paul Sartre, an up-and-coming writer whose new book, *La nausée* (*Nausea*), was sweeping France. Sartre's fatalistic plots and frustrated characters had added a new word to the language—existentialism—and now he was looking for a translator to take his work to a bigger audience. Frank jumped at the chance, and within a few weeks had translated about fifty pages of *La nausée* into English. He was all set to send them off to publishers in Britain and the United States; if things went well, he would work on translating Sartre's next book. The first responses were disappointing (neither Random House nor Faber and Faber showed any interest in the manuscript), but another good friend of Frank's, Girija Mookerjee, offered to help find a publisher. Mookerjee was the European correspondent for a newspaper in Delhi, and had been introduced to Frank at a dinner at Kay Moore's; he had friends at Allen & Unwin, the renowned English publisher, and sent two chapters of *La nausée* to London for their consideration.

All in all, Frank's mood was buoyant, despite continuing stomach trouble (which may well have been imagined) and wisdom teeth that were acting up and eventually had to be pulled. The fact that he still relied on Jack for money gnawed at him, and occasionally he fell into a funk as he considered his still-uncertain future. "I can't get rid of a haunting fear of (a) unemployment or (b) being a bank clerk or something; & also a feeling . . . that I'm not justifying my existence and ought to be working," he wrote to Jack. When friends wrote to him about their work, he was seized by pangs that he was living "in a rather useless and butterfly fashion" and not doing anything of substance. But most of the time, he wrote, "I still think . . . that some day I may be of use."[11] So he made the most of being a penniless student in Europe, and looked at every experience as material for his career in journalism. In the summer of 1939, he decided to head east, to get a better handle on the situation in Poland. It wasn't his favourite country—the language was impenetrable and Canadian newspapers didn't seem too interested in stories about Poland—but he took it all in stride. "I'm going to stick it out in Yurrup to the last ditch," he wrote to Jack's new wife, Margaret, from Poland. It was the experience of a lifetime, and the bumps along the road gave him no reason to reconsider what he had written to Jack that April: "I've never had such an exciting and happy year I don't think, & I see no reason for it not continuing like that."[12]

Only one thing stood in his way. On 27 July 1939, not long after reaching Poland, Frank had written a cheerful letter to George Ford. He talked about the future of Danzig and East Prussia, Polish ambitions, and the conduct of British Prime Minister Neville Chamberlain. It was all fascinating stuff and, with his usual perceptiveness, he predicted another grave crisis in early September: "I suspect it will be war this time."[13]

Four

The Darkness Descends

The blow fell while Frank was in Poland. In the last week of August, the drift toward war started to seem inexorable. On the first of September, German divisions swept across the frontier into Poland; days later, they had advanced hundreds of miles and were threatening Warsaw. By then, Frank was long gone. He had left his lodgings in Kalisz, west of Warsaw, as soon as the situation began to deteriorate, and when he got to the Polish capital, the advice from the British Embassy was unequivocal: get out now. There was no way back across Germany, so Frank took a train south to Romania in the hope of getting some sort of press accreditation that would allow him to travel easily in eastern Europe. The British consul in Bucharest was just as adamant; he told Frank that such permits were available only to journalists working for specific press outlets, and put him aboard the Simplon Express, bound for France. On 3 September 1939, the day that Britain entered the war and nine days after leaving Warsaw, Frank reached Paris.

He was taken aback by the transformation of the city he loved. The first thing he noticed, as he described in an article written later that fall, was a stunned silence that had settled over Paris. The metro was packed, even more than it usually was, but there was an "inexpressible gloom oozing up out of the subway's heat." People carrying gas masks hurried along the sidewalks, past shops that had been closed up because of the impending mobilization. They whispered to each other with grave concern about decrees that they put aside three days' worth of provisions in case of emergency and keep their windows and shutters closed. Even politics had ceased to interest that most politically minded race. All they could think of was the present catastrophe. Even so, "There was more than tragedy about the Parisians' faces that day; it was vaguer than tragedy. They all looked as though they had been hit by a blunt instrument." Frank, whose mood had been sombre for some time, was infected by the general pessimism. He spent a lot of time with Kay Moore and Madeleine Probert at the Hotel Lenox (Frank moved in there too, because the Maison Canadienne had closed for the duration of the war), but there was little merriment in his visits. "God, I feel dismal," he would mutter as he threw himself into an armchair. "And he would look dismal," recalled Madeleine, "even to the lobes of his ears."[1]

Poland capitulated at the end of September and then . . . nothing. France didn't feel the hammer blow, nor did Belgium, or Britain. In Paris, people began filling the sidewalk cafés again. Shops reopened, and lines started forming at the cinemas. The shock was passing, and Parisians were getting back to normal. Perhaps things wouldn't be as bad as we had feared, they allowed themselves to think. They even started talking politics again. But it would take more than a few weeks of normalcy to return Frank to an even keel. As he wrote to Jack, he had suffered "the general collapse in the space of a few days of every idea private and personal or political that I may have had."[2]

And his hopes of finding a way to make a living were thrown into disarray. A university job suddenly seemed very unlikely, although it had never looked very promising. The week after the war began, Jack had put Frank's name in for a position at Dalhousie University, but nothing came of it. There was talk of him finding work with the Department of External Affairs—he passed the civil service exam with ease and External was prepared to rush him to London to take a French competency exam—or running the information service that the Canadian Institute of International Affairs was setting up (another opportunity engineered by Jack), but neither appealed very much to Frank. He candidly admitted that if he joined the diplomatic corps "it would be with the intention of getting out, into writing at the first good chance I had." He had hopes of being called up by the French government for civil air defence work or of joining the Red Cross as an ambulance driver, but nothing panned out. The only firm offer of employment he had was from a Paris dairy looking for someone to drive a milk truck—something that excited him because it would allow him to write articles "from the inside and under by a Parisian working man."[3] But a job like that would require him mastering the mysteries of automobiles, something that had never been his strong suit back in Canada.

The most promising avenue still seemed to be freelance journalism. Frank had travelled widely, had an excellent grasp of French politics, and was shaping up to be quite a first-class writer. He spent hours banging away on his typewriter, then sent (or rather Jack did, acting as his copy-editor, secretary, and literary agent) articles to dozens of newspapers and magazines—the *Winnipeg Free Press, Harper's*, the *Louisville Times, New Republic*, the *Baltimore Evening Sun*. But writing turned out to be a more frustrating career path that he had imagined. *Saturday Night* paid $22 for an article on German politics and the *University of Toronto Quarterly* paid $25 for "The French Press and War Aims," but most media outlets he approached were a tough sell; many of them never even responded to his inquiries. The Paris press association, Opéra Mondiale, commissioned him to write a series of articles on Canadian issues, then had a change of heart and stopped returning his calls. The *Vancouver Sun* published a few essays in September 1939 but never paid for them, while the *Winnipeg Free Press* sent Frank a cheque that was refused by the bank. All the tantalizing leads that he turned up—doing a short broadcast for CBC radio on Paris in war-time, translating the work of a Czech journalist from German into English, working for Radio Paris Mondiale—disappeared into thin air as quickly as they emerged. Frank was right back where he started from—relying on cash advances from the Canadian Legation in Paris to meet his living expenses (Jack had joined the staff of Prime Minister Mackenzie King's office in 1937, a position that came with many advantages, not the least of which was that any British or Canadian consular office would advance cash to Frank on the strength of Jack's promise to pay), and asking Jack if he would continue to support him.

Logically, Frank should have gone back to Canada for steady work but personal attachments were holding him in Paris. "My friends over here mean as much if not more to me than my Canadian ones," he wrote to Jack, and one was especially important to him: a young woman named Odette Schwartz, who worked in a bookstore that he frequented. Frank, with his intensity of emotion, had a history of falling hard for women who attracted him, and neither war nor poverty changed that. He referred to Odette as "le beau visage de la France," and admitted that to leave Paris at that time would be "to put it mildly difficult." Later, Odette of the bookshop was supplanted in his heart by Fleurette, the sister of his good friend Marc Maurette. "I've got it awfully bad this time," he wrote to Jack, "and she's absolutely eclipsed anything else in the female species that I've ever encountered."[4] The problem with Fleurette was that she was engaged to another of Frank's good friends, Henri Robillot. But regardless of how much he was infatuated with Odette and Fleurette, his attachment to France was even stronger: "Paris and its population since the outbreak of war have convinced me in a fashion absolutely personal and sincere (not theoretical) that this country = everything decent, human that is going." He found himself becoming a French nationalist, for whom "the eclipse of France seems like the end of the world." To leave when France's fate was hanging in the balance was unthinkable: "Je suis si plein de honte et de dégoût qu'il faut que je fasse quelque chose—sans ça, je n'en reviendrais jamais." ("I am so full of shame and disgust that I must do something—if I don't, I could never come back.")[5]

But Frank's inability to find anything useful to do fed a feeling of impotence that slowly turned into bitterness and anger. He tried to work out his emotions in his letters home, confessing to his state of mental uncertainty and despair, only to feel guilty the next day for burdening Jack and Sara with his complaints. A series of health problems (some of them real, some of them probably imagined), including bouts of stomach trouble, liver problems, impacted wisdom teeth, and a cold that never seemed to go away, made things worse and frustration began to consume him. He was in no hurry to get into uniform—"I'm not going to make the world safe for democracy unless I have to," he wrote to Sara Pickersgill, insisting that he would wait to be conscripted rather than enlist—but was growing increasingly angry at his enforced idleness. His strongest emotion, though, was a determination to do almost anything to avoid leaving France: "When I think of these people I know & these towns I know it almost makes me scream. I've got to make every conceivable effort to stay in France until this war is over. I think now if I were in Canada I'd go stark staring nuts from wondering what was going on & what was happening to certain people . . . The only solid & sure thing I feel is that I'd be prepared to do anything to stay in France so long as this thing lasts . . . Please God let me stay in France at least until this war is over."[6]

In April 1940 the Phony War finally ended when the Nazis occupied Denmark and invaded Norway. The Norwegians put up a stout defence, but the issue was never really in doubt and within a few weeks, the Third Reich controlled the North Sea coast of Scandinavia. It was only a matter of time before the Nazis turned westward. Frank happened to be visiting the Canadian Legation on 15 May 1940 when shocking news came in from the front lines: German divisions, which had rolled through the Low Countries five days earlier, had broken through French defences at Sedan, just south of the Ardennes forest. Unless they were stopped, they would punch a corridor through to the English Channel, isolating over 300,000 French and British troops in the Pas de Calais and coming within easy striking distance of Paris. Over the next couple of weeks, the mood in the French capital was sombre. As Georges Vanier, appointed to head the Canadian Legation in Paris just a year earlier, walked to work each day, he couldn't help but notice how much the people had changed: "At the café tables on the boulevards, the faces were grave and there was no gaiety." By the beginning of June, French armies had launched a number of counterattacks but none of them gave more than a momentary check to the German advance. As the panzers closed in on Paris from the northwest, the smokescreens that preceded them were carried into the city. The smoke lay over Paris "like a black pall," wrote Vanier. "It carried with it the smell of cordite—it was the smell of the battlefield again . . . Thick rolling clouds were pushed on by a strong wind which raised dust and smoke into swirling eddies: papers in the streets flew about in a crazy fashion—nature responding to man's folly."[7] On the ninth of June, Vanier learned unofficially that the defeat of the French armies was only a matter of time and that plans were in train for the government to evacuate the capital. That was enough for him—he put his staff to work preparing to move the legation to the Château de l'Hérissodière at Pernay, near Tours. Just before midnight on the tenth, he left Paris with the last of his staff.

The following day, Frank made his way to the legation. The previous week, an interview with legation staff for a job with External Affairs had gone well, but with every passing day he became more certain that his place was in France: "If I do get into the war I would rather be with the French than anyone else—because I'd get along better with them and there would be more reality about it," he wrote to Brock King on the ninth of June. "I am completely seduced by the French people and by the country and am going to do everything in my power to stay here at least as long as I can . . . Coming back to Canada would be a last resort."[8] After much soul-searching, he decided that it was time to leave Paris and wanted to pick up one last cash advance before making his escape. But the building was empty, with only a note pinned to the door: "Following a communication received from the Ministry of Foreign Affairs, the Canadian Minister and the personnel of the Legation have left Paris. The Ambassador of the United States has very kindly consented to take over the responsibility for the protection of Canadian Nationals and property. For any information required, please apply to the American Embassy, Place de la Concorde."[9] The concierge, who knew Frank well from previous visits, said that the legation had moved to

Pernay, southwest of Paris, so Frank decided that the best thing was to set out in pursuit. He used most of his remaining money to buy a bicycle and pedalled out of the city with just fifty francs left in his pocket.

It took him four days to cycle the 140 miles southwest to Pernay, only to get the worst possible news: the legation staff had left the day before, for Bordeaux. With only a couple of francs left, he was reluctant to chase Vanier—he would quite likely get there to find that he had already left. So Frank decided to look for help from his friends. Jean Pouillon had suggested that he head to Angers and find refuge with the Pouillon family, but the house was boarded up when he arrived. The city of Rennes was next on his list, but roads in that direction were clogged with refugees and impassable, so he headed for Plouvérin, where his waiter friend Jean Jezequellon had been posted with his infantry unit. But, on the way, Frank fell victim to fifth-column hysteria. A mob of terrified villagers, reinforced by a few equally terrified gendarmes, took him for a German parachutist and were all set to lynch him. Only with the greatest difficulty did Frank convince them to telephone Jean Jezequellon, who vouched for him but advised that he make for the coast of Brittany, where he just might be able to find a boat that was escaping to England. Jezequellon told him to call on his brother, a fisherman living near Quimper, who he thought might be able to provide shelter. But when he reached his destination on 19 June 1940, Frank found that the fisherman lived in a tiny cottage with barely enough space for his own needs and certainly no room for a boarder. So he decided to go to the *mairie* (town hall) in Quimper and ask for assistance. All he got was more bad news: the last Allied evacuation ship had left that very day.

It so happened that a young woman named Philippar was also at the mairie that day, and she learned of Frank's plight. The Philippar family lived in Paris, but they had a three-acre property with a small cottage in the nearby village of La Forêt-Fouesnant. They had bought it as a summer house, but relatives had encouraged them to leave Paris before the Germans arrived and take shelter in a safer location. Not long after, two other refugees arrived at their cottage: two boys, aged twelve and fifteen, the sons of a Parisian lawyer friend who also wanted to get his family as far away from the occupiers as possible. The Philippars gladly took them in, and were happy to offer Frank a haven as well.

After days on the run, La Forêt-Fouesnant was a very welcome respite for Frank. He spent his time cycling around the area, swimming and playing with the Philippars' daughter and the two young Parisians (even offering them some lessons in English), and working in the family's vegetable garden. He was able to get a small cash advance from American consular officials, but not enough to buy a sufficient number of cigarettes to feed his voracious nicotine habit. Knowing that he couldn't hide in Brittany forever, he started to make inquiries about getting permission to travel to Bordeaux in the unoccupied zone, in the hopes that the Canadian Legation staff was still there (he couldn't have known that Georges Vanier, the last Canadian official in France, had left St. Jean de Luz on the twenty-fourth of June aboard the British cruiser HMS *Galatea*). By now the German occupiers had arrived in Quimper, and Frank made no effort to conceal his identity from them; after all, he had already registered at the mairie as a refugee, and once the Germans began going through those lists, they would find him anyway.

In fact, the new rulers of France had already started on that. Not long after the British withdrawal from Dunkirk, German field police units fanned out across occupied France to make a census of all British Empire citizens living in the country. The Third Reich decided to intern some of these enemy aliens, and the arrests of all males between the ages of sixteen and sixty began. On 3 August 1940, Frank's idyllic existence at La Forêt-Fouesnant came to an end when three uniformed Germans arrived in a car driven by a local innkeeper, from whom they had requisitioned it. They were very polite, telling Frank that they had orders to take him to Quimper and giving him time to collect his belongings. He was allowed to go unescorted into the Philippars' house, and came out a few minutes later with a knapsack and an old quilt. After a few quick words of thanks to his hosts, he climbed in the car and was driven off to captivity. Half an hour later, the car pulled into Quimper and stopped in the courtyard of the Caserne de la Tour d'Auvergne.

The guards led Frank into the central building and down the stairs, to the dank and medieval-smelling cellblock, or *cachot*. He was pushed into a cell and, for a few minutes, couldn't see a thing. When his eyes finally got used to the dark and could make out a few shapes, he quickly wished that he was still blind. There were five cells, three that were only large enough for a single inmate (one of these was left empty), one that might accommodate four men, and one that could fit eight. Frank found himself in this last cell with nine other internees; altogether, there were twenty British civilians in the cells. There were no beds, just a stout wooden table that took up most of the space in the cell and served as the bed for everyone. The only saving grace was that the cell doors were left open, even at night, so that the odd beam of light filtered down from the main door to the cachot. The prisoners were allowed to move around as they wished, and could go into the fortress's courtyard or visit the washrooms. However, they couldn't communicate with the French prisoners of war who made up the bulk of the camp's population (Frank caught a glimpse of his old friend Jean Jezequellon, who had finally fallen afoul of the occupiers). For someone who was young and strong, like Frank, it wasn't too bad, but his fellow internees were much older and one was ill and unable to walk; for them, the eight days spent in the *caserne* (barracks) were a nightmare.

Their last night in the cachot was the worst. It was nearly eleven o'clock and the lights had been turned off, plunging the cells into complete blackness. Just as the internees were settling in, the door to the cellblock banged open and, in the beam of light, two German field policemen, apparently drunk, could be seen dragging in a French soldier whose jacket had been torn from him. They pushed the prisoner into the empty cell and began to beat him, evidently to extract some information. Whatever the Frenchman said wasn't good enough, because the policemen grew more outraged and the beating became more furious. The internees listened helplessly to the sickening sound of blows and kicks raining down on the soldier until finally the cachot grew silent again. One of the Germans grunted that the fellow was dead, and the murderers stumbled off, leaving the mess to be cleaned up by someone else.

The next day, 11 August 1940, the British colony of la Tour d'Auvergne was put into trucks and driven to an internment camp at Montreuil-Bellay, south of Angers. Anyone who imagined that the poor treatment in Quimper had been an aberration was quickly disabused of the notion. The camp had been established in 1938 to accommodate Republican refugees from the Spanish Civil War; when Frank arrived, there were still about thirty Spanish civilians there, although the Germans eventually shipped them to the island of Jersey, to labour on the underground fortifications there. In January 1940, the French government had taken over the camp to house workers at a nearby munitions factory, but in June, when the occupiers arrived, the huts were ringed with barbed wire and used to house French POWs and Allied civilians who had been swept up in western France.

It was a grim spot. The camp sat in the middle of a barren, treeless plain, and the wooden huts offered no protection from either the cold winter winds (only two buildings, the chapel and the school, were heated) or the blistering summer heat. The inmates, nearly 900 in number, were a mix of some fifteen different nationalities. Aside from the Spaniards, there were nearly 200 British internees, 100 or so German Jews, 250 Moroccans, 150 Indo-chinese, and a few dozen French soldiers waiting to be transferred to a POW camp. Some were bedridden, but the rest had to work ten hours a day in pointless menial labour projects. For sustenance, they were given a cup of hot water in the morning, a plate of thin soup made from mouldy potatoes at lunch, and a small chunk of bread and some pork fat in the evening; the prisoners' misery was merely increased by an outbreak of dysentery and by the camp commander's subsequent order that no one was allowed to visit the latrines at night. Small wonder that Frank lost forty pounds in his first two months in Montreuil-Bellay. The only bright spot was a friendship he struck up with Jean Boucher, a local contractor who was supervising some building work in the compound. They chatted whenever it was safe to do so, and Boucher complemented Frank on his command of the language; he also joked that Frank was far too English-looking to be mistaken for a Frenchman. In time, Boucher took to smuggling in bundles of food for Frank—a few vegetables one day, a small loaf of bread the next. It wasn't much, but it helped Frank's morale as much as his health.

Fortunately, the time at Montreuil-Bellay was short, for on 9 September 1940 the German military authorities decided that all British civilians in northern France should be collected in one camp, in the Paris suburb of St. Denis. There, in the middle of a working-class district of crumbling block tenements, stood La Grande Caserne, a military barracks dating from the French Revolution. Its new name was Frontstalag 220. Frank arrived on a brisk morning in early October 1940, and was registered by the camp adjutant. With that, he took on the first of many new identities: British Internee 1135. He then scanned the courtyard for a familiar face and was about to give up when he glanced at one of the caserne windows and saw Girija Mookerjee, whom he hadn't seen since before the war. Frank waved his arms madly, but Mookerjee simply looked puzzled; he later wrote that Frank looked so thin and dishevelled that he didn't recognize his old friend. But soon the penny dropped and Mookerjee rushed outside to welcome Frank and show him around.

The caserne was a four-storey fortress whose stonework had been blackened by decades of urban grime. At first, there was plenty of space for all the internees in the old barracks, where the large rooms had been furnished with double bunks and tables and chairs made from packing crates. But by late 1941, as the camp population approached two thousand, the Germans built six flimsy huts on the wire-enclosed exercise yard. Unfortunately for the inmates, the French labourers brought in for the project worked as they always did when under contract with the Nazis: as slowly and sloppily as possible. The result was barrack huts with gaps between the boards that made up the floors, walls, and ceiling, gaps through which dust in the summer and icy drafts in the winter flowed with ease. Frank had first-hand experience with the discomforts of the huts, for in July 1941 he was moved out of the caserne and into one of the new barracks.

As such camps went, the other amenities were quite good: a library with four thousand volumes and plenty of study space (Frank used it once to organize a discussion session on St. Augustine); sports equipment, including three billiard tables and two table tennis sets; flower and vegetable gardens; a theatre and a number of musical ensembles, including a choir, a classical orchestra, and a dance band; even weekly bus excursions in the countryside. Inmates could have visitors for thirty minutes every two weeks, and local aid organizations had arranged for surrogates to visit internees who had no friends or relatives in Paris. The latrine facilities were adequate, and there were enough shower facilities for each inmate to shower four times a week. Everything was managed by a Committee of Internees, which handled internal camp organization and relations with the Germans. But a prison is still a prison, no matter how good the entertainment.

An inmate's first concern is usually food, and on that score St. Denis was adequate if not generous. When the camp first opened in July 1940, the food was deplorable, but things had steadily improved since then. The rations were at the same level that German civilians received, and higher than those of French civilians, but in the spring of 1941, the prisoners began receiving a Red Cross food parcel every two weeks. With that, the British cooks who staffed the kitchen were able to prepare relatively nourishing, if dull, meals. Breakfast was a chunk of bread and coffee made from roasted malt with some real coffee mixed in, lunch was bread and vegetable soup (with meat three days a week), and dinner was usually coffee and bread with jam and butter. Sunday meals had cheese, baked potatoes, and extra meat; less welcome was lunch on Wednesdays, when the meat was usually lung. There was, however, a canteen where the prisoners could purchase fruit, vegetables, figs, sardines, cakes, vinegar, beer, lemonade, wine, and cigarettes. This last item was, for Frank, one of the most important. Still "un fumeur irréductible" (a diehard smoker), as fellow internee and Canadian architecture student Édouard Fiset wrote (the two had struck up a friendship after Frank gave

Fiset a pair of tennis shoes that he had received from home in exchange for a few packages of cigarettes), Frank spent most of the three hundred francs that the Swiss government provided to each prisoner every month to buy cigarettes and books.[10]

No matter how good the amenities and food, St. Denis wasn't a happy camp, because of conflicts among the inmates. The Committee of Internees was self-appointed rather than elected, and looked out for the interests of its own first. In practice, that meant that the British, Canadian (the majority of whom were priests or seminarians from Quebec), and Australian prisoners got first crack at any extras that were made available, while everyone else—the Maltese, the Cypriots, the Mauritians—had to make do with what was left over. Frank wasn't the only internee to notice that the members of the committee got on a little too well with their captors, and that the other prisoners suffered as a result. One day, while Frank was hanging around the main gate talking with passersby, a local curé arrived with a parcel of food intended for the Canadian prisoners. Frank immediately introduced himself and promised to share everything around, but when the curé asked him how they had enjoyed the last parcel he had brought, Frank was puzzled. He later learned that the parcel had been accepted by one of the French-Canadian priests, who had kept it for himself and his friends rather than dividing it up among all the Canadians. And the Germans did whatever they could to exploit these divisions, or create new ones. In 1941, a German officer appeared in the camp offering the French Canadians a chance to broadcast a message home to their relatives. A number of the priests were delighted and urged everyone to accept the offer, but Frank and a group of Canadian internees protested: the offer should be extended to all Canadians, or none. Seeing the dissent this caused, the Germans tried it again in 1942, raising the possibility that the rest of the French Canadians in the camp might be released. Again the priests were enthusiastic, but again Frank and the other Canadians spoke out: they would agree only to a release of all Canadian internees, not just a few based on ethnicity.

Frank quickly settled into the tedious routine of prison life. Breakfast was at 7:30, and then the prisoners were put on work details for the morning. Mostly, this involved tidying up the compound, emptying the garbage containers, sweeping out the huts, or trying to scrub the centuries of dust from the floors in the caserne. Frank and Girija Mookerjee found themselves chopping wood—Girija later recalled the German assumption that not even journalists could bungle that task. Frank loved the chance to return, at least in his mind, to happier days spent at Highbrow House, but he also enjoyed shovelling coal, although for a different reason: it gave him a chance to steal a little extra for his room. After lunch, often the beef and rutabaga stew that was the house specialty ("les odeurs assassinent les appétits les plus tenaces"—"the smells killed the most persistent appetites"—recalled one inmate[11]), the prisoners were free until 5 p.m. roll call. After dinner, they were free again until lights out. The afternoons were Frank's favourite time, because there were enough unusual characters in the camp to satisfy even his insatiable curiosity. In the summer of 1941, there were about twelve hundred men in the camp (around a hundred in their sixties, and perhaps twice as many teenagers), from all parts of the British Empire. At one time, there were more than a hundred Canadians in the camp, but many of the French-Canadian priests or seminarians were gradually released. Georges Savaria was a Canadian studying music in France, while Jean-Philippe Dallaire of Hull, Quebec, had been studying art in Paris (he later worked as an animator with the National Film Board). James Ashworth was the business manager of the continental edition of the London *Daily Mail* in Paris, and Arthur Briggs had played with some of the best known jazz bands in Germany before the Nazis decided that jazz was too decadent and should be banned. There was a British Army officer who had given up his commission to become a Trappist monk and whose brown cassock and flowing white beard, combined with his unfailing good humour, gave him an air of almost saintly goodness, and a Sikh soldier who had stayed in France after the Great War, despite the fact that he was illiterate and could speak only his own dialect. There were no end of stories to hear in St. Denis, and

Frank spent hours chatting with his fellow inmates, getting into the habit of drinking endless cups of tea in the process.

And the camp certainly knew how to celebrate the holidays. For Christmas 1941, Frank and another inmate wrote a musical comedy that was performed to appreciative crowds. For Christmas dinner that year, everyone in Frank's hut pooled their resources and came up with a meal that would have done any chef proud: oysters, moules marinière, chili con carne (Frank's own contribution), four bottles of good wine, and two bottles of gros rouge. New Year's dinner of coques and beefsteak frites, which would have been a treat at any other time, seemed positively plebeian by comparison. Even more than the special occasions, Frank looked forward to every other Thursday, when he was allowed visits from friends. Jean Pouillon, Marc Maurette, and Robert Lapassade visited him at every opportunity, bringing small packages of food (saved from their own rations, which were hardly generous) and any little comforts they could manage, from darning supplies to a mouth organ. Jean Jezequellon, who had been released from captivity, brought him pastries and sweets that weren't available at the canteen, and the two chatted about their meeting in Brittany in 1940. His old friends would soon prove to be much more useful.

For weeks, Frank had been mulling over ways to get out of the camp. He thought it might be possible to disguise himself as a priest and walk straight through the main gate, and even went so far as to look for the proper clothing. He approached his friend William Moran, to whom he had been teaching Latin, and asked if there was any way he could get a curate's robe and collar. Moran knew many divinity students in Paris and was able to get a contact to smuggle the clothing into St. Denis. When Frank put it on, Moran decided that, if he weren't quite so tall, he could pass for a typical French parson. But it quickly became apparent that a tall, balding priest was far too conspicuous and would certainly arouse the interest of the guards on the gate. Then, Frank struck up a friendship with Whitmore Hicks, a British subject who was raised in Paris and whose first language was French. Hicks's father and brother were in St. Denis as well, but he had never considered escaping for fear that reprisals might be taken against his mother and sister, who were still living in Paris. But when a few internees broke out of the camp and Hicks learned that no action had been taken against their families, he resolved to give it a try himself.

Hicks had friends on the Committee of Internees who got him a job cleaning the offices in the German administrative building, outside of the barbed wire but inside the high brick wall that surrounded the caserne. He always did the cleaning on Saturday afternoon and, because there wasn't another roll call until Monday morning, it would allow a good thirty-six hours' head start before his escape was discovered. But how to get over the wall? In snooping around the offices as he cleaned, Hicks immediately saw the possibilities of the camp censor's office, in one corner of the compound. It was farther from the guard posts than any other building, and had a barred window that looked out over the street. One of the camp officers lived in a flat above the office, but he left every Saturday at noon to stay with his mistress in Paris. Their plan, then, was simple: Hicks would get Frank posted to the work detail, and some Saturday they would hide in the officer's flat instead of returning to the compound after work. Once night fell, they would return to the censor's office, saw through one of the bars, and climb through the window to freedom. Eventually, they would make their way south, to Vichy France. When the French government had capitulated in 1940, one of the conditions was that only the northern part of the country would be occupied; the south would exist as a "free" enclave administered by a Nazi-sympathizing government at Vichy. There, Frank and Hicks would be beyond the reach of the German occupiers.

Hicks had no problem getting Frank assigned to his detail, and for a few weeks they cleaned the offices together, coming and going at the proper times and making sure that the guards got used to seeing both of them in the administrative building on Saturdays. All they needed now was a hacksaw and the key to the officer's flat. This is where Frank's friends proved to be indispensable. The officer was careless with his key and Hicks took it from the lock while he was cleaning the building. He had in his pocket a small box with some modelling clay in it; it took only a few seconds to make an impression of the key in the clay and return it to the door lock. On the next visiting day, Frank slipped the box to Robert Lapassade and two weeks later Robert returned with a freshly made key that he palmed to Frank as they shook hands. Lapassade also agreed to find a hacksaw, which he would mail to Hicks in a large loaf of bread (because Hicks was in the parcels office so frequently, the Germans had lost interest in searching his mail and it was unlikely that the saw would be discovered). They had already decided to make their break as soon as the hacksaw arrived; Frank had seen an escape plan betrayed by a prisoner at Montreuil-Bellay, and he had no faith that their secret could be kept. And they already had almost everything they needed. The pair had sold their belongings to collect as much money as they could. Frank really needed a pair of good, strong boots—he had asked Jack to send him a pair the previous summer and watched his incoming mail eagerly—but when Hicks dug a hacksaw and three blades out of a loaf on Friday, 6 March 1942, Frank knew he would have to make do without the boots.

The following day, Frank and Hicks tried to go about their business as usual, doing their chores and having their meals as if it was a day like any other. After lunch, they drew their cigarette ration for the month and, at about 2:30 in the afternoon, presented themselves at the gate with their work passes. As they had hoped, the guard barely looked at them as they strolled casually toward the censor's office, fighting the temptation to turn around and see if they were being watched. Once they were safely inside, Frank crossed the room to the window and looked anxiously up and down the street: Lapassade had promised to come to the prison every Saturday at 3 p.m. and, if he saw Frank in the window, tell him where and when they should meet. Sure enough, a few minutes after three, Frank spotted his friend in a shop across the street. With barely a glance at the window, Lapassade and his girlfriend walked away from the shop and past the censor's office. As they passed Frank, Lapassade said in a low but distinct voice, "Gare du Nord, onze heures." Seconds later, the couple disappeared around the corner.

Hicks got right to work on the window bar, but the hacksaw made such a racket that they decided to wait until well after dark to saw their way to freedom, to make sure that the street outside the office was deserted. So they had some time to pass. Frank and Hicks locked themselves in the upstairs flat, took the liberty of brewing some tea, and made themselves comfortable. It was after midnight before they decided it was safe to begin work again. They returned to the censor's office and Hicks started on the bar. The saw made a terrible noise and every time it squealed against the metal they both listened intently for the sound of approaching jackboots. The hours passed—the iron bar was proving to be more stubborn than they had expected—but a little after 4 a.m., Hicks finally cut it through. They waited a few more hours until there were some pedestrians to blend in with and, as soon as the right moment presented itself, they heaved themselves through the window into the street. The last thing Hicks did was put the bar back in place. He thought it might throw the Germans off their trail for a few hours, but it worked much better than that. At Monday morning's roll call, the camp staff discovered that two prisoners had escaped but had no idea how or in which direction. Weeks later, a guard happened to pull on the window bar and was surprised when it came loose in his hands.

After eighteen months in captivity, walking through Paris as free men was a joy; Frank later wrote that it was the most intensely thrilling experience he had had in years. It was a beautiful spring morning and soon the sidewalks were filled with people, none of whom gave a second look to Frank and Hicks. They didn't speak to each other, but simply enjoyed the sensations of liberty. Everything was exciting—the workmen talking about recent bombing raids, the gruff conductor on the bus they boarded, even the stale fug of the metro station. When they reached the Gare du Nord, Robert Lapassade was waiting for them. The group from the Maison Canadienne had made everything ready for them. Jean Pouillon had the keys to his father-in-law's vacant apartment, so they had a safe place to hide for the night. Lapassade had arranged a dinner party at a local restaurant; for Frank, it could have been any evening in the spring of 1939, save for the two Nazi storm troopers seated at a table near them. And they had also taken care of the last part of the escape: crossing out of the occupied zone of France. The frontier between the two zones, known as the demarcation line, was policed with varying degrees of intensity, and it was best to have the help of a local to cross safely. An acquaintance knew a French soldier who was escaping to Vichy the following morning, and it had been arranged that Frank and Hicks would go with him. After a light breakfast, the whole group went to the Gare d'Austerlitz to see them off. Taking advantage of the anonymity provided by the weekday morning crowds, Frank thanked his old friends for their help, and the escapers climbed on the train with the fleeing soldier. They spent all day on the train, and it was after dark when they pulled into Dax, close to the Spanish border and not far from the demarcation line. Because Frank and Hicks had no identity papers, a hotel was out of the question so the trio's only option was to spend the night in a field. It wasn't a new experience for any of them, but a heavy rain kept them from sleeping. They were relieved to board the bus for Vichy the next morning.

About nine miles from the line, the bus wheezed to a halt. A bunch of passengers got off and a French policeman got on. This was the moment of truth—would he ask for papers, or simply walk up and down the aisle and get off again? He hesitated for a few agonizingly long seconds, then, to Frank and Hicks' horror, began to ask people for their identification. The game was up. Then, the unthinkable happened. The policeman gave the pair an intent, meaningful look, then promptly turned his back on them and bent down to talk to the people in the seats across the aisle. His meaning was unmistakable: "Get off the bus now and we'll say nothing more about it." Looking as nonchalant as possible, the two fugitives left the bus and started walking down the road.

The sympathetic gendarme had given them a break, but they were still in trouble. Without the French soldier to guide them, they had no idea where they should be going. All they could do was keep walking in the same direction. But within a few minutes, they got another unexpected break. With a few honks, the bus pulled up beside them; the driver opened the door and said casually, "It's all right now, he's gone. You can get back in." As Frank and Hicks went back to their seats, they noticed that all the other passengers were smiling broadly. It soon became apparent that everyone—from the driver to the passengers to the gendarme—was familiar with the routine. About a mile from the frontier, the bus stopped again and everyone filed off, trudging through the field in the direction indicated by the driver. They came upon a farmer taking in his hay and he happily guided them to the line, even doing a quick reconnaissance first to make sure there were no German guards about. In minutes, everyone from the bus was safely in Vichy.

For Frank, the relief was overwhelming. He walked a few more yards, then collapsed. The French soldier tried to get him to eat some bread and pâté, but he couldn't swallow anything; Frank just slumped by the side of the road, his body wracked by sobs. The stress of his flight to Brittany, hearing the French soldier being beaten to death in Quimper, the squalor of Montreuil-Bellay, the sometimes poisoned relations among the inmates at St. Denis—all of it flooded out of him. It was some time before he could collect himself and carry on. They stopped at a farm and were again received warmly, this time by a woman who gave them some wine and invited them in to rest. But they could stay only for a few minutes before setting off again. They walked for another six miles and when they came to a public telephone, rewarded themselves by calling a taxi to take them to Pau. The French soldier went his own way while Frank and Hicks, growing more confident all the time, booked into a hotel and the next morning took a train to Trélissac, in the Dordogne. There, Paul and Arlette Maurette, the brother and sister-in-law of Frank's friends from the prewar days on the Left Bank, threw open their home to the escapers and helped Frank and Hicks negotiate the administrative obstacles, including getting their identity papers, ration cards, and clothing tickets. Until they had everything squared away, they had no choice but to rely on the charity of the Maurettes, who had their own family to support. One of Frank's first jobs was to write to Jack, asking for underwear, shoes, money, and advice—in that order.

The first priority was to secure residence permits from the Vichy gov-ernment—despite the fact that Frank and Hicks were fugitives from an ally of Vichy, the regime in unoccupied France liked to assert its independence from its masters in Berlin. It wasn't in the habit of returning escapers to Nazi jails; so long as Frank and Hicks completed the necessary paperwork, they would be left alone. With the help of Jean Varille, another of Frank's friends from the Maison Canadienne, the pair soon had their residence permits and could begin the long process of obtaining the proper forms to get out of France. Varille and Maurette had done all they could for Frank; he now turned for help to U.S. consular officials in Lyons. Throughout his internment, Frank had relied on diplomats from the neutral United States to supply him with cash advances (which were ultimately covered by Jack). The U.S. had entered the war in December 1941 after the Japanese attack on Pearl Harbor, but still had a diplomatic presence in Vichy, which clung to a fig leaf of formal neutrality. Now, Frank's guardian angel was Constance Harvey, a young assistant at the American Legation. She moved him into an old country place she had rented, did what she could to fatten him up, found him some clothes (he had to make do with the shabbiest suit, because the better clothing went to people who were likely to be stuck in Vichy), and loaned him a bicycle, which he used to visit his friends in the area. She even found him some war work to do, in the way of translating news bulletins for local distribution.

But that was hardly what Frank had in mind. During the months of imprisonment in France, he had nourished the hope of escaping to England, where he could do something positive and tangible to help liberate France, and the friends who meant so much to him, from the Nazis. Spending months in idleness in Vichy had never been in his plans, and the low-level propaganda work that Constance Harvey found for him wasn't a signifi-cant contribution to the war effort. Getting to England was the first step toward a return to France and Frank was desperate to hurry the process along, but consular officials strongly advised that everything be done by the book. If the Vichy authorities discovered that Frank was of special interest to anyone, they would inevitably start asking difficult questions. On the other hand, if they went through the proper channels, Frank could get a non-combatant travel visa (on account of his damaged ears) for travel to Portugal and be out of Vichy within a few months. It was sound advice, but it was hard to take. Pleasant as it was to cycle between friends' houses or spend an afternoon with Gertrude Stein and Alice B. Toklas (who, with much of the Paris literati, had deserted the capital for the relative safety of the French countryside) at their farmhouse near Lyons, Frank chafed at having to wait for everything to fall into place. Such was his anxiety that he didn't even feel much like writing.

•

In his office in Rhodes House, C.K. Allen tried to suppress his annoyance as he reread the letter from Ken Macalister, written in the small village of Tourneville in western Normandy on 22 September 1939. Macalister freely admitted that he didn't know what to do. He had stayed in Tourneville when the war began because it seemed the safest thing to do, and in a week's time he was planning to move in with friends in Lisieux (he didn't mention the Lucases by name). Continuing his studies seemed out of the question, given the international crisis—"I cannot spend the coming year as planned . . . My sense of duty would not permit it," Ken wrote—but the French army wasn't accepting foreigners into its ranks (he neglected to mention that he had tried to volunteer for the French army, but had been sent away when he failed the vision test). Could Professor Allen offer any advice?[12]

Allen's advice was short and sharp: get out of France. The port of Le Havre wasn't far from Lisieux; Ken should make every effort to get a boat across the Channel from there. Until his student was back in England, Allen didn't feel he could offer any useful advice. But in a letter to the warden of New College, Allen revealed his frustrations. Before the war began, he had advised all Rhodes Scholars on the Continent to return to England as soon as possible—Allen and his family had fled from France themselves, getting a steamer from Le Havre on the eve of war. He couldn't understand why

Ken hadn't heeded that advice, or at the very least contacted the college to explain his situation. Allen, recalling earlier suspicions of Ken's motives for requesting permission to spend a term in France, was losing patience with the promising young Canadian; a year at l'Université de Paris was now impossible and finishing his degree at Oxford seemed pointless, Allen told the warden. The best thing for Macalister was to begin his professional career, either in England or in Canada.

A week later, Ken wrote to Allen again, to explain why he hadn't left France when he had the chance. "I had hoped for some miracle which would make peace possible," he confided earnestly, if rather naively.[13] On a practical level, he had moved all of his belongings to France and couldn't easily get them back to England. Furthermore, the war had disrupted train service and travel was very difficult, especially because Ken didn't have a proper identity card of the kind that any foreigner residing in France for more than two months had to carry. Apparently, the local administration had lost his application, forcing Ken to start the entire process again, something that could take up to a month. He had written to the Canadian Legation in Paris for assistance and information about possible work with the federal government, but hadn't received a reply. Finally, he had sprained his ankle and still found it difficult to get around.

However, to make the best use of the time while he was stranded in France, Ken proposed to continue studying there over the winter and return to Oxford for the Easter term to take his bachelor in civil law (BCL) examinations and bar finals. He had already been working on improving his French, because he had heard that the French government was in need of translators, and intended to take a course at l'Université de Caen until Christmas. Then, he would come back to England and prepare for his examinations with David Boult. Needless to say, Ken didn't expect the Rhodes Trust to pay his stipend for the period he was in France. Perhaps assuming that Macalister would do as he planned regardless of their response, the Rhodes Trustees agreed to his proposal.

In November 1939, Allen received a more encouraging letter from

Ken. He had enrolled at the university in Caen, where he was taking a short course in French language and literature and attending lectures on international and administrative law. Lincoln's Inn and the Council of Legal Education had agreed to waive their regulations so that Ken didn't lose his standing in the profession, but a letter from Georges Vanier at the Canadian Legation in Paris had revealed that the government was not hiring Canadians abroad, so that avenue was closed. With this new information, the Rhodes Trust decided to reverse its earlier decision; since Macalister was obviously continuing his studies while away from Oxford, the trustees decided that he would receive his full one-hundred-pound scholarship for that term. For Ken, who was relying on the charity of his French friends, it was an enormous relief. He continued to send occasional notes to C.K. to tell him of his progress. He was enjoying the law courses at l'Université de Caen—"I hope some day to be able to do some serious work in the field of comparative law," he wrote—and had also taken up bookbinding as a hobby.[14] Later, Macalister sent a copy of a classic treatise on French law that he had bound especially for Allen, almost as a kind of peace offering. The warden was delighted, but couldn't help wondering if there was more behind it.

By early 1940, as Frank was enjoying the last few weeks of Paris's freedom, Ken was back in England. In contrast to what he had said in his earlier letters, he reported to Allen that he had had no trouble getting out of France, and he was now looking for some useful work to do. The Ministry of Information, the Ministry of Economic Warfare, the Admiralty, the military police, Canada's Department of External Affairs—Ken was willing to consider anything. Again, Allen's advice was short and sensible: focus on completing your exams, and then consider the future. Perhaps for the first time in his Oxford career, Ken buckled down and showed what he was really capable of: he passed the bar exam with first class standing and was awarded the Certificate of Honour, given to the best examinee of all candidates, and then took an easy first in his BCL in June. For David Boult, who had earlier expressed reservations about his student's potential,

Ken's performance was a revelation, "a fitting climax to a very distinguished academic record." Macalister's three years at Oxford had "done an almost extraordinary lot of good to him," wrote Boult. "They have humanised him to a remarkable degree, and his whole attitude had changed from one of suspicion and aloofness to one of genial and friendly amiability. When he goes I personally shall miss a very good friend."[15]

C.K. was more than a little surprised by the results that placed Ken first in his class of 142 students, and in July 1940 all of his lingering suspicions about Ken's time in France were confirmed. "I have a confession to make," Macalister wrote to his mentor before describing what had really kept him in France. While he was staying with the Lucases, he had met Jeannine Lucas, the daughter of the law professor. She was five feet tall with blonde hair and soft, grey-blue eyes, and Ken was instantly smitten. The two became engaged (Ken wrote that it was with the blessings of both families, but it seems unlikely that Celestine's approval, if it was ever given, was particularly enthusiastic) and on 31 October 1939, when Jeannine was just nineteen, the couple had married in Lisieux; before long, Jeannine was pregnant. All of the excuses Ken had given for not leaving France—the troubles with his identity card, the problem of moving his possessions, travel difficulties—had been invented to avoid revealing to the Rhodes Trust his breach of the scholarship regulations, which prohibited married men from holding the award. But his conscience had been nagging him since his return to England and now, "so worried about the situation in France with my wife expecting a baby in the beginning of September, in German occupied territory, and with all means of communication cut off," Ken felt the only way to deal with his guilt and calm his deteriorating nerves was to come clean.[16]

Macalister must have been intensely nervous when he was summoned to Allen's office; not only had he broken the regulations governing his scholarship, but he had persistently lied about it to the one man who, more than anyone else, had been like a father to him in England. And the warden was not impressed. He emphasized the gravity of Ken's offence and his continued deception, admitting that it was mitigated by Ken's character, his excellent academic results, the anxiety of being separated from his wife, and the fact that she was trapped in occupied France and expecting a child in September. Still, Allen said that he had no choice but to report the matter to the Rhodes Trustees and leave it in their hands.

The warden's response was entirely reasonable, but it was a sign of Ken's fragile mental state that he took everything the wrong way and was outraged. Rather than seeing the interview as exactly what it was, a reprimand for a clear and admitted misconduct, he took it as an attack on his integrity, and Jeannine's. Unable to put his emotions into words, he stormed from Allen's office and returned to his lodgings to write a bitter letter to his mentor. He accused Allen of casting aspersions on Jeannine's character and implying that she wasn't good enough for him, and even took from the reprimand the notion that Allen was glad the couple would be separated indefinitely. As to Allen's accusation that he had all but stolen one hundred pounds from the Rhodes Trust (an accusation that was entirely the product of Ken's troubled mind), it was insulting and hurtful.

Fortunately for Macalister, Allen was at his best in such situations. The man who looked like a stiff and stern army officer now revealed his deep understanding and compassion. He allowed some time to pass and, just as he expected, a letter soon arrived from Ken. After thinking about things for a few days, the young man was now mortified by his conduct, not only in France but toward Allen, and begged the forgiveness of the man who had done so much to help him. He put his outburst down to his nervous deterioration, made worse by the knowledge that his wife was now living under Nazi occupation, and wrote that his spiteful letter to Allen represented "exactly the mental state I was in at the time, desperate, ashamed and resentful . . . I hope that never again shall I find myself deliberately entering into a course of conduct that I know to be wrong."[17]

When Allen reported the incident to Lord Elton, the historian and general secretary of the Rhodes Trust, the letter made it clear that C.K. understood Ken better than the young man understood himself. He had suspected all along that Ken was staying in France for personal rather than educational reasons, and concluded that "having begun a course of duplicity, he, doubtless, found himself more and more involved." "I may mention," Allen added, "that he is a Roman Catholic with somewhat strict ideas of guilt and penance and this has increased his distress of conscience." As to the accusatory letter, it simply "showed that he was evidently in a state of profound agitation and simply not himself," so all had been forgiven. They had patched things up, and the offending letter had been returned to Ken to destroy. Allen had made one request to Macalister, however: when he became successful in the future ("as I have no doubt he will if he survives the war," he told Elton), he should help some young man in need of an education, in the amount that he received from the Rhodes Trust while he was in France. Ken immediately agreed. In late July 1940, the Rhodes Trustees met to consider Ken Macalister's fate, and it became clear that Allen's appeal for leniency carried weight. Their verdict was brief and to the point: "Mr. Macalister should be informed that they would forget this breach of the Scholarship regulations and that they wished him well for the future."[18]

FIVE

IN UNIFORM

I f Ken had his way, his future would be spent in uniform. Being rejected by the French army because of poor eyesight had been annoying, but it was nothing like what he was experiencing now that he was back in England. After passing the bar exam in June 1940, he made the rounds of every military unit he could find, but the answer was always the same: there was no place in the forces for a man with such bad eyes. Finally, in July, he had an interview with the Field Security Police (FSP), a shadowy unit that employed unconventional people in a variety of intelligence duties. Ken had no trouble with the required foreign language test—he was accepted and told to await his call-up papers, which might arrive within a week but certainly before the month was out.

Two months later, Ken was still waiting, and growing more agitated by the day. Without his stipend from the Rhodes Trust, he had no source of income and would soon have to rely on the charity of friends. But much worse was the inactivity. He fretted at being cut off from his family in France and was tortured by the thought that his baby would soon be born under Nazi occupation. His only comfort was a growing sense of certainty that he must help to liberate them, not in the abstract sense of becoming a small cog in the Allied war machine, but by taking a direct role in working to free France. Everyone else seemed to be pitching in. The men of the Royal Air Force fought daily duels with the German Luftwaffe over the skies of southern England in the Battle of Britain. Civilians across the British Isles were rallying together in a show of defiance against the German bombers that were targeting London and cities as far north as Birmingham and Manchester. Veterans of the last war, known colloquially as Dad's Army, were preparing to meet the German invaders, who might cross the Channel at any time. Even the Allens were doing their bit, C.K. as an air-raid warden and Dorothy working in a soldiers' canteen at the railway station. And all the while, Ken tried to keep himself busy as he waited to be called to join his unit. In desperation, he wrote to C.K. "They have treated me very badly," he confided, adding that he didn't appreciate the Field Security Police making him wait after the promises he had been given. Allen had once offered to do what he could to help Ken get into uniform; now he asked his mentor to intercede on his behalf.[1]

Allen duly wrote to Captain G.P.D. Maufe, who was in charge of local recruiting for the Field Security Police, and received a puzzled reply. Maufe referred to a letter from Ken in early August, in which he had asked to be released from his obligation to the unit; assuming he had enlisted in another branch of the service, the FSP agreed and duly informed Ken that he had been struck from the unit's rolls. Did Allen's letter mean that Ken had changed his mind? If so, Captain Maufe could have him called up immediately. Now it was Allen's turn to be puzzled. He talked to Ken, who assured him that his letter had been only an inquiry, not a request for release. As to Maufe's offer to enrol him immediately for active service, Ken accepted, apparently with gratitude, and Allen, who was a civilian member of the Oxfordshire recruiting panel, assured him that he could speed the process along. Still, Allen sensed that something was wrong with his former student.

In mid-September 1940, things came to a head. Two letters reached Ken at his Oxford lodgings: one was the expected call-up notice from the Field Security Police; the other was from his University of Toronto professor N.A. Mackenzie, offering him a lectureship in law. With only a few hours to decide, Ken opted to present himself at Winchester and be attested into the Field Security Police. But the following day, he received two more messages: a cable from Mackenzie, who was about to leave Toronto to take up the presidency of the University of New Brunswick, asking for an immediate response to his offer; and an airmail letter from Celestine Macalister, who claimed that her heart was weak and might not be able to withstand the knowledge that her only son was on active service. She begged him not to enlist, and to return to Canada instead. It was apparently not the first such warning she had sent.

Ken, whose nerves had been sorely tried by the events of the past year, was thrown to the verge of hysteria, torn between his deep devotion to his mother and his equally strong sense of duty. His first instinct was to find a way out of the army, so he asked his landlady if she could do anything to help; with all the implacability of someone who had spent a lifetime dealing with upper-class Oxford students, she took herself to Winchester and presented Ken's case to the commanding officer of the Field Security Police depot, but even she couldn't win his release. So he went to see C.K. Allen and poured out his frustrations. Allen, greatly disturbed by Ken's agitation, agreed to do what he could, although he wasn't hopeful; it was unlikely that he would be released from his unit, and if he simply left the country, he would be classed as a deserter. As they talked, Ken paced the room like a caged animal, getting more agitated by the minute. As Allen later wrote to Lord Elton, Ken's "mental stress was greatly and unnecessarily increased because there was violent opposition from one member of his family to his joining the forces in England . . . He had stern and lonely battles to face, and he was, in any case, a very highly strung man."[2]

Fearing for his emotional health, Allen decided that the only option was to reach out to the Macalisters, but not directly; they suspected that he had something to do with Ken joining the army, and were not likely to listen to anything he had to say. Instead, Allen wrote to E.C. Young, the president of the Guelph *Daily Mercury* and Alexander Macalister's friend, describing Ken's travails in a compassionate and moving letter. The boy "was in a deplorable condition of nerves," he wrote, because the die was cast; he was now in the army and could no longer accept the Toronto post, even if he wanted to. "I am terribly sorry for him," Allen went on. "He has had more to stand in the past year than a young man of his sensitive disposition can well endure; part of his troubles have been due to his own impetuousness, but we do not expect perfect wisdom of youth . . . The only thing that matters is that he should win through, and it is going to be a great test of character whether he does or not." He hoped that once Ken was forced to concentrate on his military duties, it would take his mind off his anxieties. "If he cannot do that, then I fear a serious break-down, but there is plenty of tough fibre in him and I don't see why he should not come through the test." The key was the attitude of his parents:

> He will be perturbed to an extent which would make me fear for the consequences if he is going to suffer reproach and remonstrance from his parents . . . I would say frankly that I think it very wrong of parents to make it difficult for a son of full age to do what he conceives to be his duty. I understand that Mrs. Macalister is in indifferent health and that she has conveyed to her son that his going into the Army may be too much for her. He even hinted to me that his parents would be disposed to renounce him if he accepted military service . . . If the parents take that attitude it will be extremely cruel to the boy himself and will add enormously to the worries which he already has to conquer.

Allen, deeply affected by Ken's predicament, asked Young to intercede with the Macalisters. "If you can do anything to avert what I most fear, you will have done this promising lad a great service. If he could be assured that his parents were content to abide by his mature decision and were resigned to the inevitable risks which he must run, I am sure it would be a tremendous comfort to him, and it would be the best contribution which the parents could make to their son's happiness and usefulness . . . If he breaks down, he is another of the unhappy casualties of war, but if he wins through, he will always be infinitely the better man for overcoming his difficulties. I beg you at all costs to prevent his parents from making his lot more difficult."[3]

We shall never know what Young said to the Macalisters, but it had the desired effect. Two weeks later, a greatly relieved Allen received a cable from Guelph: "Words of pride devotion and encouragement cabled by parents yesterday whose relief was emphatic thousand thanks bless you all writing. Young."[4] Even so, the words of encouragement were obviously not as unconditional as Young believed; the following week, Ken wrote to Allen that his parents were now "fairly reconciled" to his service. It was hardly the ringing endorsement that the young man needed, but on the whole Ken wasn't unhappy with his lot. He had received a letter from Jeannine written in July indicating that she was well; "this comes as a tremendous relief and I am really a new man," Ken told Allen. "I now have something to live for and which keeps me generally hopeful." He admitted that the first few weeks of life in the army had been trying, but he was getting used to it, and particularly enjoyed the strange collection of people in his unit. As to the missed opportunity to teach at Toronto, that was now water under the bridge and he had cabled his regrets to Professor Mackenzie (the lectureship went to Bora Laskin, who went on to become chief justice of Canada). Ken remained concerned (and probably a little insulted), however, that someone of his educational achievements was languishing as a private in the security police. He didn't see any chance of receiving a commission in his unit, so was looking into a transfer to the Canadian Army, where the "remuneration will be more adequate."[5]

In a subsequent letter to Young, C.K. Allen put his finger on Ken's state of mind. He couldn't say that Ken's letter was "enthusiastic or very effusive, but, on the whole, it is cheerful and it is quite clear that he has been much encouraged by the message he has had from his parents." The military life, observed Allen, "must all be very strange and probably harsh to him at first, but I shall be surprised if it does not strengthen and develop him in many respects and probably make a better and more self-reliant man of him . . . I have vivid recollections of my own first experiences in the extremely unaccustomed surroundings of the army and I have never felt any doubt that whatever one had to go through at times, the balance was far more on the credit than on the debit side and I have never regretted a moment of the experience." With the Macalisters apparently tamed and Ken now in service, it was finally all up to him: "This young man must now work out his own destiny and I have enough confidence in his character and endurance to believe that he will come through victoriously if he is only spared from the ordeal."[6]

As Allen realized, Ken (he was known as John Macalister after enlisting, the British Army evidently having decided that his parents chose John as his first name for a reason) was finding army life a disorienting experience, although he at least had the comfort of being with like-minded individuals, including the musician and composer Humphrey Searle, and three star graduates of King's College, Cambridge: Noel Annan, John da Silva, and Peter Webber. The FSP recruits were housed in the unit's depot in Winchester, in what had once been King Alfred's College, an old teacher training institution. There, they were given the full training regimen, not by just any drill sergeants but by men of the Guards Division, renowned for having a high standard of discipline. As Humphrey Searle put it, the army evidently assumed they were all "formerly long-haired intellectuals who needed to be licked into shape," and licked into shape they were.[7] They lived by the old army dictum "If it moves, salute it—if it doesn't move, paint it white," and slowly but surely they were transformed into soldiers.

But it was also obvious that they weren't normal soldiers. Every so often, a sergeant would appear in their barracks and pin up a list of those volunteers who had indicated a knowledge of certain foreign languages and who were to present themselves for fluency testing. Not that the tests were especially challenging. Peter Webber was tested four times in the first few months he was there, and was asked to translate the same phrases every time: in French, it was "Tell him to wait until I come" and in German, "I was at the meeting when the speaker was speaking" and "I ought to have done it," all of which were designed to test him on the grammatical complexities of the languages.[8]

Still, the difficult drills and constant evaluations kept them busy, which was just as well for Ken, who was growing worried about Jeannine. The Battle of Britain continued to rage and a German invasion remained a distinct possibility, so communications with the Continent were still very uncertain. But C.K. Allen was not without influence, and he did what he could to get news of Jeannine and the baby, which was due in September. He got in touch with the U.S. Embassy in London, which had been trying since the summer to find out what was happening with Jeannine, and in early November the first news in months reached Allen in Oxford. The U.S. Embassy in Paris had received a letter from Madame Lucas saying that Jeannine was in good health at Tourneville, and would be returning to Lisieux shortly. Sadly, the letter went on, "after a difficult accouchement, [Jeannine] was delivered of a female child which has since died."[9]

It fell to C.K. Allen to deliver the sad news to Ken, who bore it stoically. He admitted that he had begun to fear the worst and that the news had come as "a combined relief and shock." He had begun to grow very fond of the unborn child "but, of course, it would have been much more terrible to lose my wife. At least when a baby dies," he added in a comment that gave away something of his own torments, "if it loses the opportunity of knowing the joys of life, it misses the inevitable suffering that is part of life." In a letter to Dorothy Allen, Ken was a little more open: "As to the child, although I never saw it I feel a strong sense of loss. I wanted a girl very much. I am also sure that it will cause Jeannine to suffer much more than I." All in all, Ken was grateful that the rigours of training left him little time or energy to dwell on his loss: "I think it is a very good thing in some ways, particularly for people like myself who have been spending years bent over books. One has to smarten up to survive."[10]

At the end of every course at Winchester, a sergeant would appear in their barracks with another list, this time indicating the units to which the graduates had been posted. The decisions didn't always make sense.

Humphrey Searle recalled, "As I could speak reasonable French and German, I was naturally sent to the Highlands of Scotland where the only language of any use was Gaelic"; he was assigned to protect a number of camps between Fort William and Mallaig, and one of his chief duties was to meet the train from Glasgow every day to watch for suspicious-looking characters. Noel Annan, who would go on to become vice-chancellor of the University of London, was disappointed to be posted to the Intelligence Corps, and was scarcely consoled by John da Silva's observation that the unit had quite a nice cap badge. In February 1941, Ken's name came up. He, too, was posted to the Intelligence Corps, to the 64th Field Security Section, then stationed at Guildford, in Surrey. He was billeted with an elderly couple on the outskirts of town, and found the kind of domestic tranquility that he hadn't known since Lisieux. "We tried to make more of him than a friend, being such a long way from home and worrying terribly about his wife," wrote Allan Evans of Ken's stay with them. "We invited him in and he accepted with great appreciation; our home was his home at all times."[11]

Ken kept up his correspondence with C.K. Allen, although he said little about what he was doing. After one visit, however, the professor remarked upon a change coming over the young Canadian: "He has been going through a hard discipline, but has taken it very well and I feel no doubt that, as I had greatly hoped, he has benefited by it physically and psychologically. He looks ten times better in health and he has been kept at it so hard that he has not had time to dwell upon his own worries."[12] He still harboured hopes of a transfer to the Canadian Army (which had started to assemble in England in December 1939), even though it was by no means clear what Canadian units might be called upon to do. Allen encouraged Ken to write to his old University of Toronto classmate (and academic rival) George Ignatieff, then working as a junior diplomat at Canada House, the Canadian High Commission in London. At the same time, Allen spoke to Lester Pearson, another Oxford graduate and Canada House staffer, and a future prime minister, on Macalister's behalf, but the answer was discouraging: transferring was a gamble, because Ken might drop to the bottom of the ladder again, facing a long wait before anything suited to his talents came up. If he stayed with the Field Security Police, at least he had a foot in the door and stood a better chance of getting a commission somewhere interesting. For his part, Ignatieff found it "unthinkable that a man of his [Ken's] calibre should remain a Lance Corporal permanently without any prospect of commission in the Field Security Service." Still, he had to agree with Pearson: the situation in the Canadian Army was even worse, and the best that Ken could hope for there was a reversion to the rank of private and a long wait for advancement. Things were resolved once and for all in April 1941, when Ken learned that the Canadian Army in England was authorized to enlist only those with a Grade I medical category; Ken's poor eyesight had dropped him to a Grade IIa, so a posting to the Canadian Army was out of the question. He was philosophical about the setback: "I am disappointed, but am finding my present work interesting, though almost certainly without any prospect of advancement barring some extraordinary piece of luck."[13]

He continued to value his relationship with Allen—"It has been a pleasure to write to you about things which you will understand but which are Greek to the people with whom I spend my time," he wrote in June 1942—and never lost his interest in the big picture. "I am still well and truly embedded in the mud, but I mustn't 'grouse.' I am kept busy and continue to learn a lot about men and mice." Ken had a growing interest in postwar reconstruction, and saw enormous potential for the world that would be when the war was won: "I shouldn't think many people over twenty-five are going to like the new world. But what a glorious mission there will be for those who are prepared to make the peace work this time! I am accepting without bitterness that the British Army should keep my light under a bushel, but once peace comes I am going to fight like hell for an opportunity to be really useful . . . The post-war organization is going to require a young well-trained personnel. Most of the best material will be found in the forces, if not killed off by that time." One area in which he believed he could be useful was in improving relations between French and English Canadians. "The attitude of Quebec is partially the fault of English-speaking Canada," he wrote to Allen. "Our case has never been properly presented. Too few people have taken the trouble to master French and to become familiar with the traditions of Quebec and sentiments of its people." His motivation lay as much in his love of Canada as in his love of France: "I have had much contact with French soldiers here, and in spite of everything, I remain Francophile. For me as most Frenchmen France is still 'une terre sainte.' If we invade I hope that I shall have the chance to be among the first. There will be need for much skill and tact."[14]

But until then, there was much to be done with the Field Security Police, and Ken worked hard, as much to keep his mind off the separation from Jeannine as anything. He still lived with the Evanses in Guildford but spent many of his leaves with the family of Harry Rée, a friend in the security service whose mother and sisters virtually adopted Ken as a second son. But those friendships, important as they were to Ken, couldn't dull the pain of being separated from Jeannine. They were able to exchange brief and infrequent messages through the International Committee of the Red Cross and once she was able to smuggle a letter out of the country, but that only made things worse; she told Ken that she was desperately short of money, sending him on a frantic search for a way to get money to her through the Swiss consulate in Paris. Then, in September 1941, he was promoted to sergeant—"now risen to the glory of *three* stripes!" he wrote Allen gleefully.[15] Ken took it as a sign that things might be starting to turn in his favour.

•

Frank Pickersgill knew about inactivity too—for four months, he had been putting in time in Vichy, socializing and doing busywork. But in September 1942 he finally reached Lisbon via Madrid, thanks to the intervention of the British and U.S. embassies in Portugal, the U.S. Embassy in unoccupied France, and the Portuguese Consulate in Lyons—it paid to have an influential relative. If Vichy had been a welcome change from St. Denis, Lisbon was like another world. British Embassy officials told Frank that almost every intelligence service in the world had agents in the Portuguese capital, but in other ways it seemed as if there was no war on at all. The Clippers, Pan-Am's luxurious flying boats, still made regular flights between Portugal and New York, just as they had done in peacetime. There was no blackout, and the streets were filled with cars and trucks of all sorts. And the food made a particularly powerful impression on Frank: "The idea of going to breakfast and having rolls made with white flour—*and* having as many as I want without the horrid feeling that I won't have any tickets left at the end of the month—*and* of being able to smoke—oil and butter à volonté, and potatoes, real *frites* at every meal—is overwhelming and I still think I'm dreaming," he wrote. The other attraction of Lisbon was a young woman named Jacqueline Grant, who had been interned in France with her mother before escaping to Vichy and, eventually, Portugal. Both Frank and Jacqueline were on emotional highs because of their escapes, and perhaps it was inevitable that they would fall in love. "We couldn't get married until I start paying my debts and put myself on a business basis," Frank wrote to Jack in his rational, younger-brother frame of mind, "but I suspect . . . marriage is in the offing in the not too distant future."[16]

But soon Frank felt himself being pushed in a direction that he didn't want to go. Jack was trying to pull strings to secure travel papers and a berth on the Clipper to bring him back to Canada. U.S. officials, who controlled the flights, were assured that Frank's presence was urgently desired by the Canadian government in Ottawa, to whom he "would no doubt have some report to convey."[17] In other words, the Pickersgills were keen to get Frank out of the war zone (and, given Frank's history of falling hard for women, perhaps out of a hasty marriage of the kind that wars inevitably produce) and back to Canada, where his skills could be put to good use for the war effort. Frank had other ideas. On the first of October 1942, he wrote to Jack that he intended to go to England, and that the British Consulate in Lisbon was working on arranging a flight for him. He didn't say what his plans were—only that once he got to London, he would try to join the army. Jack responded with a telegram urging him to return to Canada, but Frank wouldn't be moved. "I'm terribly anxious to see Mother," he wrote to his brother, "& will be relieved to have her see no pieces are missing—and of course would give anything to settle down to a long world problem-solving séance with you," but his motivation to get out of captivity in France was that he would one day return and continue the fight. The longer he had waited in the occupied zone, the more determined he was to go back to France, and he had already made contacts in Lisbon who could put him in touch with "the right people" and arrange a posting that would suit his talents and experience. It would also avoid difficult medical questions, for Frank was hardly a perfect physical specimen. His childhood brush with scarlet fever and infected mastoids had left him deaf in one ear and permanently affected his balance, giving him the trademark lopsided walk that one old friend referred to as his "whiffling mode of locomotion."[18] Frank would have been delighted to spend a month in Canada with the family before joining the fight, but feared that once he was back at home, "I'd have the devil's own time getting back to Europe." He hoped above all else that his family would understand his decision: "I've seen & done some things which have rather radically changed my outlook. After seeing a French soldier clubbed to death by German cops at Quimper, after starving in a gravel-pit at Montreuil Bellay and getting blood-poisoning through being made to put up barbed-wire entanglements without any gloves on, and after sawing my way out of St. Denis through a barred window, and spending four months in Lyon doing illegal propaganda for the Americans and not quite sure from one day to the next when I might be 'repéré' and arrested— well, I'm afraid I'd find it pretty difficult to settle down to pushing a pen in an Ottawa office for the duration of the war and trying to convince myself that it was 'useful work.'"[19]

Now a more committed francophile than ever, Frank simply couldn't desert the country he had grown to love. "I'm feeling too belligerent to be happy 4000 miles away from the Nazis," he wrote to Celine Ballu in

Winnipeg. His strongest sympathies lay with the poor farmers, the humble merchants and tavern-keepers, the industrial workers ("railwaymen—what a marvellous lot of people!" he wrote to Jack in December 1942)—the kind of people he had known in occupied France who had so little but were willing to risk it all to help a stranger. He hadn't been impressed by the rich and powerful people he had met while interned.[20] "St. Denis was a place where the wealthy members of the Paris British Colony made themselves comfortable at the expense of the poor devils, by toadying to the Germans and by the most outrageous black-marketing," he wrote in late 1942. But the common people of Europe filled him with hope: "Something is forming there underneath Nazi domination and I don't think it is anarchy. It may be labelled communism by fools, but it's a damned sight more patriotic than any of the so-called nationalist movements which, in each and every country in Europe, sold out to the Germans." His most fervent wish was to help build the new Europe. As Leonard Brockington, a civil servant friend of Jack Pickersgill's who had tried to get Frank a job with the National Film Board in Canada, put it, "His reactions to his continental experience make it psychologically necessary for him to undertake important work in this country."[21]

On 23 October 1942, Frank finally got his wish and reached Britain, after a gruelling flight spent mostly with his head in an airsickness bag. It was his first visit to England since his European tour in 1934, and it hardly seemed like the same country. German air raids on British cities were now few and far between, but evidence of the Blitz of 1940–41 could be seen in the ruined buildings and piles of rubble that were everywhere. The southern counties resembled an armed camp, filled with soldiers and military equipment of a dozen nationalities, and it seemed as if half the population was in uniform. But gone was the sense of foreboding of the early years of the war, when a German invasion had seemed likely. Now, an air of optimism prevailed. The United States had been drawn into the war by the Japanese attack on Pearl Harbor in December 1941, and the first of millions of American servicemen had started to pour into Britain a few months later.

The Red Army, after halting the German attack just short of Moscow, was starting the slow and painful job of pushing the invaders out of Mother Russia. It was not yet the beginning of the end, British Prime Minister Winston Churchill would say famously in a speech given a few weeks after Frank arrived in England, but it was certainly the end of the beginning.

The rest cure in Lisbon hadn't yet overcome the effects of eighteen months of privations, and Frank's friends were surprised by the physical condition of the thin, pale, and nervous young man who started whenever he saw a policeman. One friend said that he displayed all the symptoms of a former captive; Frank didn't think that was a good sign, so he chose to look on the bright side: his internment seemed to have cured his chronic stomach troubles. More important, friends saw the strength of his desire to be useful. The little bit of translating he had done in Vichy hardly counted for much, and Frank was determined to take up more than the pen in this war. He took a flat at 118 Brompton Road in southwest London, and quickly went about finding the right people—or rather, they quickly went about finding him. The day after dragging himself off the Lisbon flight, Frank was summoned to an interview with some unnamed government officials who decided that he could indeed be useful, and shouldn't go back to Canada. Just five days later, he was the subject of a request by MI5, the military intelligence branch of the War Office that dealt with security operations. It noted that he had been in Paris in 1940 studying for the diplomatic service, had been captured and interned by the Germans, and had escaped through unoccupied France. Such a person was of great interest to the British government, and that same day Frank sent a telegram to Jack in Ottawa: "War Office has offered job of extreme importance and direct value in war effort as British officer. Propose to accept, subject your blessing. Cannot overemphasize certainty this is the right course."[22]

Frank's excitement came through clearly in the telegram—the posting, although he didn't yet know the specifics of it, seemed to be everything he was looking for. It promised, not incidentally, a steady pay. Since before the war began, Frank had been living on cash advances from Canadian, British, or American diplomatic offices, the Protecting Power, or the International Committee of the Red Cross. He even needed to draw an advance of seventy-five pounds from Canada House to cover his clothing and living expenses during the first weeks back in England. But whatever the source, all of the advances were covered by Jack. Not that his elder brother ever begrudged him anything—quite the opposite—but Frank had long been bothered by not having any permanent means of support. Of course, there was more to it than that. One of his Canadian friends from Paris later remembered Frank as "a man who was looking for his place in life, who had not yet decided what to make of himself." Brock King confided to Jack that "this business of finding a niche for oneself bothered Frank, for he didn't fit into life that way."[23] Now, the long search for a place, something that had nagged him for years, was at an end. Like Ken Macalister, Frank Pickersgill had finally found something useful to do.

Still, Jack was tempted to marshal the considerable political influence at his disposal to have his brother returned to Canada, and he did make inquiries with his colleagues in External Affairs, with Canada House, and with Prime Minister Mackenzie King. Norman Robertson, the undersecretary of state at External, was satisfied that the work offered by the War Office was important: "They are probably in a better position than we are to make direct and effective use of the special knowledge his experience over the last two years have given him," he wrote to King with his usual clear-sightedness.[24] Jack wanted to get the prime minister's opinion before communicating with Canadian authorities in London and, while there is no record of that conversation, it seems likely that King was swayed by Robertson's sage advice. External Affairs reported to Vincent Massey, the Canadian high commissioner in London, that "we have plenty of useful work for Pickersgill to do in Ottawa but feel that he must make his own decision as to where his services can best be used"; if he did take the War Office assignment, however, he should be informed that Ottawa could always make use of his talents if the opportunity arose. In any case, it soon became clear that Frank had made his own decision, independent of any of the inquiries being made on his behalf: he would accept the War Office assignment. As Massey wrote to External Affairs, "He has consulted me in the matter and I feel that he is fully justified in this decision in view of the importance of the work offered him."[25] Jack, saddened that they would continue to be separated but also proud of his brother's conviction and determination, gave his blessing.

A month later, Frank received a cryptic invitation to a meeting on 27 November 1942 at 10 a.m. at the Hotel Victoria, an enormous nine-teenth-century pile that sprawled along Northumberland Avenue in central London. Commandeered by the War Office in 1940, the Victoria's corridors buzzed with officious-looking staff officers carrying file folders and rolled maps, each with an air of supreme importance. Frank signed in at the front desk, which was watched over by a one-armed messenger who proceeded to lead him through the building to Room 238. If he was expecting a plush suite that befitted the splendour of what had once been one of London's largest hotels, he was disappointed; the door was opened to reveal a small, shabby room that looked out onto a small courtyard. Anything that had once made the room comfortable had been removed, to be replaced by a plain wooden trestle table covered with a prickly grey army blanket, two wooden chairs, and a filing cabinet (empty, as Frank later discovered). Draped gracefully on one of the chairs was a middle-aged man exquisitely dressed in a very expensive suit and the finest pair of shoes Frank had seen in years. He could have been mistaken for a rather louche playboy, but for the keen, dark eyes that sized the Canadian up in the few seconds before he smiled a greeting. This was the man who had invited Frank to the Victoria, Captain Selwyn Jepson, a Great War veteran and military intelligence officer who was better known to the British public as the author of bestselling crime novels. He also had an uncanny knack for spotting the right people for the jobs he had in mind.

Frank took an uncomfortable seat across the table, and the two began chatting. Jepson started in English, but after a few minutes switched to French. He evidently knew a fair bit about Frank already, but wanted to hear the full story, from his childhood right through to his experiences in France. Every once in a while he would toss in a question that, were it not for those sharp eyes, Frank might have taken for a complete non sequitur. Jepson didn't say much about the organization that he represented, only that it was involved in secret work on the Continent and that it had a particular need for people who knew France, spoke the language well, and were committed to putting those skills at the disposal of the war effort. Frank probably knew more about the organization than he let on, for even when he was in Lisbon he dropped broad hints about the kind of work he might be asked to do, telling Jack that "there are certain jobs I can do better than anybody else but a handful of people . . . That such jobs would be dangerous is just one more thing in their favour."[26] He was adamant that this was precisely the kind of job he was looking for. After an hour or so, the two parted, with Jepson promising that someone would contact him in due course. Frank didn't think that being asked to wait was a good sign, but in fact Jepson had come away from the meeting very favourably impressed: "Has interesting linguistic and geographical qualifications which should prove to be of great value operationally," he noted in a confidential report. In fact, Jepson (whose predecessor in the job had been Lewis Gielgud, brother of the actor John Gielgud) was the chief recruiting officer for one of Britain's secret intelligence organizations, and the short interview convinced him of Frank's suitability for the organization. And the work that Jepson had in mind for Frank? "Agent in the field after training."[27]

But not even the War Office could go around poaching the subjects of other countries for special duties. Frank had to be commissioned into the Canadian Army and attached to Canadian Military Headquarters (CMHQ) in London before his transfer to the British forces could be considered. Then, the War Office would submit a formal request for the loan of Lieutenant Pickersgill's services for a period of one month. If that initial trial period went well, the loan would be formalized. And so Frank Pickersgill, a man who was just as far from the martial ideal as Ken Macalister, found himself in the uniform of an officer of the Canadian Army. He was profoundly uneasy about saluting, and was known to cross the street to avoid having to give or receive a salute. Nor did he ever quite grasp the subtleties of an officer's uniform—he was once hauled away by the Military Police for wearing a blue shirt and a brightly coloured tie with his battledress, and had to be told which end of his tin helmet was the front. The protocols of caring for and wearing a Sam Brown belt remained a complete and utter mystery to him. However, he got a kick out of how people responded to him. Once, after hurting his knee in a training exercise and being forced to go around with a cane, he met an elderly woman on the bus who insisted that he take her seat, in the mistaken impression that he must have stopped a load of Nazi shrapnel during a fierce firefight.

He had less patience with military formalities. An intelligence test that involved identifying pictures of miscellaneous tools and gadgets infuriated him—"I do not know the name of this gadget in French or in English, but I used one to escape from prison with," he wrote scathingly on the paper, which may explain why the test results concluded that his intelligence level was very low.[28] Still, he quite enjoyed the comradeship of military life. In the company of Mervyn Sprung, another officer and an old friend from Winnipeg, he visited some Canadian Army bases to meet the men and talk about life in occupied France. The troops were still grumbling that Canada's only significant land operations through more than three years of war, the dispatch of two battalions to Hong Kong in late 1941 and the raid on the French coastal town of Dieppe in August 1942, had been unmitigated disasters, and many of them were bored enough to wonder if a visit from an escaped internee was the closest they would get to France. But for Frank, the afternoon was a tonic. The experience "warmed my heart terrifically," he wrote to Jack. "I hadn't realized what a pleasure compatriots en masse can give—occasionally," he added, a hint of how much of a francophile he had become. Spending an afternoon with the men of the Régiment de Maisonneuve was a delight—"I began to wonder if I hadn't been wrong about French-Canadians"—but didn't fully erase the memories of "the sinister things" that the French-Canadian priests in St. Denis had gotten up to.

All in all, though, he loved the short time spent with fellow Canadians. It "gave me the illusion of being back home for awhile," he later recalled.[29]

On 28 January 1943, the War Office contacted CMHQ with the request that Frank's loan, for a period of six months, become effective 1 January 1943. Assent was promptly given. One of the final formalities was for Frank to sign a declaration of secrecy:

> I declare that I will never disclose to anyone any information which I have acquired or may at any future time acquire as the result of my connection with this Department, unless such disclosure is necessary for my work for the Department.
>
> In particular I declare that except under the conditions aforementioned, I will in no circumstances give away any information concerning:—
>
> 1. The name, alias description, identity, location or duties of any past, present or future members of this Department.
> 2. The name, alias description, identity, location or duties of any member of the staff, or any persons working with this Department, either as a member of the forces or as a civilian.
> 3. The nature, methods, objects or subjects of instruction of this Department.
> 4. The location or name of any establishment of this Department.
> 5. The past, present or future location, movement or employment, either potential or factual, of myself, any member of or any person working with this Department.
>
> I declare moreover that I understand that I am personally responsible for any disclosure of such information I may make and that disciplinary proceedings under the Official Secrets Acts 1911 and 1920, the Treachery Act 1940, or the Defence (General)

Regulations 1939 may be taken against me if I at any time or in any way contravene the terms of this declaration.[30]

From now on, Frank was bound to a code of silence that prevented him from telling even his immediate family the details of his work. There would be long periods when they would not hear from him, but that shouldn't necessarily be taken as cause for alarm. Whatever the situation, they would receive occasional notes from the War Office, with the return address given as Room 238, Hotel Victoria, saying that "we hear excellent news of him" or some other such platitude. They could expect nothing more for the foreseeable future.

The organization that had recruited Frank was not in fact MI5, but an obscure unit that had been seeking out people with specific language skills for some months. It was also the unit in which, unbeknownst to his family or even to C.K. Allen, Ken Macalister had been working for nearly two years. Since 1 February 1941, the 64th Field Security Section had been attached for duty to an outfit known as the Inter-Services Research Bureau. It went by other, equally meaningless names—the Joint Technical Board, Special Training Schools Headquarters, MOI(SP) in Room 055A of the War Office, NID(Q) of the Admiralty, AI10 of the Air Ministry. Its official name, rarely spoken in public, was the Special Operations Executive. Those who worked there usually just called it The Firm.

PART TWO

INTO THE FIGHT

Six

THE FIRM

From the Baker Street underground station in the summer of 1942, a short walk south would take you to the fictional home of the great Sherlock Holmes, at 222B Baker Street, and farther along, toward Portman Square, to a series of dreary office blocks: Norgeby House, at number 83; St. Michael House, at number 82; Montagu Mansions; and 62–64 Baker Street. Their windows were covered with the same sort of curtains that graced a thousand other office buildings, and the stone and brick was stained by decades of coal dust and city grime. There was nothing to reveal what went on behind those walls except a small black plaque that read "Inter-Services Research Bureau." It was affixed to the doorway of 64, a five-storey building that was every bit as depressing inside as it was outside. Dark, narrow hallways were lined with stuffy, tired offices, the elevator heaved and groaned as if every ascent was its last, and the less said about the plumbing the better. Until recently, the building had been the office of the prison commissioners, but by 1942, it was part of the Baker Street complex, the nerve centre of the clandestine war against the Axis powers, where nearly seven hundred people worked to bring down the enemy from within. Secret organizations need nondescript offices, and it would be hard to imagine anything less noteworthy and more suitable than the home of the Special Operations Executive.

The Firm could trace its roots back to the prewar years, to a number of covert intelligence organizations established by the British government. The Foreign Office had created two units: one, known variously as EH (after its headquarters at Electra House) or CS (after its head, Sir Campbell Stuart), to investigate methods of influencing German opinion; and Section D, an offshoot of the Secret Intelligence Service (SIS) that was responsible for investigating "every possibility of attacking potential enemies by means other than the operations of military forces."[1] At the War Office, the general staff had created an office known as GS(R), a research section charged with investigating the conduct of irregular operations. But none of them were very large. GS(R), which was renamed MI(R) in the spring of 1939, originally consisted of one staff officer and a single typist.

SOE's more immediate roots could be found in the earliest days of the Second World War. British strategic planning envisaged defeating Germany not on the battlefield, but through selective attacks against its economy: a naval blockade to cut off its imports, a strategic bombing campaign directed at economic and industrial targets, and covert operations within Germany and German-occupied territories to destabilize its economy further. The basic assumption underlying this strategy—that Germany was riven by internal weaknesses and divisions just waiting to be exploited—was entirely mistaken, but that didn't stop the British government from basing much of its planning on it. Flawed though it was, the strategy seemed to be all that Britain had available in the late spring of 1940, with the Nazis in control of Poland, Denmark, and Norway and the blitzkrieg slashing into the Low Countries and France. The military outlook was dim when the Chiefs of Staff met on 19 May 1940 to consider the threat of a German invasion and the implications of an Allied defeat on the Continent for future British planning. With a naval blockade and a bombing campaign being the only military tools at hand to attack the German economy, covert operations in occupied Europe emerged as a potentially powerful weapon to bring Europe to the verge of revolt. "In the circumstances envisaged we regard this form of activity as of the very highest importance," concluded the Chiefs of Staff. "A special organization will be required to plan and put operations into effect . . . [It] should be proceeded with as a matter of urgency." They envisioned a three-pronged strategy of ships, aircraft, and secret agents: "Germany might still be defeated by economic pressure, by a combination of air attack on economic objectives in Germany and on German morale and the creation of widespread revolt in her conquered territories."[2]

A week later, after the British cabinet asked the Chiefs of Staff to refine their strategy for carrying on the war, they reiterated their conclusions. With more optimism than the situation demanded, the service chiefs wrote of achieving air superiority and putting pressure on Hitler's economic resources, neither of which Britain had the military capacity to achieve, and added, "The only other method of bringing about the downfall of Germany is by stimulating the seeds of revolt within the occupied territories."[3] The French army was close to the end of its rope, while the British Expeditionary Force had just started to evacuate from the Continent, leaving most of its heavy weapons and transport behind. The only way to deliver the coup de grâce to Germany after it had been fatally weakened by economic measures was through covert operations in cooperation with popular resistance movements in occupied Europe.

The idea quickly won supporters in cabinet, especially after June 1940, when the capitulation of France and the evacuation of the British Expeditionary Force from Dunkirk left Germany in control of most of western Europe, from the Pyrenees to the Soviet border. On the second of July, in a note to the foreign minister, Lord Halifax, Minister of Economic Warfare Hugh Dalton wrote that there were plenty of precedents for what they should be trying to achieve: "We have got to organize movements in enemy-occupied territory comparable to the Sinn Fein movement in Ireland, to the Chinese Guerrillas now operating against Japan, to the Spanish Irregulars who played a notable part in Wellington's campaign . . . We need absolute secrecy, a certain fanatical enthusiasm, willingness to work with people of different nationalities, complete political reliability." Dalton's enthusiasm got him something he might not have expected: the job of running the non-existent and unnamed organization, much to the chagrin of the Foreign Office and the War Office, both of which assumed that the task would fall under their purview. On 19 July 1940, a cabinet memorandum laid the groundwork for the establishment of an organization "to coordinate all action, by way of subversion and sabotage, against the enemy overseas," under Hugh Dalton; it was approved three days later by Prime Minister Neville Chamberlain.[4]

But SOE didn't spring to life fully formed. At first, the memorandum resulted in the establishment of two distinct organizations: So1, to be engaged in so-called black propaganda, the creation of subversive material that purported to come from the enemy; and So2, which brought together the War Office's MI(R) and the Foreign Office's Section D to coordinate sabotage and subversion in the occupied territories. But on 27 August 1940, Dalton's fiefdom was reorganized. So1 merged with the Ministry of Information and the propaganda wing of the British Broadcasting Corporation to become the Political Warfare Executive; and So2 was renamed the Special Operations Executive. To run SOE as its executive director, Dalton appointed Sir Frank Nelson, once a merchant in India, a former Conservative member of Parliament and British consul at Basel, and a veteran of the Bombay Light Horse and military intelligence during the Great War. Nelson saw SOE through its early days before he retired due to ill health in early 1942, to be replaced by Sir Charles Hambro, the youngest ever director of the Bank of England and an old Etonian with a Military Cross earned while serving with the Coldstream Guards in the First World War.

The other key figure who was with The Firm from its earliest days was Colin Gubbins, who was appointed director of operations and training on 18 November 1940 (he later succeeded Hambro as SOE's executive director). The son of a Scottish diplomat, Gubbins had seen action with the Royal Field Artillery in France, Belgium, and Russia in the First World War and had fought Irish insurgents in the early 1920s and Indian insurgents in the late 1920s. When the Second World War broke out, Gubbins, like Frank Pickersgill, was in Warsaw, escaping from the Polish capital hours before the German invasion. When he arrived at SOE, it had just finished relocating from Section D's old offices in St. Ermin's Hotel in Caxton Street to Berkeley Court, a block of flats opposite the Baker Street railway station, where it occupied a couple of grubby apartments. When SOE moved further south down Baker Street, Gubbins set up shop in Norgeby House.

But at the time of Gubbins's arrival, it still wasn't entirely clear what SOE was intended to do. It was all very well to speak of subversion and sabotage, but where would the personnel come from? How would they be trained? Who would decide what their targets would be? How would they get to occupied Europe? The answers to these questions lay in the future. For now, Hugh Dalton put forward a proposal to the Chiefs of Staff that his house of subversion and sabotage should be recognized by all fighting services as a fourth arm, independent of the other three services. This idea was clearly a non-starter—the services always resisted giving any legitimacy to underground armies and were profoundly suspicious of agents running around and blowing things up—but the chiefs accepted, even if unwillingly, that covert work was one of the few tasks that could be undertaken with the resources available.

So on 25 November 1940, they prepared a memorandum entitled "Subversive Activities in Relation to Strategy," which demonstrated both their willingness to accept SOE in principle and the enormous gap that separated their thinking from the realities of occupied Europe. "The process of undermining the strength and spirit of the enemy armed forces, especially those in the occupied territories, should be the constant aim of our subversive organization," read the memo. To that end, the first priority should be attacking Italian morale and interfering with communications; the second, interfering with communications and supplies in northern France, Belgium, and Holland; and the third, preparing underground organizations to cooperate with Allied forces in the likely invasion areas of France.[5] However, there was no indication that Italian morale was in any way vulnerable, nor was it laid out precisely how interfering with communications and supplies should be achieved. Finally, fostering resistance movements was a laudable goal, but there was really nothing to foster in most of Europe; only in

Scandinavia and Poland (neither of which was mentioned in the plan) was there anything resembling the roots of a resistance movement that could be coaxed along.

At the same time, SOE was formulating more realistic proposals based on the organization's potential. Dalton's early dream, that The Firm should (or could) keep occupied Europe in a state of constant revolutionary ferment, had been supplanted by the notion that it should help build, slowly and carefully, secret armies to support a future invasion of the Continent; they should maintain pressure on the occupiers with selective acts of sabotage, but should stay underground and avoid significant engagements involving large partisan armies. To achieve that, Gubbins drew up an ambitious plan in May 1941 based on the conventional wisdom that Britain couldn't produce an army large or strong enough to defeat Germany in the field; the only alternative was to undermine Germany's war economy and morale by subversion. Gubbins argued that civilian morale was ripe for uprising in Norway, Czechoslovakia, and Poland, but that France was "spiritually unready for revolt" and needed much more preparation and propaganda. So Allied forces in Britain should be retrained as paratroops and dropped onto the Continent to help form sabotage groups and secret armies. They would lay the groundwork for a revolt in occupied Europe, but the task would require the full-time use of four hundred aircraft flying eight thousand sorties if the goal was to be achieved by the spring of 1942.

The Joint Planning Staff seemed to endorse Gubbins's plan, recognizing the value of assisting the occupied peoples to rise up when the time was right and observing that, with proper training, supplies, and timing, "we should be able overnight to produce the anarchy of Ireland in 1920 or Palestine in 1936."[6] But the request for four hundred aircraft was outrageous. Nineteen forty-one had been a disastrous year so far, with Commonwealth armies being pushed out of Greece, Crete, and large parts of North Africa. In June, the Nazis had turned east to invade Russia and every week brought them hundreds of miles closer to Moscow. The RAF bomber force was one of the few weapons left to the Allies, and it was unthinkable that the aircraft would start dropping spies when they could be dropping bombs. On the twenty-first of July, Dalton presented a scaled-back version of Gubbins's plan. Poland and Czechoslovakia had been removed from the list, because of the logistical problems of supplying resistance groups there, as had Norway, because Britain was unlikely to attempt an invasion of Scandinavia. Instead, the focus for subversive propaganda, serious sabotage, and the building of secret armies would be on France, which would get twelve hundred of the projected two thousand sorties flown by fifty aircraft (the rest would go to Belgium, the Netherlands, and the Balkans). By the fall of 1942, predicted Dalton, an underground army 24,000 strong could be armed and trained, to be kept in readiness until needed.

But although Dalton was a force in cabinet, he was outmanoeuvred by others around the table. The Chiefs of Staff decided that Bomber Command and the SIS should be given priority for aircraft; SOE would be third in line behind them, in the full knowledge that the Royal Air Force was loath to divert any of its aircraft to other operations. The chiefs were more supportive of SOE's material needs in the areas of subversive propaganda and sabotage, and agreed to supply everything that was required, including wireless transceiver (WT) sets for communications purposes, but only a quarter of the arms and munitions that SOE requested for building secret armies would be made available. In August 1941, the Joint Planning Staff formalized these arrangements. SOE's aim should be "to introduce in the early stages organizers and means of communication" to encourage and assist with subversive activities; secret armies might be encouraged, but only if they didn't conflict with this primary aim. Finally, the key area of operations was to be northern France, where the cross-Channel invasion would eventually occur.[7]

But before anything further could be achieved, the infighting that plagued SOE bubbled over into open warfare. The Ministry of Information didn't like The Firm because it didn't believe other agencies should be meddling in the propaganda war, while the Foreign Office regarded SOE, in the words of its first historian, as "an intrusive nuisance with an infinite capacity for diplomatic mischief."[8] This was part personal conflict, for Dalton and Foreign Minister Anthony Eden didn't care for each other, and part turf war. The SIS (which continued to send intelligence agents to the Continent) feared that SOE (which envisioned sending only organizers and saboteurs) was a hastily cobbled together organization that could ruin all the hard work it had done, if only by accident. Colin Gubbins recalled that "at the best SOE was looked upon as an organization of harmless backroom lunatics which, it was hoped, would not develop into an active nuisance. At the worst, it was regarded as another confusing excrescence . . . As a whole it was left severely alone as a somewhat disreputable child." The War Office, meanwhile, objected to using amateurs to do the job of professionals, and thought that everything should be left to its own intelligence services. As historian E.H. Cookridge put it, in the military view, "surely one could not give His Majesty the King's commission to accountants, dons, journalists or wine merchants and dispatch them with forged papers to fight a secret war in Europe!"[9]

This infighting was potentially ruinous for SOE—Robert Bruce Lockhart, the director of the Political Warfare Executive, wrote to Anthony Eden that the energy that should have been used against the enemy "has been dissipated in inter-departmental strife and jealousies"[10]—and there were even rumours that Winston Churchill, Neville Chamberlain's successor as prime minister, was contemplating disbanding his secret organization for setting Europe ablaze. However, none of the other departments relished the prospect of dealing with the various governments-in-exile, a task that had fallen to SOE. Those governments usually didn't approve of SOE work in occupied Europe because they were rarely consulted and heavy reprisals often followed sabotage actions, but still Baker Street seemed to have a knack for working with the fractious and stubborn governments-in-exile, a fact that played a significant role in the SOE's continued survival. So instead of dismantling The Firm, Churchill engineered a cabinet shuffle that sent Dalton to the Board of Trade and replaced him with long-time Conservative politician Lord Selborne in February 1942. Selborne immediately instituted an inquiry into the role and function of SOE. It helped clear the air, although the Foreign Office remained suspicious of The Firm and, in Gubbins's words, never ceased to regard its members as "nasty people who run around with explosives."[11]

When Hugh Dalton departed, he took with him the grand scheme of SOE helping to raise secret armies to trigger a rising in Europe (the detonator concept of warfare) and the combined program of subversive propaganda and action; the "fourth arm" notion was dead, leaving only the tasks of specific sabotage and persuading local resistance movements to coordinate with Allied strategy. In May 1942, SOE received its second general directive, and the first on Selborne's watch. It recommended that SOE be strengthened, but that its aim should be directed at laying the groundwork for the future invasion. It should help to build secret armies, especially in areas near the Channel coast, which would be the site of a future invasion of western Europe, but, just as important, it should work to prevent premature uprisings among the people of occupied Europe. But where exactly SOE should concentrate its efforts continued to change with the fortunes of the Allies.

Still, the RAF was prevailed upon to put two squadrons (designated Special Duties squadrons) at the disposal of SIS and SOE in England, to transport personnel and supplies to the Continent. The first, 138 Squadron, arrived at Tempsford airfield in Northamptonshire, hard by the main railway line between London and Edinburgh, in March 1942 with eighteen aircraft; 161 Squadron, which had been formed a month earlier but came to Tempsford later, had fifteen single- and multi-engine aircraft. The bombers had been modified to carry agents and the long, cylindrical containers that held weapons and supplies. Because navigation skills were critical, the pilots were sent on a training exercise that required them to find a specific location near Saumur, in western France between Nantes and Tours; if they reached the correct spot, they found a brightly lit compound, coincidentally the prison camp at Montreuil-Bellay where Frank Pickersgill had spent a few weeks early in the war. But guaranteeing the availability of these aircraft was a constant battle, for the air staff reserved the right to borrow them for bombing duties whenever a special effort was required.

While this high-level bargaining was going on around the cabinet table, SOE got down to work on an operational level. The Firm was divided into a number of sections, each dealing with a different country or region and each working in almost complete independence, even ignorance, of the other sections. Some of their missions have become legendary in the history of covert operations. The Czech section was most famous for Operation Anthropoid, the assassination of SS leader Reinhard Heydrich in Prague in 1942. The Norwegian section mounted a number of successful attacks against German atomic research facilities in Scandinavia, and SOE-led resistance cells in Italy were eventually responsible for some very successful military operations, including the capture of the city of Genoa in 1944.

And then there was France, or 27 Land, as it was known in SOE parlance. Although it usually languished near the bottom of the priority list, France soon became The Firm's most important battleground. Colin Gubbins noted that it was the most important country strategically in the entire western theatre of operations, so "SOE should regard this theatre as one in which the suffering of heavy casualties is inevitable."[12] By the end of the war, there were six separate sections operating in France, most of which were under the administration of a regional controller who ran the shows in Belgium (T Section) and the Netherlands (N Section) as well. DF Section dealt with secret movements and escape lines, bringing out hundreds of fugitives, from escaped prisoners of war and evading airmen to fleeing politicians and refugees, over the course of the war. EU/P Section was responsible for covert activities among Poles outside of Poland, the largest group of which was some half-million strong around Lille and St. Étienne. AMF Section was established after the Allied landings in North Africa in November 1942 to control operations on the Mediterranean coast, while the Jedburgh Section was set up in 1943 to send small teams of uniformed resistance organizers into potential invasion areas. But the two most important were RF Section, established in the spring of 1941 to train, supply, and transport agents chosen by the Bureau Central de Renseignements et d'Action (BCRA), the intelligence wing of Charles de Gaulle's Free

French movement (one of the claimants to being the rightful government of France), and F Section, covering all of France, which soon became the largest country section in The Firm.

F Section was intended to foster the resistance movement in France through selected acts of sabotage and the organization of underground circuits, but two factors complicated its work. De Gaulle bitterly resented the existence of an independent French section and saw no reason why RF Section and his own organization shouldn't control all subversive activities in France. Although F and RF Section agents cooperated on the ground, their masters in Baker Street were often at loggerheads. And then there was the uneasy relationship with Vichy France. Until November 1942, France was divided into two parts: the German-occupied zone in the north; and the unoccupied zone in the south, administered by the German-sympathizing Vichy regime. (Even after all of France was occupied, the Vichy civil service continued to work for the Germans, and against SOE.) And because the Foreign Office nourished hopes of winning over Vichyites, it banned SOE from undertaking any violent sabotage activities in Vichy, lest they inflame tensions. The Firm was even supposed to secure Foreign Office approval for any operations in Vichy, although such niceties were rarely observed.

Both of these problems, in addition to all of the operational ones, landed on the desk of F Section's head, Maurice Buckmaster. An Oxford graduate who spoke French, German, Italian, Spanish, and Portuguese, Buckmaster had worked as a reporter for the Paris newspaper *Le Matin* before joining the Ford Motor Company and becoming its manager for France in 1932. He returned to Britain in 1936, and took part in the Battle of France in 1940 as an intelligence officer with the 50th Division. He arrived at Baker Street on 17 March 1941, and within a few months was appointed head of F Section, a decision that was not universally approved. He was a compromise choice who rose to the top as the result of an internal dispute— Buckmaster himself admitted to being "the best of a poor bunch"—and as such he inspired strong opinions. No one seemed to be lukewarm about Buckmaster; he was either loved or hated. Those who disliked him found him to be indecisive, too ready to avoid conflict, prone to daydreaming, and too easygoing for a job that demanded difficult decisions. But those who appreciated Buckmaster's skills, his knowledge of France, his ambition for F Section, his scrupulous fairness, were fiercely loyal to him. One of them was the woman who, in practice, became almost his second-in-command, Vera Atkins.

For decades after the war, Atkins was portrayed as a typical Englishwoman who showed unusual aptitude for an unusual job. But, as her recent biographers have shown, she was anything but a typical Englishwoman. Her father was a German Jew from Kassel who had moved to South Africa when the city of Hamburg, where he had gone to work as an architect, was hit by a cholera epidemic in 1892. But he lost everything in the wake of the Boer War and left Africa to join the family timber business in Romania. The family was divided by citizenship. Vera's mother was English and her brothers were born in South Africa, so they were naturalized British citizens, but Vera was born in Romania, so when she and her mother returned to Britain in 1937, Vera was designated a foreign-born national and had to register with the police. While in Bucharest, Vera had mixed with men who were involved in intelligence circles, so despite her citizenship issues, in London she received an invitation from the Inter-Services Research Bureau (ISRB) about a possible position. She wasn't impressed by the operation at first, but agreed to stay for a month as a trial. She ended up staying with The Firm until after the war and became, quite literally, indispensable.

Under Buckmaster and Atkins, F Section began the secret war against the Nazi occupation by establishing resistance circuits (*réseaux*) in various parts of France. A réseau could be anything from a large regional network, covering half a dozen *départements* (administrative districts) and involving hundreds of operatives, to a tiny group of friends or relatives who carried out the odd act of sabotage. Some were set up with specific tasks to accomplish, while others were simply to attack targets of opportunity; many were envisioned as sleeper cells that would be activated when required. Most of them were created with the invasion in mind. Once Allied forces landed in occupied France, the circuits would devote their energies to destroying the transportation network to prevent German reinforcements from reaching the front, drawing German troops away from the invasion beaches by staging local uprisings, and sapping the morale and resources of the occupiers with random attacks. A typical F Section circuit would have an organizer, a WT operator to maintain communications, one or more couriers, and often a demolitions expert to train aspiring *résistants* (members of the resistance movement) in the art of destruction. The rest of the circuit would consist of the foot soldiers—farmers to hide the weapons that SOE would send in, guides to shepherd fugitives to safety, labourers to transport arms and equipment, saboteurs to mount the attacks. The entire circuit might be made up of local recruits, but more often the leadership roles were filled by agents trained in England and sent into France.

The first agent to be sent to unoccupied France, Georges Bégués, was parachuted to a field near Châteauroux on the night of 5 May 1941. Later that summer, in September 1941, Gerry Morel, a trilingual insurance salesman who was to spend two years as F Section's operations officer, became the first F Section agent to land in occupied France when a 138 Squadron aircraft took him to another field near Châteauroux; the shuttle flight brought to England Jacques de Guélis, who would be a key organizer in Baker Street for the rest of the war. By the end of September, twenty-one agents and organizers had gone to France and thirteen organizers had been recruited locally—significantly, only two wireless transceiver sets were in operation—and by January 1942, another twenty-seven agents had been sent in.

One of them was the legendary Jean Moulin, a charismatic politician who had been the youngest *préfet* (prefect) in France in the interwar era; he had been recruited by RF Section, and was greatly admired by Colin Gubbins. Indeed, Gubbins was becoming preoccupied by the work of RF Section and seemed to be growing sympathetic to de Gaulle's demands that it be given control of all operations in France. And there's no denying that RF Section had the greatest success in those early months. On 7 June 1941, British-trained Free French parachutists successfully attacked a power station near Bordeaux, The Firm's first significant blow struck against the occupiers. But the real goal was to establish networks in France that could do these things, not to drop random groups of saboteurs to attack specific targets. For the next three years, SOE would work slowly and painstakingly to build those networks.

•

As SOE was collecting the tinder it needed to set Europe ablaze, the Nazis were putting together the security service that would be responsible for stamping out any fires or, better yet, catching the arsonists before they struck. The Firm's agents faced two different and competing organizations in occupied France: the Abwehr, the German army's intelligence branch; and the various police organizations, including the Gestapo and the SD, run by the Reich Main Security Office (Reichsicherheitshauptamt, or RSHA) in Berlin.

The Abwehr was an outgrowth of the intelligence department of the German general staff, and in the wake of the First World War consisted of just four officers. It expanded through the interwar period, particularly during the tenure of its most famous chief, the hypochondriac former U-boat commander Wilhelm Canaris, and by 1939 was ready to take a leading role in the underground war. The Abwehr was responsible for the Secret Field Police, which apprehended suspects once they had been identified, and Section IIIF, the counter-intelligence wing whose French headquarters was in the Hotel Lutetia on the boulevard Raspail in Paris. The section's job was to find Allied agents and resistance networks, and exploit those networks by infiltrating them with German agents. The Abwehr, with nearly four hundred employees in Paris, was skilled, professional, efficient, and effective, but suffered from one affliction in the eyes of its political masters: the organization's devotion to National Socialism, and particularly that of Wilhelm Canaris (who despised Adolf Hitler but was willing to go to almost any lengths to see Germany triumph), was suspect. It was an affliction that would have an enormous impact on the work of F Section.

The Abwehr's competition, on the other hand, was resolutely Nazi. Popular culture usually refers to them as the Gestapo (Geheime Staatspolizei, or Secret State Police), of the black leather overcoats and dark fedoras, but they were only one part of a security apparatus that also included the Orpo (Ordnungspolizei), or regular uniformed police, the Kripo (Kriminalpolizei, or Criminal Police), and a larger umbrella group, the Sipo (Sicherheitspolizei, or Security Police). In fact, it is more accurate to refer to these organizations by their generic name, the SD (Sicherheitsdienst, or Security Service of the Nazi Party), because the distinctions between them were less important in the field. They all held SS rank but not all of them were Nazi Party members; some of the SD's best agents, far from being long-time Nazis, were plucked from civilian jobs early in the war. Still, they were all controlled by the SS through the RSHA in Berlin; ultimately, they were all answerable to SS-Reichsführer Heinrich Himmler.

If the Abwehr was more experienced in counter-intelligence work, the SD certainly had nicer offices. Avenue Foch was the grandest of twelve streets radiating out from the Place d'Étoile (now the Place d'Étoile Charles de Gaulle), and shortly after the Nazis moved into Paris, the SD took over 82, 84, and 86 to use as its French headquarters. The head of the Paris SD, Karl Boemelburg, set himself up in 82, but the most important work was done in 84. There, in a large room that looked out over avenue Foch and boasted puce carpeting and a glorious crystal chandelier, Sturmbannführer Josef Kieffer ran the counter-espionage operation. One of the few men in the building who had relevant prewar experience—before the war he was a police inspector in Karlsruhe—he was dogged and determined, but also creative and inventive in a way that few of his colleagues in the SD were. He was also never away from his office, for he lived in a small apartment at 84. Kieffer's subordinates were just as able. Josef Goetz, a former teacher in his early thirties who was brought into the SD from the Secret Field Police, was in charge of the wireless subsection, which was based on the second floor of 84. Goetz was completely fluent in French and Spanish, but the section also had an interpreter in Ernst Vogt, who had lived in Paris for most of the 1920s and 1930s, and was days away from becoming a naturalized French citizen when the war began. His office was on the fifth floor, across from the guardroom. Also on the fifth floor were seven small rooms, once the bedrooms of the housekeeping staff, that had been converted into holding cells for prisoners under interrogation.

The rest of the Nazi security apparatus was spread out around Paris. Perhaps the most important office was the French headquarters of the Peilfunkdienst, the German radio direction-finding (RDF) service, located at 64 boulevard Suchet. The service used three sophisticated direction finders at Brest, Augsburg, and Nuremberg that were capable of tracking a signal to within ten miles of its point of origin. Once they had a hit, they passed the signal on to a regional base, which dispatched two vans and narrowed the signal to a two-mile radius. At that point, a third van was sent out to pinpoint the signal to a triangle of about two hundred square yards. Finally, a technician with a portable set combed the streets on foot until he located the target. A skilled team could locate a WT set within thirty minutes and either arrest the operator or jam the signal, producing a high-pitched whine in the headset of both the sender and the receiver. The only bright spot from the résistants' perspective was that the SD never twigged to the fact that an RDF van stuck out like a sore thumb on the streets of France's cities.

•

Against this formidable security apparatus, SOE did indeed deploy an odd collection of accountants, dons, journalists, and wine merchants. The brains trust in Baker Street had no particular type of person in mind as an agent, and there were many surprises. Some of the most promising recruits failed spectacularly either during training or in the field, while others who barely completed the training program turned out to be enormously effective. One of the ablest couriers recruited in France was quite literally plucked "off a barstool in Montmartre." She rendered excellent service until her arrest, and when she returned from a concentration camp the only thing she wanted from SOE was a decent pair of evening shoes.[13]

There were, however, some basic prerequisites. Discretion, courage, and prudence were obviously essential, as was patience; being a secret agent is one of the dullest jobs imaginable, often involving weeks of inactivity punctuated by short periods of excitement. One had to be suspicious of everyone and everything, never accepting anything at face value; "Dubito, ergo sum" (I doubt, therefore I survive) was the motto of every successful agent, SOE historian Michael Foot has noted. Perhaps most important, the agent had to be comfortable in solitude. One of the most successful operatives was a man who had moved around Europe for much of his early life. "I was friendly with people from many walks of life but had no real friends," he later wrote. "In time I grew accustomed to a situation which made me something of a 'loner.'"[14] Solitude was safety. On the other hand, the natural human tendency to seek comfort in friends could be disastrous, for it made one vulnerable. In the shadowy world of covert operations, being under surveillance is like a disease: it is highly contagious (hence the practice of referring to an agent who had been compromised as "contaminated"). A loner didn't spread the contagion, but a gadfly did. Two agents decide to have lunch together to renew an old acquaintance and forget the stresses of their work for a few hours. One agent is unknown to the SD, but the other is under surveillance. By the time the lunch is over, the first agent, and everyone with whom he or she later has contact, will be contaminated just like the second agent.

In addition to character, experience was also critical. One SOE document stressed "the absolute necessity for local knowledge based on long experience of the country and of the people, which can only be gained by residence over a period of many years, living and working with—and speaking the language of—the people."[15] F Section actively sought out French expatriates and anyone else who had lived and worked in France for extended periods. One recruit might have been born in Calais to a

French mother and an English soldier who never went home after the First World War. Perhaps another married a Frenchman and moved to the Riviera, while a third lived in Paris selling pharmaceuticals for an English firm. France's overseas colonies were a good source of recruits, for people who came from North Africa, Mauritius, or Madagascar often had intimate knowledge of the metropolis to go along with their language skills. But for this reason, some people in F Section considered the recruitment of French Canadians to be risky; they might have the requisite language skills (although a French-Canadian accent is instantly discernible to anyone who is familiar with the language spoken in France) but many of them had never been to France and knew nothing of its people and customs. On balance, most of F Section's commanders would put their money on an anglophone who learned the language through living in France rather than a Québécois who had never been there before.

Someone like Georges Savaria might have seemed an excellent choice. A friend of Frank Pickersgill's in St. Denis, Savaria was obviously a fluent French speaker, but, most important, he had lived in France and understood the customs and habits of its people. Indeed, when the two met in London in December 1942, after Savaria's escape from internment, Frank tried to convince him to join the army and, without being specific, put his skills and experience to good use. But Georges declined, in the full knowledge that he was in no way suited for military service. Frank, on the other hand, was "un gaillard costaud et dynamique . . . qui est fort, robuste, plein de vie, et moi dont la santé est à refaire" ("a sturdy and dynamic fellow who was strong, robust, and full of life, and me, whose health needed mending").[16]

As Savaria realized, Frank had everything that F Section was looking for. So did Ken Macalister. They were both well educated and would be sure to respond well to training. Neither was a native French speaker, but both had learned to speak the language by being immersed in it, at the same time as they were gaining a deep understanding of French customs and society. And both were motivated by a strong love of France, and an equally strong hatred of Nazism. Having spent years trying to find a niche for their special abilities, Ken and Frank were committed to putting everything they had into helping to free France from the occupiers. F Section just had to train them to give them that chance.

SEVEN

SECRET AGENT SCHOOL

Frank Pickersgill had seen lots of stately homes in his travels through Europe, but none like this. Parts of Wanborough Manor looked familiar—the building dated back to the early sixteenth century, although its age was camouflaged by the vines that covered the stone walls, reaching up toward the gables and threatening to overwhelm the diamond-pane windows—but other things seemed entirely out of place. One of the trees had the fuselage of an airplane lodged in the upper branches; others had iron pins running up their trunks and stout ropes hanging from the limbs. There were two chalk quarries, which was not unusual, but one was pockmarked by deep pits left by exploding hand grenades, while the other often resounded with gunfire. There was a reason why SOE was nicknamed Stately 'Omes of England. This was no longer Wanborough Manor but Special Training School 5, a secret training base, commanded by Major Roger de Wesselow of the Coldstream Guards. And the young man who climbed out of the army truck in December 1942 was no longer Frank Pickersgill but 27V-3. He was about to start learning how to be a secret agent.

Each course of a dozen or so prospective agents would spend two to four weeks at Wanborough, where de Wesselow ran a tight ship—all letters were censored, telephone calls were prohibited, F Section students had to speak French at all meals, and the staff didn't hesitate to wash out anyone who was unsuitable. Every day started with reveille at 6 a.m. and a large breakfast, but after that, the students could expect anything. They might be sent to one of the chalk quarries to practise tossing hand grenades or firing everything from pistols to heavy machine guns. They could spend the morning climbing up the iron-stapled trees and shinnying down the ropes or jumping out of the airplane fuselage, and the afternoon in lectures on transmitting by Morse code, map reading, or signalling with an Aldis lamp. Many hours would be devoted to learning the mysteries of demolition—how to assemble a detonator, primer, and explosive, how to use different kinds of fuses and switches, how to determine just the right amount of explosive to bring down a bridge, or how best to disable a railway engine (the charge should be placed on the end of the steam cylinder, for the cylinder ends were made of cast iron and shattered easily; because that part didn't normally wear out, few repair yards kept spare cylinder ends, meaning that an engine could be out of action for weeks). There was French platoon and arms drill so that the students got used to reacting to French military commands; it was no use pretending to have been in a *régiment d'infanterie* (infantry regiment) if you couldn't answer when the SD asked you about standard infantry drill. In the daytime, there were lessons in wrestling and felling a tree so that it dropped across the road you wanted to block, rather than in the ditch beside it. After dark, there were long treks, sometimes late at night after the instructors had filled them up with heavy local ale, with only a compass for guidance, and exercises on approaching a guarded building noiselessly to surprise the sentry.

But agents also had to work in teams, so after a week of training in individual skills, the course was divided up into small groups, with each student taking a turn as leader. He or she would be given a task, and would be responsible for assigning jobs to each member of the group and devising a plan to achieve the objective. It was here that they learned how even the most minor mistake could trip them up. One agent-in-training was assigned to lay a dummy explosive charge in a heavily guarded railway tunnel and get away without being seen. He was feeling quite pleased with himself as he strolled unobtrusively away from the tunnel—then, one of the instructors appeared out of nowhere, inquired how he got grease smears on his light-coloured overcoat, and "arrested" him. After each exercise, the teachers sat down with the students for a post-mortem, telling them what they had done well and where they had gone wrong.

Through it all, Frank made a positive impression on the staff at Wanborough. "This man has very good command of idiomatic 27, good morale," Lieutenant Tongue recorded in his first report on 11 December 1942, although he noted that Frank spoke French with a Canadian accent. "In view of his stay in 27, has had protracted experience of Security there. Extremely well balanced, a perfectly reliable man from a security point of view." A week later, the report was the same: "His morale is excellent and he is still perfectly reliable, quite security minded." But there were a few causes for concern. "I understand that he talks English when he makes remarks in his sleep," noted Tongue in his first report, which suggested that Frank hadn't yet conquered his tendency to spend the nights fighting for sleep. The following week he wrote, "The position as regards his talking English in his sleep has improved with the exception of one outbreak one night."[1] It seemed like a trifle, but probably every town in France had at least one hotel manager or chambermaid who, hearing English coming from a guest room in the dead of night, would be all too happy to inform the Gestapo and collect a tidy reward for the information.

A second matter was equally troubling. After a lecture on the importance of security, Frank told Lieutenant Tongue of his fleeting fame as an escaper from Nazi captivity. In January 1941, the *Winnipeg Tribune* had published a short article (complete with a photograph) on his internment in St. Denis, and on 23 November 1942, a Canadian Press war correspondent named Desjardins had approached Frank about an interview; Desjardins had with him an article from a Canadian newspaper that featured a photograph of Frank above the caption "Recent Escape." Pickersgill agreed to talk about his breakout from St. Denis, but as soon as he learned of his posting to SOE, he tried to chase down Desjardins to quash the story. He asked that the article be sent to CMHQ for censoring but when nothing turned up, Frank called the Canadian Press office in Fleet Street, only to be told that

Desjardins had already sent his interview to Canada. There was nothing he could do to keep the story from appearing in Canadian newspapers.

Just as worrying was the revelation that on 29 October 1942 Frank had had his portrait taken at a photo studio on Oxford Street. He had sent two prints to his family in Canada, two to friends at Canada House, and the last two to "lady friends." He told Tongue that he could easily get the last two back, but the fact that photographs of him were floating around was a concern. "He has been interned in 27 land," reported Tongue. "The Germans, of course, took his passport, etc., and at the end of Jan. 1942 they took a photo of him. Various town authorities have also his photo, as well as several Police stations."[2] That the Frank Pickersgill who had escaped from St. Denis and the Frank Pickersgill who had his photograph taken in London might some day be connected by a zealous SD official might seem far-fetched, but SOE knew full well that the German intelligence network had a remarkable facility for gathering information. Many a prisoner of war got the shock of his life when his German interrogator produced a photo of him from an English newspaper. Still, F Section concluded that the risks were far outweighed by Frank's potential. Wanborough Manor was used to winnow out the men and women who were unlikely to make it in the field, but Frank passed with flying colours.

After the exhilaration of training at Wanborough, Christmas leave was bound to be a bit of a letdown. It wasn't all bad—there was Christmas dinner at the Masseys' watching National Film Board travelogues of Canada, and lunch with his old Toronto friend Nick Ignatieff and his brother George, Ken Macalister's friend and fellow Rhodes Scholar, then working at Canada House. There was also a reunion with Jacqueline Grant, who had finally reached England from Lisbon. The couple had spent a jolly weekend with the Grant family in Cheshire, but the more time they spent together, the more they realized their engagement had been a mistake. After hours of very difficult soul-searching, they decided to part, both realizing that theirs had been a relationship of the moment, as so many wartime unions were. They had been treading very carefully, and Frank admitted to Jack that there were too many things about himself that he didn't fully understand; until he sorted them out, it wasn't fair to make any long-term plans with anyone. "We didn't have much in common to talk about," Jacqueline later recalled. "I was aware of the fact that he was much too intelligent for me to . . . keep up with."[3] For Frank, the breakup was one of his most difficult experiences; he couldn't have been more relieved to move on to the next level of training.

●

Ken Macalister, meanwhile, was already well versed in the workings of SOE. In December 1940, the War Office had allocated three sections of the Field Security Police to SOE (a fourth was soon added) to assist in the training of agents. They were looking for people with "a natural faculty for assessing another man's character, quickly and without prejudice . . . [and] an expert knowledge of the languages and countries of the trainees." Each potential recruit was hand-picked and interviewed for the work by Intelligence Corps officers. Ken, with his incisive, logical mind, was a perfect choice. In February 1941, his Field Security section was one of the first to be attached to SOE. Each group of agents-in-training would be accompanied by at least one man from the Field Security Police (later known as a conducting officer), whose function in the process was critical: he was to be a kind of watchdog, shadowing the agents, reporting on their progress, and pointing out their strengths and weaknesses, their personal foibles and habits, their likes and dislikes—anything that could affect their ability to conduct covert operations in Europe (once in a while he joined a course under the guise of a student, to mix with a class and try to catch people off their guard). As the memo laying out their responsibilities said, their main function was "assisting trainees in every possible way including their contacts with the training staff." They would do all the drills and exercises that the students did, which allowed them to help their charges both in "absorbing the instruction and in adjusting themselves to the conditions of our service."[4]

One of the most important conditions was the primacy of security. On the one hand, the conducting officers had to come to a conclusion as to whether each recruit was sufficiently security-minded to be sent to the field. So that they could do this with an open mind, they were told nothing about the students before meeting them, on the assumption that the best means of evaluation was "really getting to know a person by living and working with him." Only then could they report on the security consciousness of their charges. And they were expected to be frank, sometimes brutally so, in their assessments, for in the field a single indiscreet comment or lapse in concentration could cost hundreds of lives. It took an awful lot to impress a conducting officer, as the evaluation of one trainee makes clear: "A man of good intelligence, but superficial, careless, irresponsible and lazy. Lacks the stamina to see a job through. Impetuous and acts without thinking, and when things go wrong gets muddled and finally gives up. Has had an aimless career without purpose in life which seems to have left him incapable of any serious concentration. Displayed no enthusiasm and was most of the time bored and even frivolous."[5] The conducting officers were also responsible for ensuring that the students kept security uppermost in their minds as they progressed through the training program. Peter Lee, who supervised the FSP sections for SOE, wrote that "they set out to make each trainee as security conscious as possible, in his own interest, as well as that of the Organisation as a whole." As much as the instructors, the FSP men made it "possible for the agents to do their extremely dangerous work and come out of it alive. The only way to do that was to have a very, very keenly developed sense of security."[6]

By all indications, Ken was enormously successful at the work. In June 1941, he was put on a special course of instruction that, as his Field Security Police commander said, would normally have brought him a commission; however, the project fell through so Ken was given the highest rank available, acting sergeant. Although his personal file gives no specifics, Ken may have gone through an early course at Wanborough with the expectation of being sent to occupied France, an assignment that would have come with an immediate commission. This conclusion is strengthened by Ken's reluctance to leave his unit while it was attached to the ISRB; he probably assumed that another opportunity would come along soon. His commanding officer reported that "he has worked consistently well for me and shown admirable aptitude for our work, for which he was well qualified." Every effort had been made to secure for Ken a commission within The Firm; he had one interview in October but "his diffident manner did not impress the interviewer and he was turned down." Still, Ken had enormous potential: "He is more than usually intelligent, but his qualifications and personality would, I think, be wasted if he were to be used as a Regimental officer, for instance. He is interested in Intelligence work, but again his personality fits him better for office rather than field work and I am sure that, were a post available in, say, the J.A.G.'s Department [Judge Advocate General, the military's legal arm], he would be ideal . . . He is so keen to get a commission that he would put his heart and soul into any post to which he might be appointed . . . He should if possible be placed in a position which would do justice to his undoubted mental qualities and where he would be able to serve best the war effort." Ken clearly felt the same way, and elected to stay with the FSP as a sergeant rather than return to the Intelligence Corps depot on the off chance that he might get a commission there: "He is wise enough to realise that it is foolish to take a commission just for the sake of being an officer when his services as an F.S. N.C.O. [Field Security Non-Commissioned Officer] might be more valuable than they would be if he were unlucky enough to land up as a square peg in a round hole."[7]

At the end of July 1942, part of Ken's frustration ended when the FSP men were commissioned as officers. Then, on 29 December 1942 came the long-awaited news. In spite of his commanding officer's opinion that Ken wasn't suited for field work, he was given a new identity—27-OB14—and posted for duty in occupied France. Having spent the past few months conducting agents-in-training through Wanborough himself, Ken was sent directly on to the next stage. He said goodbye to the civilized Surrey countryside, and boarded a train for one of the remotest parts of the British Isles.

In November 1940, SOE had set up shop in a huge tract of land in the western Highlands of Scotland, around Loch Morar and Loch Nevin, and by June 1941 had taken over nearly a dozen houses and hunting lodges to use as training facilities. The region offered many advantages: it was in what was known as the Protected Area, everything north of an imaginary line running from Inverness to Fort William, into which access was strictly controlled; its inhospitable terrain and climate would test the physical reserves of even the toughest student; its isolation meant that training could be carried out without worrying about inquisitive people asking prying questions; and it was deserted enough that fairly substantial demolition practice could take place without significant risk to the inhabitants. The course was intended, as one agent wrote, to turn a salesman or a secretary into someone who was "capable of blowing up a bridge, of sinking a ship, of putting a railway engine out of action in a matter of seconds with a mere spanner, or derailing an express train with my overcoat."[8] Some agents recall their time at Group A of Special Training Schools fondly; for others, it was an experience best forgotten.

SOE had established its headquarters in Arisaig House, an isolated mansion overlooking Loch nan Uamh and the Ardnish Peninsula. The other training stations were scattered around a hundred square miles of desolate and windswept heath and mountain. Special Training School 23 at Moeble Lodge was one of the remotest of the facilities, accessible only by a mist-soaked four-mile hike over the mountains. It was run by Major N.M. Maclean, Moeble's commanding officer, and chief instructor Derek Leach, a lawyer who would later be parachuted behind German lines in Italy. On New Year's Day 1943, Ken and Frank made their way north to start the course on the third of January. They probably had had nothing more than a nodding acquaintance at the University of Toronto; now they were to be partners.

The training in Scotland was as much about physical conditioning as about learning the tricks of the trade that would serve them well in occupied France. Every day began with the students being divided into pairs;

each pair picked up a stout log six to eight feet long, heaved it onto their shoulders, and carried it for a mile or two over the hills. Every other day, the students were sent on a twelve-mile mountain trek with nothing to guide them but a compass and a contour map. They were taught how to operate a railway locomotive, and were taken out onto the lochs in canoes or rowboats and shown how to haul in containers of arms and ammunition without getting a dunking. There was an exercise in which they were given a compass, a map coordinate, and a map; in one hour, they had to get them-selves to the specified coordinate, leave a message at that spot, and return to base, all without being seen by the conducting officers. One group of students was assigned to mount a mock attack on a train passing through the area, a job that required a long night trek through the mountains before they held up the train, terrified the passengers, planted dummy explosives on the engine, and disappeared into the night again.

Training in fieldcraft was the responsibility of Gavin Maxwell, better known as the naturalist and author of the international bestseller *Ring of Bright Water*. Maxwell taught them all the tricks of hiding or stalking in the outdoors—that it could take up to thirty minutes for the eyes to adjust fully from light to dark, that staring for too long at night made your vision play tricks, that you can hear better with your mouth open, and that the effects of sound vary with temperature, altitude, and terrain. He showed his charges how to live off the land if the alternative was starvation. Not without some revulsion, they learned that mussels and limpets could be eaten raw, and how to butcher everything from a seal to a jackdaw to a deer. They learned how to travel across broken ground without being seen, how to use the sun and moon to hide from a pursuer, and how to "read" a set of footprints. It all seemed absurdly simple once it was explained, but it was new to most of them.

Frank loved this part of the training—"it has been a real holiday as we've been parked in the nearest equivalent to the Lake of the Woods that could be imagined in Europe," as he wrote to Jack—while Ken found that the area reminded him of the landscapes that his father had described from his youth, when he was pushing railways through the wilds of northern Canada. It was probably far more physically punishing than either had imagined; Frank wrote to Helen Magill that it "involves pretty strenuous work I can tell you, so much so that at times I realize with a shock that I'm not as young as I once was and that twenty months in the hoose-gow did have a slightly rusting effect on my iron constitution." But it was also "about the most enjoyable piece of education I've ever received," he told Jack. "Under the influence of good food, fresh air and strenuous exercise I'm turning into the picture of health."[9] Now that he could devote all his energy to something he believed in passionately, Frank's chronic stomach problems mysteriously disappeared.

What was missing from their letters home was the other part of their training in Scotland: the art of killing, by any means at their disposal. The firearms training they had started at Wanborough became more intensive, and was also conducted by Gavin Maxwell, a man whose bookish appearance belied his toughness; to demonstrate that people could endure more pain than they realized, he was known to stub out burning cigarettes on his bare thigh in front of a group of students. Reputed to be one of the world's best marksmen (he was fond of interrupting students while they were playing Ping-Pong and blasting the ball out of mid-air with a single shot from his pistol), he had one of the largest collections of contemporary firearms in Britain. Maxwell's knowledge of guns was as encyclopedic as his knowledge of fieldcraft—name any firearm that was likely to be found in occupied Europe, and Maxwell could describe it down to the last screw. He taught students the most efficient way of killing quickly, the "double tap" of two shots fired into the torso of the victim, and how to storm a room where a captured agent was being held (avoid the temptation to spray gunfire indiscriminately—choose your targets deliberately, and shoot them systematically). Students learned how to strip and reassemble guns in complete darkness, and the art of instinctive shooting, or firing at targets that popped up unexpectedly without using the sight. And to test how well they had absorbed Maxwell's teaching, the trainees were sent into a house that had been specially modified by SOE engineers: electrically controlled mannequins popped out from behind doors or curtains and had to be shot, floors opened to reveal tunnels that might conceal other mannequins, and lights or flares went off to determine how agents reacted when they were temporarily blinded. It was a little like a carnival fun house, except that everything was deadly serious.

And if the situation demanded that an enemy be dispatched silently, SOE brought in two of the most frightening characters the students had ever met: Major William Fairbairn and Major Eric Sykes, both former members of the Shanghai police and known as the Heavenly Twins. They were the inventors of the Fairbairn-Sykes commando knife, a fearsome, double-edged weapon that would slice through a throat as if it was air, but they knew innumerable other ways to kill. Sykes's forte was strangulation, which he patiently taught to mild-mannered students as if he were show- ing them how to do a card trick. He dispassionately explained how to maul and maim—"During unarmed combat, if you get the chance, insert a finger into the corner of your opponent's mouth and tear it. You will find it tears very easily"—and demonstrated how simple it was to break some- one's arm. For Fairbairn, perhaps the leading practitioner of the martial arts outside of the Far East and reputed to be one of the quickest shots in the world, dealing death was his life—"Murder made easy" was his motto. One of the agents who trained under him left a vivid description of the man: "Off duty, his conversation was limited to two words: yes and no . . . All his interest, all his knowledge, all his intelligence—and he was intel- ligent—concentrated on one subject and one subject only—fighting."[10] Today, Sykes and Fairbairn would almost certainly be considered psy- chopaths, but many an agent survived a tour of duty in occupied Europe thanks to their teachings.

The Heavenly Twins were experts on killing silently and quickly but if subtlety wasn't an issue, there were always explosives. At Wanborough, the students had studied the theory of demolition; in Scotland, they actually got to practise. SOE used two types of explosives: 808, a pale, reddish-brown substance that resembled modelling clay; and a plastic explosive, known as PE or simply plastic. Both were very versatile—the one disadvantage to 808 was its odour, which called to mind almonds or rancid marzipan—and safe to handle. They were easy to cut or mould into shape (although 808 had to be "cooked up" in hot water to be formed, a process that accentuated the smell), and agents experimented with making different kinds of charges for different uses: strips of plastic for steel plate, small cylinders for cables, horseshoe- or clamshell-shaped pieces for railway lines. They learned to find and exploit the weakest point of any target, and the point that was most difficult to repair; it was better, for example, to blow a crater in a road than to bring a rockslide down on top of it, because it was much more difficult to repair a crater properly than it was to clear away some rubble. But one phrase was drilled into them at every lecture: the demolition must never fail.

As always, the conducting officers watched their students carefully, trying to spot any lapses in security or signs of weakness that could be exploited by the Germans. Lieutenant Tongue was still monitoring Frank's tendency to speak English when he talked in his sleep, but reported that, aside from an episode at the end of January 1943 when Frank was suffering from a toothache, he hadn't been heard to mumble in English at night. The concerns that Frank had expressed about his physical stamina were dissipating, too. "This man has courage and determination, his stamina has improved considerably," reported Tongue on 15 January 1943, and a week later his opinion was even more favourable: "His nerves have calmed down considerably since I first saw him, there is a big improvement in his physical wellbeing. A most capable and reliable man."[11] The newspaper article about Frank, which had indeed been published in Canada, remained a worry, especially when Frank received a letter from a woman in Manitoba asking for any information about her son, who had also been interned in St. Denis. Frank desperately wanted to give the woman what little comfort he could, but security demanded that he hand the letter over to the War Office and forget he had ever received it.

Both Ken and Frank received very positive reports from their conducting officers at the end of their course in Scotland. "Security-mindedness is ingrained in this student who is quiet, almost reserved, and painstaking to observe the rules of security," wrote Lieutenant Stebbing-Allen of Ken. "His general demeanour and behaviour from a security angle are excellent and it would be a difficult task indeed to obtain any important information or facts from him regarding his work. He has plenty of acumen and savoir faire."[12] Tongue was equally impressed with Frank's progress: "This man is very sound and reliable, courageous, determined, shows qualities of a good organiser and leader. He has shown great interest in all matters appertaining to 27 land, and has concentrated on reading literature about it. Very sound on security, and has had the benefit of his past experiences. His morale and physical condition have improved considerably. Since my last report has NOT spoken English in his sleep." For Frank, who had long been in a funk because he felt so useless, those were heady days: "I'm enjoying it as I've never enjoyed anything in life before. You know, Helen [Magill], I've been in a permanent state of exhilaration since March 8 last (the date on which I made my get-away) on the crest of a wave which kept getting higher and higher as each frontier was crossed, and which now, instead of subsiding, seems to be going on up. I don't know where it's going to land me, but it's damned good while it lasts."[13]

F Section hadn't yet decided where the training was going to land Ken and Frank, or what roles they would play. Frank had shown "an uncanny aptitude for morse [code] and should make a splendid operator," reported one instructor, but transmission speed was only a minor factor in determining whether one would be trained as a circuit organizer, a wireless operator, or a demolitions instructor. Personality was far more critical, and on that score Stebbing-Allen's very perceptive report on Ken Macalister was probably the deciding factor: "There is no change in the security mindedness of this student. He takes everything philosophically and looks upon his work as a mission from which he will allow nothing to divert him. He occasionally has nerve storms when under some mental stress, in which case he needs the influence of someone with a strong personality to take charge of him. He is resourceful and has plenty of acumen." Someone in F Section concluded that Frank was just the kind of strong personality that Ken needed. So a note was made to that effect in Frank's personal file: "We cannot at this stage indicate the localities in which they will work in the field but they will function as organisers . . . 27V-3 probably as Chief Organiser."[14]

By now, both Frank and Ken were thoroughly immersed in their new identities, because for weeks, each of them had been living as the person he would be in France. As far as F Section was concerned, Pickersgill was now François Marie Picard, but would be known to other agents in the field as Bertrand. Macalister was Jean Charles Maulnier, or Valentin (much to his chagrin, his third code name, to be used in F Section's internal communications, was Plumber). Each of them also had a detailed cover story, a fictional biography to commit to memory. Every cover story was fabricated by the individual agent and F Section staff. It could be entirely invented, a mixture of fact and fiction, or, in the case of French nationals, substantially truthful, with a few details contrived to explain their absence in England for training. So that the agent could be absolutely convincing under interrogation, the story should be based as much as possible on his or her own experience—someone who had been a commercial traveller before the war often took on the identity of a commercial traveller—but the most attention had to be paid to explaining recent events. As the SOE lecture on cover stories stressed, "Your recent history is of most interest to the police. It is also most difficult to invent satisfactorily. Particular care should be devoted to its preparation."[15] The identity assumed should also be based on places with which the agent was familiar. Ken would have been careful to avoid anything that might implicate Jeannine and Lisieux, but he knew Caen well enough and might have chosen that as his hometown. Frank had travelled more widely in France but was most at home in Paris and likely opted to become a native of the French capital. Sadly, neither of their biographies has survived in SOE's archives but the cover story prepared for Gilbert Norman (or Gilbert Aubin, as his documents identified him), who would play a major role in their lives, can serve as an example:

Gilbert was born on the 7th April, 1915 in Paris. His father Jean was a chartered accountant doing quite well. In 1916 Gilbert went with his mother to Barneville in Normandy, where he lived until 1919. He then went to Villers-sur-Mer, and in 1921 to Parame. They also used to go for the holidays to Biarritz.

After the last war his parents were separated and he has only a very vague recollection of his father who died in 1921 leaving his mother a certain amount of money, but the bulk of his fortune in trust for Gilbert.

Between the ages of six and nine he was taught by young Danish girls who used to come as *demoiselles de compagnie* to his mother. In 1925 they went back to Paris, and he was sent as a boarder to the Lycée Hoche de Versailles, where he stayed for four years. During that time he rarely saw his mother, and found out later that the reason for this was that she was living with another man.

In 1929 his mother, (he thinks with a view to getting him out of the way), sent him to England where he finished his education at Ongar public school.

In 1933 he came back to France, and started to work in an accountant's office. He had continued rows with his mother who thought he was not taking his work seriously enough and paid too much attention to sport. When he was twenty-one he came into quite a lot of money from his father and then had his complete independence. After a very serious quarrel with his mother on the subject of this legacy and also on the subject of his military service which his mother wanted him to postpone so that he could finish his studies, and since then he has never seen her again.

In May 1936 he did his service in the Vingt Quatrieme
Regiment d'Infanterie. He was Service Auxiliaire, and worked in
the Bureau de la Compagnie as Secretaire.

After his service he got a job as private secretary with
knowledge of accountancy with M. Jean Paul Sender, Industrial
Metallurgist, (Mines de Ste. Marie de Gravigny, Comité des
Forges), co-director of the restaurant "A l'Ecu de France," rue de
Strasbourg, Paris, and later director of the restaurant "A l'Ecu de
France, Ltd," Jermyn Street, London, and of the sweet-shop "La
France Gourmande Ltd" also in Jermyn Street, and also owner of
the "Ferme St. Lazare," Paris.

His job entailed him coming to England about once a fortnight, which he did regularly.

In August, 1939 he caught very serious bronchitis,
followed by sinus trouble, and he was unable to join the army
until January, 1940, when he went to Maison Lafitte to the
Depot 211. Nevertheless after he had been there no longer than a
fortnight, his sinus trouble started again, and he was sent back to
the military hospital at Versailles, only being sent back to Maison
Lafitte in the beginning of May. He was then evacuated through
Orleans with the depot, and was finally demobilised in Perpignan
for Paris.

On arrival in Paris he found that his old address which was
in the Avenue Clodoald, Le Val d'Or, near St. Cloud, had been
occupied by the Germans, and he went to stay in Senlis to recu-
perate a little in the country, where he took out his identity card,
12, rue du Chatel, Senlis. He later changed his ration card in Paris,
Gallic Hotel, 288, rue Vaugirard.

All during this time he had enough capital to live without
working, but now fearing to be sent to Germany he has come
down to the South of France to live.[16]

Norman's detailed cover story is revealing for the care that SOE took to avoid possible problems for agents who might be captured. Gilbert Aubin had no living relatives that he cared about, which meant that the Germans could find no one to use against him. The fact that his Paris dwelling had been requisitioned (something that had happened all over occupied Europe) gave him a good excuse for having moved around. Should he be questioned by a French policeman who happened to know something about his military unit, the fact that his most recent service had been short and interrupted by stays in hospital would explain why he knew little about the unit, and the unit knew little about him. And finally, any deficiencies in Norman's French (like many of SOE's English agents, his French had a slight English accent) could be accounted for by the fact that he went to school in England and travelled frequently there on business; his bouts with sinus trouble could also explain away any pronunciation oddities. The birthplace was always a difficult decision—should it be a big city, where there were easily accessible municipal records but dozens of people named Gilbert Aubin, or an isolated village, where documents were harder to come by but everyone knew everyone else? Sometimes, the choice was positively inspired. Had the SD been able to do a tally, it would have found that an inordinately large number of agents were born either in St. Pierre de Martinique, which was destroyed by a volcano in 1902, or Péronne, whose municipal record office was burned out during the Battle of the Somme in 1916.

•

After seven days' leave came the next stage of training, which was directed at solving the problem of getting the agents to France by one of three methods. When the Royal Navy could be persuaded, a small boat might be made available to drop an agent off at some deserted spot on the coastline of France. This method was most useful in the Mediterranean, where a small coasting vessel known as a felucca was often used to ferry agents ashore, particularly near the Spanish border, to one of the many isolated coves and beaches that were perfect for illicit landings.

More common was to go in by airplane. In 1936, Westland Aircraft Limited had developed an ungainly but extremely versatile aircraft called the Lysander, whose greatest advantage was its short takeoff and landing capability. With room for three passengers as well as the pilot, it could land on a field only 170 yards long, unload its passengers, and be back in the air within a couple of minutes; many agents were sent on a short course at Tempsford in which they practised, for hours at a time, getting themselves and their luggage on and off a Lysander quickly and with a minimum of fumbling. The main disadvantage of this method of transport was that there was room only for small suitcases; WT operators who went by Lysander had to wait for their sets to be parachuted in on another operation. Later, as SOE staff realized that these landings were much easier and less risky than they had imagined, a larger aircraft, the Lockheed Hudson (the military version of the Lockheed Electra, the most successful civilian airliner of the prewar years), was put to use. It needed a 1,000-yard field and more time to land, unload, and take off again, but it could handle ten passengers or nearly a ton of cargo. These operations began modestly, with a single Lysander flight in 1941, but soon mushroomed; in 1943, there were fifty-four landings, bringing in 103 agents and taking out 200.

But the most common method was by parachute, so all agents were posted to Special Training School 51, the British Army's parachute school at Ringway, near Manchester. So while Ken was sent to train as a wireless operator, Frank went to Ringway in February 1943 to learn the fine art of jumping out of airplanes. It all started very innocently, with the students scattered around a patch of ground and rolling to the left and to the right, then doing backward and forward somersaults, all the time with their hands in their pockets. In this way, they learned how to fall safely in whatever position they happened to be in when they hit the ground. Then they were sent into an aircraft parked nearby and took turns jumping through a metal chute in the floor, so they could get the feel of what it would be like exiting the aircraft. Next it was onto the trapeze, where they were swung, sometimes violently, to get used to the feeling of hanging under a parachute. Finally, it was on to the real thing.

The instructors worked the nervous students up to it gradually. First, they used Ringway's tower, jumping from higher and higher platforms each time. There was a funnel mounted on one of the platforms that was similar to the chute in the aircraft, so they spent a few hours jumping through that, elbows hugging their sides and legs together, always keeping stiff and straight to avoid bashing their face on the funnel as their legs were caught by the wind. Some trainees made a jump or two from a tethered balloon affectionately known as Bessie, but most went straight to the airplane. Nothing conveys the mixture of emotions in the experience better than Frank's own description of his first jump:

When we piled into the plane and the R.A.F. despatcher had hitched our static lines to the plane I felt pretty awful. We sat for about ten minutes while the plane took off and flew over to the landing park. I've never been so scared in my life. I was third to jump, and I sat there muttering to myself: 'Heads up, legs together, hands by your sides' which was about the only thing that kept me from rolling around and screaming with terror. Then the first pair went out and I had to move over right beside the hole while the plane circled round the field. Those were the worst two minutes as I was terrified that I would inadvertently glance through the hole and was sure if I did that I'd funk it. So I kept my eyes glued to the despatcher's hand. He yelled Action Stations and I got my feet into the hole and from then on I wasn't afraid anymore, which is quite curious. I was conscious of absolutely nothing but the despatcher's hand. He brought it down yelling GooooOOOOO so loud it fairly blew me out of the plane, and my only feeling as I saw myself falling through the hole was one of complete relief to be rid of the god-damned plane. Then three seconds of absolute heaven. The displacement of air made by the plane causes a 100 m.p.h wind all round the plane—this gale is called a slipstream—so that the parachutist, instead of dropping like lead when the shoot opens, finds himself carried along on this wind, in a horizontal direction, absolutely riding on air. I came out beautifully from the plane and hit the slipstream in such a way that I found myself floating along on my back in the gale, 800 feet off the ground, as though I were lying on a feather bed, watching the plane drift off. Then a very slight tug all over the body and I looked still further up and saw the most incredibly beautiful sight in the world which is a 'chute opening. I swung my arms up to take hold of the rigging lines and suddenly the gale was no longer. Absolute peace and silence. I looked down and saw the ground gently approaching from a long way off, and suddenly out of this, a still small voice saying, 'All right No. 1, a nice exit—now keep your legs together and take up a good position in the air' . . . then suddenly, 'Careful No. 1, get ready to land'—and suddenly the ground was a few yards away and coming up at an uncomfortable speed. Then WHAM and I hit the ground, rolled over, and was on my feet without feeling even a bump, and this time it was the ground that felt vaguely unreal for a split second. Then about two hours of the most intense elation—an intensity of feeling such as I've never experienced. Then complete exhaustion for the rest of the day. Such a variety and intensity of emotion within such a short time is very tiring indeed . . . I jumped well—and I must confess to feeling a bit pleased with myself, especially as I wasn't sure right up to the last minute whether I mightn't get cold feet and refuse. Some do. And it's marvellous, once you do get out of the bloody plane. It's the nearest thing to a perfect dream that could be imagined. I really feel deeply sorry for anyone who hasn't done it.[17]

Of course, getting to the right place on the ground was just as important as getting out of the airplane; unless the agent was being dropped blind, or without a reception committee, that meant hitting the drop zone that local résistants had set up. Each site was known by a code name or number, and confirmation of any operation was aired over the BBC in a broadcast known as "Messages Personnels," as part of the 7:15 and 9:15 p.m. news bulletins. Invented by SOE agent Georges Bégués and first used in November 1941, the idea took advantage of the fact that most French people who owned a radio studiously ignored the German ban on listening to the BBC. So "Messages Personnels" became a way to communicate instantly with resistance groups. Most of the messages were nonsense, but hidden among them were phrases to verify that an operation would indeed take place that night or to specify the drop zone: "Flora a le cou rouge" (Flora's neck is red) referred to a field south of Thenon, while "Le crocodile a la pépie" (The crocodile is parched) meant a drop zone near Couloumieux. When the reception team reached the correct site, three résistants held flashlights or bicycle lamps in a row along the direction of the wind while a fourth stood off to one side, to make a backwards *L*. As long as it wasn't too cloudy or foggy and the lamps weren't too dim or pointed in the wrong direction, the incoming aircraft would spot the lights and begin to circle, at which point a recognition code consisting of two letters of the alphabet in Morse code or a certain sequence of colours would be flashed. In the aircraft circling above, the navigator watched carefully for the correct signal and flashed the green light in the fuselage when it was time to jump. It was essential that the agents jump exactly when they were told, because a few seconds too late was enough to put them far away from the drop zone. When high winds meant that even the best navigator couldn't guarantee a landing on the drop zone, the agents were always given the final word: did they want to jump and try to find the drop zone themselves, or go back to Tempsford and try again another night? As the agents, and any containers of arms, ammunition, and supplies that accompanied them, floated down, each person on the reception team had to count the number of parachutes, so they knew exactly how many they had to retrieve. All things considered, such drops were not as dangerous as they might seem, either for those on the ground or for those in the air. Operations were always done during moon periods, but even with a bright full moon, pilots were often surprised at being able to wander around French skies without attracting the attention of enemy aircraft. And, at over 250,000 square miles, France was far too large for the occupiers to be watching every field; in any case, for much of the war, German patrols ventured into the depths of the French countryside at their peril, for they were up against locals who knew every forest track, gully, and creek, and could lay an ambush for them with embarrassing ease. So if everything went according to plan, the agents and containers could be collected and the drop zone cleared within thirty minutes.

•

Ken had already done the Ringway course a number of times as a conducting officer—like most people, he found it terrifying at first but was surprised (and amused) to discover that jumping became a strangely addictive joy—so he went straight to Special Training School 52 at Thame Park to attend a course for wireless operators. Thame Park, east of Oxford, had for hundreds of years been home to a community of Cistercian monks, but in the eighteenth century a grand stately home was built by a family of wealthy wool merchants. During the Second World War it was pressed into service as an SOE training academy, where agents prepared for what was arguably the most difficult and dangerous job that F Section had to offer. The wireless operator was the lifeline between the field and home base: as one agent put it, "without your radio operator you were a pigeon without wings."[18]

At Thame Park, Ken learned that everything about the job made the wireless operator vulnerable, starting with the big and bulky radio set. The standard set was the B Mark II wireless transceiver that weighed nearly thirty pounds and was squeezed into a two-foot-long suitcase (a later model, the A Mark III transceiver, was smaller, at ten by seven by five inches, and about half the weight, but was still too big to be easily concealed). The suitcase, lined with flannel or felt to protect the contents and prevent things from rattling around inside, contained all the tools of the WT operator's trade: a power pack to run the set either from the electrical mains or on battery (later sets came with an adapter that allowed the WT to be powered by a car battery), an instruction book, ten feet of grounding wire, the transmitting key, a telephone headset, twelve fuses of assorted amperages, four spare valves, and a tool kit for repairs. None of these pieces could be easily disguised, nor could the two quartz crystals that determined the frequency to be used; whenever an operator wanted to change frequencies, he or she had to change crystals. They were about the size of a postage stamp and were easy to hide, but it was impossible to make them look like anything else; any half-trained German policeman could spot a stray crystal from across the room. Finally, there was the aerial, sixty or seventy feet long, that had to be strung out before a transmission. The fact that every passerby was a potential informant meant that laying out the aerial had to be done with the utmost caution.

To lessen the risk of detection, operators were advised to find a number of safe locations (ideally in the suburbs, where there were fewer RDF vans at work) so they never transmitted from the same place for two consecutive sessions. This was especially important because they were tied to scheduled transmission times, usually three per week, when the signals staff back in England would be monitoring their frequency and waiting for them to come on the air. But habit is the enemy of the undercover agent and being tied to a transmission schedule meant that, over a period of time, the Germans could home in on an operator; more than one agent was discovered because of being tied to fixed transmission schedules. Choosing the site for a radio post was also tricky. Because the key taps could easily be heard in an adjoining apartment (a metal building magnified the sound of the taps even more), the reliability of all the neighbours had to be investigated as well. And moving around meant that the heavy wireless set had to be camouflaged and carried from place to place. In theory, the operator was not supposed to move his or her own set, but was to rely on a courier to transport it; after all, a wireless set and courier were easy to replace, but a highly trained operator wasn't. In fact, the operator should not be used for any other work at all, and should not transmit for other circuits except in extraordinary circumstances. In such cases, other agents were to make contact not directly, but always through intermediaries; even contact between the operator and his or her own organizer should be kept to a minimum. And in general, the operator should have as little to do with the rest of the circuit as possible. The ideal operator was known to only one or two members of the circuit; in the shadowy world of the resistance, the wireless operator was supposed to be little more than a rumour.

One aspect of the training appealed to Ken's sharply analytical mind more than most: initiation into the mysteries of coding. Eventually, part of his job would be to encode all of the messages that Frank wanted to send to England, and decode the incoming messages. SOE used a number of codes, the most common of which was the poem code, in which each agent chose a poem or song lyric that could be easily remembered. For every message to be sent, the operator would select five words at random from the poem, give each letter a number (the transposition key), and then use the numbers to encode the message; the process would then be repeated using five different words. A sequence of five letters, known as the indicator group, at the beginning of each message told SOE which words from the poem should be used to decode the message. The flaw with the code was that agents tended to choose common verses, such as passages from the Bible or Shakespeare. If a well-read German cryptographer cracked a single message, or even broke a couple of words, it was fairly easy to determine the poem code, which would provide the key to deciphering all of the operator's future messages. In a variant known as double transposition, the operator had to memorize two sequences of six or seven letters each; the message would be written out under the first sequence, then again under the second. This was much more secure than using a poem, but too many agents, reluctant to trust their memory, wrote down their codes, which could then be used by the enemy if they were captured.

To complicate matters further for the WT operator, two security features had to be included in every message: a bluff check and a true check. Each was a deliberate mistake introduced into the coding—for an agent sent to the Netherlands, for example, one of his checks was to replace every sixteenth letter of a message with the letter that preceded it in the alphabet. The rationale for two checks was simple. If SOE received a message with both checks, it was authentic. Operators were told that they could reveal their bluff check under torture, but that they should not under any circumstances disclose their true check, or reveal that there were two different security checks. So if a message came in with only the bluff check, it meant that the agent had been captured and the message was sent either under duress or by the Germans. As a last resort, SOE was prepared to send specific questions to any agent, either asking for personal information that only he or she would know or demanding a certain response that had been agreed upon beforehand. The correct response, of course, was never what might be expected. For example, the proper reply to "Do you need cigarettes?" might be "Do you need matches?"

But the fact that coding and transmitting involved a large measure of chance made the operator's job even more difficult. When a message reached England, it might be garbled because of any number of factors: German jamming, atmospheric conditions, a weak signal, errors in coding (a single incorrect letter or number in the coding process could render a message all but indecipherable), the stress of trying to transmit in the full knowledge that RDF vans could be in the neighbourhood, or even a simple slip of the hand. The women who staffed SOE's coding centre would spend hours trying to interpret a garbled message, particularly by looking at the kinds of coding mistakes the operator had made in the past, and the vast majority of "indecipherables" were eventually cracked. But for an operator in the field, the worst message to receive was "Last transmission indecipherable please resend."

●

The last stage was Group B of Special Training Schools, better known as Beaulieu, in the New Forest. Today, Beaulieu is one of Britain's top tourist attractions, home to the National Motor Museum, a magnificent stately home, a medieval abbey, and, on any given day, hundreds of busloads of visitors. Before the First World War, its owner, the 2nd Baron Montagu, had invited a number of his friends to lease parcels of land on his massive estate and build private residences to use as retreats from the bustle of London. Between 1905 and the mid-1930s, nearly a dozen homes were built, from the tiny Hartford House, designed for three or four people, to The Drokes, a thirteen-bedroom mansion with two cottages on twenty-four acres of property. But when the Second World War began, many of the owners went into uniform and an SOE officer who lived near Beaulieu suggested to Gubbins that, because they were isolated and could be easily guarded, some of the houses could be requisitioned as training stations. Gubbins liked what he saw, and by early 1942, SOE had taken over nine of the houses, some for administrative offices, lecture rooms, and instructors' quarters, and others for students from the various national sections, who were usually segregated during the final stage of training. For its headquarters, SOE chose The Rings, a thirty-nine-room mansion built in 1910 and, in 1939, leased to a prominent London heart specialist. At its peak, Beaulieu would be home to as many as four courses of trainees at one time.

In April 1943, Ken Macalister and Frank Pickersgill came together again at what was colloquially known as The Finishing School. They were probably stationed at Boarman's, built in 1935 by a naval commander and favoured by F Section for training purposes. With the physical conditioning of the Highlands behind them, the students now engaged in intensive study of the other parts of a secret agent's job: deception, guile, secrecy, disguise. There were usually about fifteen instructors on staff at Beaulieu, each of them an expert in something that might one day mean the difference between life and death in the field. Peter Follis, who had been trained by one of Max Factor's cosmetics experts, taught them how to alter their appearance using hair dyes, cosmetics, or balls of cotton wool placed in the cheeks or nostrils. Hardy Amies, later the dressmaker to Queen Elizabeth II, lectured on the structure of the German army and police, particularly on how to recognize what kind of enemy you were dealing with by the uniform and rank badges. Kim Philby, who would come to fame as a Soviet mole in Britain, instructed them in propaganda techniques and on how to undermine the authority of the occupiers by subtle means. William Clark had spent twenty-two years in the British Army before embarking on a second career as a gamekeeper at the royal estate at Sandringham, and taught them how to live off the land if they were forced to flee to the countryside. He knew only one French word—*braconner*, to poach—but he taught them that a hedgehog could be cooked on a smokeless fire, that rooks, jays, and wood pigeons made a terrible racket when disturbed, that sheep would huddle together and stare at whatever scared them, and that geese made lots of noise and tried to chase any intruder. There were people to help them perfect their cover stories, to show them how to bury a parachute so that it would leave no traces, and to pass on countless bits of arcane and unusual advice—like the fact that many Germans had a deathly fear of infectious diseases. If a policeman approached, you should bite your lip, cough noisily, and spit bloody saliva on the sidewalk; it might just convince him that you had tuberculosis and should be avoided.

One of the most important series of lectures dealt with the principles of setting up cells of résistants, which would be Frank's job. The first lesson was that it didn't matter what motivated the potential recruit—patriotism, hatred of the Nazis, politics, greed, love of adventure, or something else entirely. Someone who was in it for the money could be just as useful as someone who did it for purer motives; what mattered was their reliability, their discretion, their sense of security, and their skills. Recruiting agents was a tricky business, especially if there was no skeleton of an organization to build on. The ideal résistant might be anywhere—French railway workers were known to be solidly anti-Nazi, but religious groups or fraternal organizations were also fertile ground. Whatever the situation, enlisting a recruit meant treading carefully, gently testing the candidate's reliability and opinions, revealing as little as possible about the work to be done, and backing off at the first sign of reluctance. It was better to go through a dozen fruitless interviews waiting for the right person than to enlist someone about whom one had doubts.

But the organizers were also taught how to build safeguards into their network in case one of their recruits turned. Ideally, a network should be made up of a number of cells, each of which was almost completely independent of the others; only one member of the cell should know the identity of the organizer (or, even better, the identity of the organizer's second-in-command) for whom the cell was working. Contact between cells was to be maintained through intermediaries, known as cut-outs. Circuit heads should have as little contact with each other as possible, and ideally should never be seen in public together. The job of the cut-out was to be the link between circuits. The work might not extend beyond delivering messages, or it could mean playing a more active role in the organization. Either way, the ideal cut-out was someone who had an excuse for mingling with all ranks of society and who blended into his or her surroundings, like a taxi driver, shopkeeper, or mail carrier. Another key element in organizing cells was to set up a number of letter boxes (*boîtes-aux-lettres*), places where messages could be left to be collected by another member of the network. The owners might know the nature of the messages, but it was safer if they were ignorant. For example, a bookshop could be a very effective boîte-aux-lettres; messages could be left in a certain book (preferably one that was unlikely to sell) to be picked up by another agent, and the owner would be none the wiser. Finally, the organizer had to find a number of safe houses, where incoming agents could rendezvous and where anyone whose cover had been blown could hide until being helped to safety. Those addresses, of course, had to be communicated to London using an elaborate code that had been arranged to ensure their security. For addresses in Paris, for example, the telephone book was the key: "You will pick the 9th street after the real one in volume 2 of the 1939 directory, add 9 to the number of the street, put that figure both before and after the name of the street, and omit the name of the town entirely."[19] If sufficient care was exercised, cut-outs, boîtes-aux-lettres, and safe houses would go a long way toward keeping a resistance circuit secure from infiltration and collapse.

But carelessness came in many forms, so the expert on local customs tried to get the students to remember a thousand and one minor details, each of which could avert disaster in the field. Never try to buy cigarettes without a tobacco card. In a restaurant, don't ask for café noir, because there was no other kind of coffee available in occupied France, or a pastry, because butter rationing had consigned them to the black market, and never fall into the English habit of pouring the milk in your teacup before the tea. As you are finishing your soup, don't tip the bowl away from you, in the English custom, but toward you, as they do in France. When pausing in a telephone conversation, don't say "Tenez la ligne," as an English person might, but "Ne quittez pas l'écoute" or simply "Ne quittez pas." Be aware of the risks of certain kinds of travel. In Paris, the metro was the quickest way to move about the city, but there were many security checks; walking or cycling was slower, but immeasurably safer. Even travelling by train had its risks. You should always avoid lining up to buy tickets or to board a train; the police often watched queues, because it was easy to spot people who looked nervous or out of place. And many large railway stations had just one exit open, so all passengers had to pass through a security cordon to reach the street. You should resist the temptation to give up your seat on a train or a bus for a woman, even if she was elderly or infirm, because it was never done in wartime Europe. In the countryside, it was best to travel by bicycle unless one had access to a commercial vehicle with the necessary travel permits; civilian cars were rare in rural areas, and sure to attract attention. Learn how to comb your hair and leave your cutlery on your plate in the French manner. Agents even had their teeth inspected and, if necessary, the English fillings were removed and replaced with dental work done in the French style.

All of these little details came under the heading of personal security, the single most important consideration for an agent in the field. A failure to take basic security precautions could lead not only to one's own arrest, but to the collapse of an entire circuit. But SOE realized that security was difficult to teach, because some people were naturally less careful and cautious than others. So it considered security to be "a frame of mind attainable through self-discipline and self-training that will make the taking of precautions a 'habit.'"[20] All sorts of things had to become second nature. Commit things to memory instead of writing them down, and burn any written material as soon as it was no longer needed. Keep your lodgings as neat as possible; it's much easier to discern evidence of a police search in a tidy, spartan room than in a cluttered one. Avoid doing anything, in terms of appearance or conduct, that might attract attention—the most effective agent was the person about whom there was nothing distinctive. Plan for any eventuality, particularly by ensuring that you knew an alternate exit to any building you entered. Be aware of the people around you at all times—a face or voice seen or heard more than once could mean you are being tailed. In one exercise, an instructor came into a room of students for five minutes; when he left, they each had to write down a detailed physical description of him. Most of them were surprised at how poorly they did, until they were taught how to approach the subject systematically and logically. They were also taught to observe what was happening in the distance. If you could spot a police checkpoint a block ahead, you could avoid it; once you got too close, turning around would arouse suspicion. Another tip was to avoid confiding in people as a way of easing mental strain. Running a resistance network was an enormous burden, but it was a burden that had to be borne alone. To give in to the temptation to tell people more than they should know, to get something off your chest, was to risk compromising the entire organization. If the most effective agent was the one who was indistinguishable from the crowd, SOE's lecturers repeated time and time again, he or she was also the loner with an anti-social streak.

But for many of the students, the most disturbing part of the course was the mock interrogations. Specialists had lectured them on how to conduct themselves under questioning, telling them that the first principle was never to give anything away. But the reality was that the enemy was known to resort to terrible torture and not everyone had the same capacity to resist. So the rule of thumb was to reveal nothing for at least forty-eight hours, to give your contacts time to escape, and there were a few simple principles to help them through those two long days. Most people aren't very convincing liars, especially in a tense situation like an interrogation, nor can they remain expressionless through any eventuality (one exception was an agent whose father had bought horses from a slaughterhouse, cleaned them up, and sold them as quality animals—from his teenage years, the agent became adept at convincing people that a knackered-out old mare was really a fine hunter). So instructors showed the students how to be evasive, dissembling, and downright unhelpful without infuriating an interrogator. Speak slowly and, no matter what the question, get into the habit of pausing before answering, to give yourself time to think about the more difficult questions. Make your answers as short and simple as possible, and ensure that they don't open up more questions. Deny everything you cannot explain, rather than trying to change your story in midstream to get around problem areas. Don't try to appear clever, but rather aim to create the impression of someone who is rather stupid but honest and eager to be helpful. Don't express personal interest in or affection for anyone. Be aware of all the old tricks, like the interrogator who tells you that he knows everything about your operation already so you might as well cooperate.

But the mock interrogations were different from sitting through a lecture. They might occur at any time, although the conducting officers were fond of turning the students out of bed early in the morning, the very time that the Gestapo liked to stage raids because it was the time when people's resistance was typically at its lowest. The students weren't allowed to go to the washroom or get dressed, but had to sit or stand, sometimes with their hands above their heads, while their "interrogators" fired questions and yelled threats of dire punishment at them. All the while, they had to stay in character and stick doggedly to their story. Occasionally, two or three of them were separated, placed in a room, and given a few minutes to come up with an alibi for some act of sabotage that had occurred. This test of quick thinking and the ability to stick to a plausible story was much harder than it sounded. One group of students came up with a very good story that, while the attack was taking place, they were having lunch at a local doctor's house. Each of the three was then questioned individually, and they almost passed the test impressively. But they were tripped up by the most mundane of questions: was the table they ate at round or square?

Each course at Beaulieu finished up its training with a three- or four-day exercise in which students were instructed to study a target, such as a munitions factory or the Manchester ship canal, find some way of getting close to it, determine how best to disable it, and do it all without raising any suspicion. Not only did they have to dodge the real police, who were not informed in advance of the exercises, but SOE also planted operatives along the way who would use any means possible, from sex to alcohol, to try to infiltrate their group. It was gratifying for F Section to discover that its agents were rarely seduced by sex and alcohol; they usually fell victim to much more prosaic things. One team was sent to Portsmouth, where their leader was to get a job in an aircraft factory and find the best part of the plant to sabotage in an effort to cripple production. He achieved all of that with ease, and then wrote a letter, ostensibly from his wife describing her sudden illness, to explain why he had to leave his job on a few hours' warning. It was a good idea, but he failed to camouflage his handwriting enough; the factory manager noticed that the husband and wife had suspiciously similar handwriting and called the police, and the agent-in-training was arrested. Another student got the better of his teachers. Sent to Sheffield with a list of names of possible contacts, he was instructed to set up a resistance cell; the trick was that the contacts, all SOE plants, were not all reliable, and some had been given the role of traitor to play. But the agent quickly realized the dangers in the exercise, tore up the list, and made his own way around Sheffield finding people he deemed trustworthy. F Section's instructors had to admit that they had been bested at their own game, and had the city police arrest their clever student.

Regrettably, their personal files are silent on how Ken and Frank fared at Beaulieu. We have only the report of Lieutenant Holland, Ken's last conducting officer, which again is a very perceptive assessment of the man and his motivation: "This student is now approaching the end of his training. The appearance he presents to the world is deceptive, giving the impression of easy-going urbanity, whereas he has in reality a particularly tough scholar's mind, logical and uncompromising in analysis. He is interested in general ideas, in involving a sort of practical philosophy of living in society, and he sees the German menace as a canker which calls for drastic surgery and consequent willingness for sacrifice on the part of those who are to be the instruments of it. His idealism is no weaker for being based on ideas rather than on instinctive love of country, for example. He is the type of man who analyses a situation, places it in relation to the wider background of the development of mankind, arrives at the only solution of the problem by deductive reasoning, and then pursues it with unswerving intellectual conviction."[21] At the end of it all, Ken and Frank were pronounced ready. Fully trained, both physically and psychologically, all they could do was wait to see what F Section had in store for them. When their assignment came, it would tie their fate to a man who would become one of the enigmas of F Section.

EIGHT

PROSPER

In the early fifth century, an obscure layman from the south of France rose to prominence in the church on the strength of two letters he wrote to St. Augustine of Hippo, "On the Predestination of the Saints" and "On the Gift of Perseverance." Prosper of Aquitaine would become secretary to Pope Leo the Great, a poet and historian of some ability, and, eventually, a saint. Fifteen hundred years after his death, his name would be adopted by one of SOE's most important agents.* Frank Pickersgill would have been quite familiar with Prosper from his research on Augustine, but Francis Suttill, thanks to a solid classical education at Stonyhurst College in the north of England, also knew of St. Prosper. He may have been attracted to him because of his defence of perseverance. Ironically, predestination would become the defining characteristic of Suttill's work in France.

In many ways, Francis Suttill was exactly what F Section was looking for in an agent. He was born in 1910 near Lille, a rough-and-tumble cloth city in northern France, to a French mother and an English father who was managing director of a large textile firm and president of the city's chamber of commerce. His parents sent him to England for a public school education, but he took a degree in law at l'Université de Lille and was called to the bar at Lincoln's Inn (the same inn with which Ken Macalister was affiliated) in

---

*Every agent was given a code name but I shall refrain from using them, to avoid confusion. Ken Macalister shared his code name with one other agent, while Frank Pickersgill shared his with at least three. In the early days, every wireless operator going into France was given the code name Georges.

1936, with a specialty in international law (again, Ken's great passion). When war broke out, Suttill was commissioned in the East Surrey Regiment but soon came to the attention of SOE and was brought into The Firm in 1941. Suttill was an impressive man—charismatic, good-looking (perhaps a little too good-looking to blend in with a crowd), intelligent, strong-willed, and ambitious. And he was given an important task, perhaps the most critical that faced F Section in 1942: rebuilding the shattered remains of its first forays into covert operations.

F Section's great empire in France had begun with a single circuit, Autogiro, led by the formidable Pierre de Vomécourt. If ever there was a man with reason to hate the occupiers, it was de Vomécourt. He came from a distinguished military family that had suffered heavily at the hands of Germany: his great-grandfather had been tortured and murdered by the invaders during the Franco-Prussian War and his father, despite being over-age, enlisted at the beginning of the First World War, only to be killed in action within weeks. The shock of the loss sent his mother to an early grave, leaving the five de Vomécourt children orphaned. The eldest, Jean, joined the Royal Flying Corps and was grievously wounded in 1918; the other two boys, Pierre and Philippe, were too young to serve. Their chance to exact revenge on the Germans would come in the next war.

Only one of the brothers escaped from occupied France and, after extremely rudimentary training with SOE—"no one's very sure what sort of training we ought to be doing," he told his brother Philippe—Pierre de Vomécourt parachuted back into France on 11 May 1941. He travelled under his real name, carrying papers confirming that he had been demo-bilized from the French military in North Africa, and before long, he had assembled Autogiro, made up of dozens of networks that he directed from his home in Paris. At the same time, Philippe de Vomécourt was run-ning covert operations in unoccupied France, while Jean was setting up resistance cells along the frontier between the two zones. It was a potent organization—Philippe de Vomécourt claimed that he could mobilize as many as ten thousand résistants when orders and arms came through—but therein lay the problem. The circuit's growth was stunted because Pierre was cut off from his masters in London; he had no access to a WT operator in the occupied zone, so every time he needed to communicate with F Section in London to get instructions, he had to make the trip across the demarcation line into Vichy France. This was a potentially dangerous journey, for crossing without the proper travel permits was punishable by imprisonment, but in fact it could be more inconvenient than risky. The German guards along the line were assiduous in their duties but, as Frank Pickersgill and Whitmore Hicks had discovered during their escape, often the French were interested in the letter more than the spirit of their instructions. They had been instructed to examine papers, so they examined papers; many of them had not, apparently, been told to detain anyone. So when a busload of civilians carrying large packages pulled up to the border, the French guards duly examined everyone's identification, then watched blithely as the passengers piled off the bus and hurried over the fields across the demarcation line. Still, it was enough of an annoyance that de Vomécourt was relieved when, in September 1941, Autogiro finally received its own operator, who was installed first in a suburb of Paris and then in Le Mans. But after sending a message in November 1941, the operator disappeared. It was later discovered that he had been denounced as a Jew, arrested, and summarily executed.

The situation was little better in the unoccupied zone. On 6 September 1941, Ben Cowburn, a tough Lancashire engineer; Michael Trotobas, a young Anglo-French lawyer who had lived in northern France before the war; Jean Bougennac,* a journalist from St. Eloi (the following night, as Jacques de Guélis's assistant, he would be part of the reception committee that met F Section's operations officer Gerry Morel when he landed in France for a reconnaissance of resistance circuits); and three other agents were dropped near Châteauroux in an operation with the colourful code name Draughtsman Autogiro Downstairs Vestige Tropical Ukelele. Within

---

*Bougennac served under the name François Garel.

two months, most of them were in custody. Bougennac was arrested in the garage where, according to his cover story, he worked as a mechanic, while another agent was picked up in early October while waiting to meet Georges Bégués, F Section's only WT operator, to make a transmission. The same week, four agents were dropped west of Bordeaux, only to be arrested within ten days. Then Bégués himself was captured on 24 October 1941, and Trotobas soon after.

With Bégués in custody, Autogiro was again left with no means of easy communication from either zone of France. In desperation, de Vomécourt eventually found Mathilde Carré, who claimed to have access to a WT through a Polish resistance network in Vichy called Interallié. What de Vomécourt didn't know was that Carré was also working for the Germans. When he discovered her duplicity, he tried the same game by convincing her that her interests were best served by working for the Allies. Still, de Vomécourt was canny enough to know that someone who had been turned twice could probably be turned a third time, so he carefully prepared to evacuate from France every one of his agents with whom Carré had been in contact. De Vomécourt himself returned to England in February 1942, conferred with the brains trust at SOE, and convinced them to send him back, on the grounds that his presence might be the only way to save Autogiro. Still, if he was willing to risk his own life, he wasn't willing to risk those of his operatives, so he urged SOE to accelerate plans to withdraw his agents. Regrettably, F Section wasn't in a position to do anything very quickly in those early days and before the evacuations could be organized, de Vomécourt was arrested, on 25 April 1942, followed by many of his key people. Autogiro, upon which F Section had pinned its hopes and lavished its attention, lay in ruins, even before it was able to achieve anything of substance. Buckmaster's office was right back where it had started, with no organized circuits in occupied France and no presence in Paris.

But the force of de Vomécourt's personality had one positive effect: it succeeded in improving Gubbins's opinion of F Section, even if the results had fallen far short of what was hoped for. The SOE chief, who had made little secret of his preference for RF Section, suddenly became interested in helping Buckmaster's office. And Buckmaster had a very promising lead that, in de Vomécourt's absence, might be more successful than Autogiro. In the south of France, a smooth talker named André Girard had established a network called Carte, and was making great promises that whenever London desired he could mobilize a secret army of 250,000 resistance fighters. It sounded a little too good to be true, but F Section had few other options. Buckmaster, still new at the job, was in no position to evaluate Girard's claims, so he elected to rely on assessments from the field. Nicholas Bodington, a former journalist and F Section staff officer, was sent to Vichy in July 1942 to meet with Girard and his deputy, Henri Frager, who had first fought the Germans as a seventeen-year-old during the Great War, and report on Carte. Bodington returned full of praise for the operation, and SOE was sufficiently impressed to believe that Carte was indeed the fabled secret army, or at the very least a private venture closely related to it. Either way, the situation was promising enough for The Firm to send in a liaison officer, a former international ice hockey player named Peter Churchill (no relation to the British prime minister), and start experimental arms drops to Carte agents.

Churchill would be sorely disappointed. He discovered that Girard was a planner, not a doer, and that his great passion was compiling card indexes of people who might one day join the secret army that existed only in his head. His administrative talents were prodigious, but his complete disdain for even the most elementary security precautions was alarming. One reception committee he organized consisted of at least nineteen people, who proceeded to walk to the drop zone along the main street of a village at 3 a.m., in full moonlight and just a few metres from German sentries. Girard did nothing to discourage such conduct, considering it to be a trifle that was unworthy of his attention. As an F Section report put it, Girard had begun "to assume almost Ministerial rights over his subordinates, of whose welfare he was, in fact, completely careless."[1] It was perhaps inevitable that a bitter rift would grow between Girard, who was content to shuffle his index cards and make big plans, and Frager and Churchill, who wanted Carte to begin actual sabotage activities. Eventually, Churchill convinced SOE that the Carte leader was mad and, in March 1943, Girard was brought back to England "for consultation." He would not return to France before the war's end.

But there were enough members of Carte at large who shared the spirit of Churchill and Frager for SOE to work with. The decision was made to divide the circuit's territory into three parts: Frager would operate in the region east of Nancy, Paris, and Chalon-sur-Saône, running a circuit known as Donkeyman; Churchill would be responsible for southeastern France; and a circuit called Jockey, in the southwestern part of the country, would be put under the control of Francis Cammaerts, the son of a Belgian poet. Cammaerts had studied at Cambridge in the 1930s and had been well known there for his pacifist leanings, but his views changed when his brother was killed in action while serving with the Royal Air Force. After F Section training under the watchful eye of Ken Macalister, his conducting officer, he was sent back to France with two million francs and instructions to pick up the pieces of Carte in his region.

It looked good on paper, but F Section would have done better to make a complete break with everyone connected with Carte and start from scratch. As it was, things started to go wrong almost from the beginning. Henri Frager's Donkeyman had been infiltrated by Hugo Bleicher, an Abwehr sergeant who claimed to have secret sympathies for the Allies. Bleicher was a clerk with a Hamburg export company in 1939 when he received a letter asking for volunteers to serve the Third Reich by censoring mail. Unfamiliar with the army saying that you should never volunteer for anything, Bleicher agreed, only to find himself in the uniform of the Secret Field Police. He spent time in the backwaters of Caen and St. Lô before being transferred to the resistance hotbed of Cherbourg; it was there that he cracked an agent who led him to the Polish network Interallié, which in turn won him a promotion to the Paris office of the Abwehr's Section IIIF.

By 1942, he was an experienced agent with a gift for cultivating turncoats—he had taken Mathilde Carré as his lover as part of his plan to convince her to work for the Nazis—and while Frager was away in England for rest and consultation, Bleicher turned his most senior lieutenant, Roger Bardet, to the German side. Donkeyman was compromised almost from the beginning, although Frager refused to admit the possibility.

If Frager was blind to what was going on around him, at least others weren't. Cammaerts quickly sensed that all was not right with Donkeyman and broke contact with Frager, making his own circuit entirely independent. Other new agents sent in by F Section in 1942 kept the same careful distance. In May, Charles Grover-Williams was parachuted in to establish a small sabotage circuit, known as Chestnut, near Paris. Once the chauffeur to painter Sir William Orpen, Grover-Williams had been one of the greatest racing drivers of the era (often competing under the name W. Williams, so his parents didn't know that he was involved in that most lethal of sports), winning the first Monaco Grand Prix in 1928 and the Belgian Grand Prix three years running. He refused to use Carte contacts, preferring to recruit people he knew personally, such as his friend and fellow racing driver Robert Benoist. The two had gone head-to-head many times before the war, with Benoist's fame eclipsing that of his English friend. A multiple Grand Prix winner and twice victor of the 24 Heures du Mans, Benoist was the first driver to be dubbed world champion. But, more important for Chestnut's purposes, he was a director of the Bugatti company and the owner of a small transport firm, both of which gave him access to trucks and permits to drive at night. Claude de Baissac, a thirty-five-year-old Mauritian who had once been the publicity director for a French cinema chain, and his WT operator, Harry Peulevé, a British officer of Huguenot origins who lived on the French Riviera before the war, were dropped blind on 30 July 1942 to establish a circuit named Scientist in the Bordeaux area. Both of them were injured in the drop and, while Peulevé's injuries were sufficiently severe to force him to retreat over the Pyrenees and back to England, de Baissac carried on. But he wanted nothing to do with Carte members, preferring to build Scientist with people he found on his own.

Still, the modest early successes of Jockey, Chestnut, and Scientist in establishing footholds in their districts couldn't compensate for the disappointments of Autogiro around Paris and Carte in the south. Autogiro's last agent, Christopher Burney, was dropped blind on 31 May 1942 from the same aircraft that brought in Grover-Williams, but he immediately realized that he had no contacts and no organizer. In a remarkable display of resourcefulness and courage, he remained at large for eleven weeks before being picked up. In August 1942, John Starr was dropped near the Riviera to make arrangements for feeding Carte's massive, if notional, army. Starr had trained as a graphic artist in France, married a Frenchwoman, and settled in a suburb of Paris with their young son. Like Ken Macalister, he had joined the Field Security Police in 1940; it is even possible that the two ran into each other at King Alfred's College in Winchester that fall. The FSP had been a stepping stone to covert operations, and Starr had entered F Section's training program; his brother was also a very successful F Section agent in the south of France. But John Starr's mission was a failure. He did what he could to stockpile dried bananas, wheat, chocolate, and anything else he could lay his hands on at the wharves of Marseilles, but Girard showed no interest in using the supplies that Starr had carefully husbanded. Starr was also suffering from nephritis, so Peter Churchill sent him back to England in November 1942.

By that time, it was painfully clear that F Section's grand schemes had been stillborn. Autogiro had ceased to exist and Carte, far from being a quarter-million-strong secret army, was merely a few small, if modestly successful, circuits. It was critical for SOE to fill the void as quickly as possible, ideally by establishing a large network with a solid footing in Paris and connections throughout the occupied zone. This was to be Francis Suttill's task. Travelling as François Desprez, a dealer in agricultural products, he was to establish a base in or near Paris, gather together any remaining pieces of Autogiro and Carte, and set up new circuits in northern, eastern, and central France. Then, he was to bring them together into a huge umbrella network called Physician,* which would stretch some three hundred miles from the Ardennes to the Atlantic. Such a task would require the very perseverance that St. Prosper had valued so highly.

•

Over the space of five weeks in the autumn of 1942, the Physician team came together in France. On the night of the first of October, Francis Suttill was dropped into a field near Blois, southwest of Paris, with a WT operator to begin building Physician. Their mission had an inauspicious start. The Halifax bomber reached the drop zone to find it shrouded in fog, and the Czech pilot began to circle to make sure they were in the right place. Finally, on the fifth circuit, the crew spotted the proper signal light and the two men jumped, with Suttill coming down hard and wrenching his leg. One of the people who helped him away was the woman assigned to be his guide, Andrée Borrel, who had arrived the previous week. She had also had a difficult trip in; her first attempt had been aborted because the wrong signal light was flashing. The RAF tried again the following night, and this time everything went smoothly, with Borrel coming to ground in a field east of Blois. Borrel, whose working-class roots gave her politics a distinctly left-wing flavour, was a tough young woman of enormous strength and endurance whose sister referred to her as *un garçon manqué* (tomboy).[2] Before the war, she had worked at Boulangerie Pujo, in Paris's fashionable sixteenth arrondissement, but she was anything but a demure shopgirl. She frightened at least one of her fellow agents-in-training by saying that if she encountered an unarmed German, she would wait until he was asleep and kill him by stabbing a pencil through his ear; the alarmed agent, who described Borrel as a Paris street urchin, "rough, tough and a bit of a hooligan," had little doubt that she meant what she said.[3] At the end

*Many accounts use the code name Prosper to refer both to Suttill and to the network he managed. The fact that the network's actual code name, Physician, is often missing from accounts suggests the degree to which Suttill became personally identified with his network.

of October came Gilbert Norman, who parachuted to a field northeast of Blois. Norman's original assignment had been to land on Corsica to handle WT communications for Carte agents there, but his orders were changed and he was sent to join Scientist. Claude de Baissac had no need of an extra operator, so he hung onto Norman for a few days and then sent him to Suttill. Born near Paris in 1915 of an English father (the senior partner in a firm of international chartered accountants) and a French mother, Norman was educated in England and France, articled at the London office of his father's company, and held a commission in the Durham Light Infantry before joining SOE in 1942. In France, he would be known as Gilbert Aubin, a travelling toilet-paper salesman. Finally, in December 1942, a half-Armenian, half-French agent named Jack Agazarian parachuted into the Seine valley southeast of Rouen to act as a second WT operator for Suttill, because Norman was having trouble establishing contact with F Section. With Agazarian's arrival, Physician's inner circle was complete. From now on, everything would revolve around four key people: Suttill, Borrel, Norman, and Agazarian.

It was an impressive group of agents but, as historian Michael Foot has pointed out, for all his strengths, Suttill was no replacement for de Vomécourt. He was, after all, half English and couldn't easily pass as a local—another resistance leader described him as "a tall distinguished looking man desperately trying to look like a Frenchman"[4]—so he needed Borrel (posing as his sister) to shepherd him around and protect him from making basic mistakes. Also, de Vomécourt had built up Autogiro with his own friends and contacts, on whom he could rely. Ben Cowburn, one of F Section's earliest and most successful agents, did the same; recruiting from his prewar friends, he sized them up on the basis of their character, rather than their politics. The principle never let him down, not even when he brought into his circuit a man whom he had known before the war as a staunch anti-British pacifist. Suttill, on the other hand, had to create Physician using agents sent from England or résistants left over from Autogiro or Carte; his first job upon arrival was to visit, with Andrée Borrel, the contacts in Blois, Romorantin, Chartres, Compiègne, and St. Quentin, mostly remnants of Carte, that Baker Street had given him. Unlike de Vomécourt or Cowburn, he often had no personal knowledge of their reliability or suitability.

But F Section had great faith in Suttill, and in the six months after his arrival he was followed by dozens of agents assigned to establish subcircuits around Physician's heartland. Some of them were veterans—Michael Trotobas and Jean Bougennac, who had escaped from a Vichy prison camp in July 1942, were on their second tour, while Ben Cowburn came in for his third mission—and others were young men in their early twenties. There were Frenchmen, Britons, Mauritians, and another Canadian, Gustave (Guy) Bieler, born in France but a resident of Montreal since 1924. Through the winter of 1942–43, they established circuits in Lille, St. Quentin, Châteauroux, Troyes, and Dijon, putting together a resistance network stretching across northern France and well to the south of Paris. Linking everything together was Suttill. Some of the circuits had almost no contact with him, while others worked very closely with his inner circle. Physician was becoming an immense spiderweb—or perhaps a house of cards.

•

One region would become particularly important in Physician's work: the Sologne, southwest of Paris in the Loire-et-Cher département. As historian E.H. Cookridge described it, the Sologne was ideal resistance country:

> Bordered by the rivers Loire in the north and the Cher and the Yeuvre in the south, it is richly wooded, while some of its parts are marshland. Much of it is covered by dense shrubs which in spring produce a vast carpet of dazzling yellow flowers, while in autumn the lilac heather is a magnificent sight. Main roads by-passed the Sologne and tales were still alive of people getting themselves lost in the forests and marshes. It is an ideal hunting country.

For these reasons, resistance in the Sologne was especially successful, and especially difficult for the Germans to control. As one SS officer wrote, "The Resistance terrorists in this area are the most dangerous and difficult in the whole of France."[5] It was critical, then, that the Sologne be in good hands, and Suttill could find none better than Pierre Culioli and Yvonne Rudelatt.

They were an unusual pair. Culioli came from a military family; his grandfather fought in the Crimea and Mexico, and his father won the Légion d'honneur in the Great War before dying of wounds received in battle. Pierre was educated at the Legion school at St. Denis, then went to work with the French finance ministry, hardly a fitting post for someone from a family of warriors. So even though his slight physique and bad eyes made him a less-than-impressive physical specimen, Culioli decided to enlist. The air force rejected him on medical grounds, so he joined the infantry instead, becoming a platoon commander with a motorcycle unit. He was badly wounded and captured in May 1940 in the Pas-de-Calais, and sent to a prison camp in eastern Germany. But he would not spend long there. Rather than hold millions of French soldiers as POWs, the Germans began releasing some of them on medical or compassionate grounds. Culioli, whose wife had been killed when Italian bombers attacked his village, was freed on Christmas Day 1940. The Germans might well have wished they had kept him in custody because for the next two years, Culioli criss-crossed France trying to find ways to get back into the fight. Finally, by luck more than good management, he got in touch with an SOE circuit known as Monkeypuzzle, which had been established around Tours. It never amounted to much, thanks in part to its organizer's erratic behaviour—in September 1942, Culioli had to reschedule Andrée Borrel's arrival because the organizer had botched the first attempt by flashing the wrong signal light—but it did bring together some remarkable individuals. France Antelme had been sent in to work with Monkeypuzzle, although he eventually left to build his own circuit. And then there was an agent who did not fit the F Section model: a forty-seven-year-old grandmother named Yvonne Rudelatt.

One of ten children, only two of whom survived childhood, Yvonne had left Paris while a young woman and travelled to London, taking a job in Galeries Lafayette, a French-owned department store in Regent Street. In 1920 she married a waiter at the nearby Piccadilly Hotel, but the marriage was not a happy one. He was nine years her senior and they had little in common; the union produced a daughter but not much else, and dissolved in 1935.* She had none of the typical connections that would bring her to the attention of SOE, but in the spring of 1941, after taking a job at a club frequented by secret service types, Rudelatt was summoned to the same shabby room in the Hotel Victoria that Frank Pickersgill had visited. She sufficiently impressed Selwyn Jepson that she was called back for a second interview with Buckmaster, and was then moved into an SOE-owned flat to await training. In July 1942, after graduating from Beaulieu in the first course of women to train at Boarman's (a group that included Andrée Borrel), she and three other agents were landed by felucca on the French Riviera; from there, she headed north to join Monkeypuzzle, and Pierre Culioli.

The tall, matronly Rudelatt and the slight, awkward Culioli might not have looked like typical résistants, but they soon demonstrated enormous ability. One of Culioli's great skills was understanding the lay of the land. As a native of the Sologne, he had a knack for locating ideal drop zones and organizing drops. Rudelatt, for her part, had developed a fondness for sabotage. Her conducting officer had observed that "the first impression of fluffiness is entirely misleading. Her air of innocence and anxiety to please should prove a most valuable 'cover' asset," an assessment that proved to be remarkably prescient. As Suttill later reported, she "cycles about at night with her plastics and is extremely handy when it comes to blowing up things. Her explosives are stored under her bed."[6]

Suttill's confidence in Culioli and Rudelatt was such that, when Monkeypuzzle's organizer was summoned back to London in March 1943,

---

*To make ends meet, the Rudelatts rented rooms, and a host of literary luminaries passed through their houses as tenants or guests, including playwright Joan Littlewood, Hugh Porteus (later literary and art critic for the *Times*), the poet and writer Ruthven Todd, T.S. Eliot, and Ezra Pound.

he asked the pair to take over responsibility for the Sologne. It was, after all, Culioli's home turf, and he could draw on family members and old friends to help create the subcircuit that would be known as Adolphe, in honour of the toothbrush moustache that Culioli cultivated to mock the German leader. Publicly, Culioli and Rudelatt were known as Monsieur and Madame Leclaire, who had been bombed out of their home in Brest; as refugees, they could be expected to move frequently, something that fit perfectly with the security needs of a resistance circuit. But privately, they were hard at work setting up cells. The largest, at Romorantin, was run by Roger Couffrant, a dealer in electrical parts; the smallest was one man, a seventy-year-old poacher who lived at Chaumont-sur-Tharonne. Soon, Adolphe had some three hundred operatives, and it organized more than twenty drops of arms and agents in its first three months in operation.

Adolphe's success went hand-in-hand with Physician's. On the night of 13 May 1943, Francis Suttill left for England in an operation that brought in four agents. Suttill was in high spirits, looking forward to a much-needed rest after a period that saw Physician's agents receive some 240 containers of arms and explosives, many of which were destined for Suttill's friends in Communist resistance groups in the "red belt" around Paris. The circuit, which now covered twelve départements and had access to thirty-three drop zones, had been active in sabotage, mounting sixty-three attacks in April 1943 alone and destroying thousands of gallons of fuel, derailing trains, and killing or wounding more than a hundred Germans in the process. Suttill had even done a bit of sabotage himself: on 25 April 1943, he, Norman, and a group of friends sabotaged a small power station. It wasn't a very good job—all they did was knock down a few pylons and power was restored that same day—but it was something. He told his superiors that he needed more arms, more munitions, more organizers, more wireless operators—more of everything, so that Physician could be ready for the cross-Channel invasion that was sure to come soon.

•

One of the teams being prepared for Physician consisted of Frank Pickersgill and Ken Macalister. They had been in limbo since finishing their training, having been told only that they would receive a telephone call when it was time for them to leave. Jack would happily have arranged a quick flight back to Canada for Frank, but Frank and Ken had very little free time, and usually spent it in the same place. As soon as he had reached London from Portugal, Frank had looked up his Paris friends Kay Moore and Mary Mundle, who were sharing a house at 54A Walton Avenue in Knightsbridge with Alison Grant, a Toronto art school graduate. They lived in three floors above a dairy that was managed by Mrs. Lewis, a garrulous woman whom Frank found quite intimidating and tried to avoid at all costs (Ken, however, had quite a way with her, and she blushingly slipped him an extra pint of milk, off the ration, whenever she had one to spare). The main floor was a large living room/dining room with pale green walls, yellow leather chairs, a big fireplace, and scads of books. Upstairs, Kay and Mary shared the larger bedroom, decorated in cream, old rose, and chintz, while Alison slept in a small study with built-in bookcases. The attic had been converted into a third bedroom for guests (including Ken and Frank), and also gave onto the roof, which was quite good for sunbathing, now that the worst of the German bombing was over and the V1 rocket bombs hadn't yet started to trouble Londoners. There was also a tiny bathroom halfway up the stairs from the dairy that was cold and damp in the winter and stuffy and damp in the summer. The Canada House Annex, as it came to be known, was a home away from home for Ken and Frank during and after their training, and they and the three women quickly became inseparable. Kay and Mary both worked for RF Section of SOE and Alison for MI5, so Ken and Frank found it a comfortable environment. Because 54A had been approved by SOE as a safe house, it was frequented by all manner of agents looking for a few days' rest before leaving for (or returning from) the Continent. The standing rule was no shop talk, and often visitors were known only by their aliases. In fact, Ken and Frank were the only agents whom the three women knew by their real names.

During training, Ken and Frank spent most of their free time at Walton Avenue, with each of them kicking in a pound a week to help with expenses. Occasionally they went out for a night on the town. The decision to see a film about a double agent in occupied France was perhaps not the wisest, but usually they had great fun. In early June 1943, Kay and Alison treated Frank to dinner at a swank London restaurant called Prunier's. The waiter appeared scandalized when the two women picked up the bill, and Frank jovially wondered aloud if he looked like a kept man. They were all much happier with the house's fireplace and endless cups of tea (which Frank drank in enormous quantities, a habit he picked up in St. Denis)—that was all they needed for the hours to fly by in discussion, debate, argument, and storytelling. Frank, always gregarious and chatty, had an insatiable curiosity and eagerly devoured every article in back copies of the *New Yorker* that the women had found in a closet; other nights, he toddled off to a cinema in some distant corner of London to see a film he had missed while in captivity. He was a fount of pointless information about everything from the chemical composition of cow's milk to Tibetan religious practices, and was .always keen to start a noisy and turbulent argument on anything from post-war reconstruction to French politics to the latest Bob Hope film. Frank was still mulling over a career in External Affairs and his brother Jack still exerted an enormous influence on his life. He talked a lot about his mother, and also about two other people whom he regarded as his greatest influences: Celine Ballu and St. Augustine. Without knowing it, he already had a link to the man who would be his chief in occupied France.

Ken was by far the quieter of the two. He always seemed uneasy in uniform, and his black, round glasses and what Alison called "his most beautiful large sad eyes" made him look a bit like an awkward schoolboy. He was more domestically inclined than Frank and was quick to volunteer to help haul coal for the fire, stand in line for the groceries, or wash the dishes. But his kindly wit was never far below the surface and he and Alison happily joined forces, as fellow Ontarians, in friendly debates against Frank, Kay, and their friends from the University of Manitoba who were frequent visitors—Ken loved to get under their skin by referring to them jokingly as Winnipeg nationalists. He didn't talk much about his family (everyone knew that on the occasions he retreated into his own thoughts, they were of Jeannine), but loved to discuss the new world order that would emerge once Nazism had been defeated. With his incisive, almost clinically logical mind, he carefully analyzed the European situation, the role of Canada in the world, and the growing influence of the United States.

The two made a formidable pair, but their energy and hunger for intellectual stimulation made their visits as exhausting as they were enjoyable. "Breakfast with both of them is somewhat of a ritual," Kay wrote to Sara Pickersgill, "and in their opinion should last about two hours with the conversation ranging to extraordinary subjects." Frank complained bitterly that the flat didn't have a tea samovar, which meant that he was constantly bobbing up to put the kettle on, and grumbled when anyone excused themselves from the conversation, even to fetch the next course—"how he thinks meals appear unless we prepare them I do not know," Kay mused. One weekend in April 1943, Ken and Frank were both on duty and the three women were left in an empty house. "Both Alison and I find it delightful not to have them underfoot," wrote Kay. "They talk so much, both of them and demand your undivided attention at all times." Fortunately, they had an ally in Mrs. Frost, who came in every day to do the beds, dishes, laundry, and grocery shopping. She quickly became devoted to Ken and Frank, and had infinitely more patience than the three women in ensuring that their clothes, about which they were both quite fussy, were properly cleaned, pressed, and folded. And if Kay had feared a reprise of the heated arguments of the Hotel Lenox days, she needn't have worried; Frank and Mary quickly got over their mutual antipathy and became firm friends. As Alison later wrote, "They were great days, days of long arguments, tremendous gaiety, good food, fun and altogether something to look back on with great happiness."[7]

One of Ken and Frank's last tasks was to get outfitted in clothing that matched their cover stories. SOE's master tailor was Claudia Pulver, a

Jewish refugee from Vienna, who ran a small operation in Margaret Street near Oxford Circus. Each agent went there to be fitted with clothes that were made in England but looked continental. Nothing could be left to chance, for a keen eye could immediately tell the difference between a French-made shirt and an English-made one—the side seams, the cuffs, the plackets, even the position of the buttonhole under the collar were all distinctive. Pulver would also search out other refugees to trade their battered continental-made suitcases, hats, or scarves for new ones, and cut any French, Belgian, or Dutch labels from their clothing; then, her workers would make identical labels in the Margaret Street shop, and sew them into their creations. At the same time, a company in Northampton had been contracted to make continental-style shoes, for reasons that it was never told. Finally, it was up to Ken and Frank to wear in the clothes—some scuffs on the shoes, perhaps a smudge or two on the trousers, frayed cuffs and shiny elbows on jackets and overcoats. After all, a sharp new suit in occupied France generally meant that the wearer was up to no good. In short order, Macalister grew quite attached to the suit that he, as Jean Charles Maulnier, would wear in France (although he was told in no uncertain terms that the tartan tie he cherished would have to stay in England), but Pickersgill never stopped complaining about the dull and cheap-looking suit that SOE's tailors had carefully made for him.

On the eighth of June, Ken and Frank visited a London lawyer to prepare their wills. Frank arranged for bequests to Marc Maurette, Jean Pouillon, and Jean Jezequellon, the friends who had helped him so much during his internment and escape, while Ken left everything to Jeannine and named C.K. Allen as his executor. Five days later, Frank wrote a short letter to his brother Jack to say that his training was finished and that he had put his affairs in order. Even with such gloomy formalities, Frank wrote that he was "in very good form and raring to go."[8] Saul Rae, who had known both Ken and Frank at the University of Toronto, had lunch with Pickersgill and found that he had suffered no negative effects from his internment and escape; on the contrary, "his conscience has been brought to a fine point and he is much preoccupied with the fate of France." Kay Moore recalled that Ken and Frank were "in tremendous high spirits, relaxed and not nervous, not apprehensive, deeply content and sure of [their] mission" as they made their final preparations.[9] Days later, the expected telephone call came, summoning the pair to their final briefing at the Orchard Court apartment.

Anyone who might have been there—Maurice Buckmaster, Vera Atkins, Jacques de Guélis, Gerry Morel—is now dead, but we can imagine what transpired. The papers of Maulnier and Picard, their new identities, would have been carefully prepared—identity cards, ration books, the employment certificates that, after March 1943, all men between the ages of eighteen and fifty had to carry, the work card that was required to collect mail at the post office (not that agents were expecting much mail, but for a salesman to be missing the card that would allow him to pick up his mail would immediately arouse suspicion), and anything else that F Section thought they needed. Someone would have given them last-minute bits of advice or information gleaned from recent wireless traffic, and also the briefing paper with full details of their mission, which was to establish a new circuit, called Archdeacon, near Sedan in the Ardennes. There was already a small subcircuit known as Gaspard III based in the town of Hirson, but its head, a poet and writer named Armel Guerne, lived in Paris and was finding it difficult to travel to the area every time a parachute drop was expected. SOE thought that Gaspard III showed enough potential to be converted into a major circuit, so Guerne would get Ken and Frank settled in the area, arranging a number of safe houses from which to transmit and putting them in touch with a few local résistants. Then it would be up to Frank to build the subcircuit, travelling around the villages and farms and carefully finding people who were reliable, discreet, and unobtrusive. In time, F Section would send them arms, ammunition, explosives, and more agents, to act as demolition instructors and help coordinate Archdeacon's sabotage work. Frank and Ken would be operating in a region of considerable importance to the Allies, for it was a potential transit route for Nazi reserve units coming in from western Germany to meet the anticipated cross-Channel invasion. So, in addition to targeting the railway engine repair facilities and marshalling yards at Mohon and Lumes and a textile mill in Sedan, Archdeacon's saboteurs were to do whatever they could to damage or destroy the rail lines running through a number of small towns around Charleville. Frank read the last paragraph of the briefing paper ("You have had our general training and been given our general briefing. You have also read the foregoing, have had an opportunity of raising any questions on matters that have not been clear and have had a trial viva voce of the methods outlined"), signed the bottom, and returned it to Vera Atkins.

Then it was off to Tempsford. Frank and Ken would have been taken to an old farmhouse known as Gibraltar Farm to make their final preparations; there, in a building that had been carefully constructed to look like an ordinary, rundown barn, Ken picked up a wireless transceiver, crystals, codes, and a moneybelt stuffed with French banknotes to finance Archdeacon. The pair were likely a study in contrasts, Ken overflowing with nervous energy that was kept in check by his utter conviction in the job he was about to do, Frank casually joking with anyone who would listen but always with stern determination in his eyes. As he always did, Buckmaster would have reminded Ken and Frank of the long odds facing all of F Section's agents in the field and given them one last chance to opt out of the mission; he left the pair with no illusions as to the dangers they faced, telling them that they were headed for "a lion's den," but neither wavered in his determination to go ahead. Buckmaster probably also brought along a parting gift—perhaps a set of gold cufflinks for each of them—that served as a reminder of F Section but could be sold for hard cash if they ran out of money. Vera Atkins was there too, checking over everything they wore and carried to ensure there was nothing British to give them away; she would also have passed along a few items from her large collection of souvenirs—Paris metro tickets, dry cleaning stubs, visiting cards, French matches, tailor's tabs, theatre tickets, newspaper cuttings—to lend an extra bit of authenticity. Their conducting officers would have given them a few final words of encouragement, double-checked everything that Atkins had already checked, and probably turned out all of their pockets to vacuum them, in case some shreds of English tobacco were lodged in the corners. Each man was handed a packet containing four pills: a sleeping pill; a Benzedrine tablet to keep them awake; a pill that induced a painful but temporary stomach ache; and a suicide pill. It had a rubber coating and, if swallowed, would pass harmlessly through the digestive system. When crushed between the teeth, however, the cyanide was released and death followed in minutes. Then, Frank and Ken collected their parachutes from the old barn and climbed into the waiting Halifax.

They were instantly transported back to the parachute school at Ringway, for everything in the fuselage of the bomber seemed so familiar: the hard and unforgiving benches that would jar their bones for the four hours or more it would take them to reach the drop zone; the crewman who would act as the despatcher, hooking their parachutes to the static line that would open them automatically when they jumped, reminding them of the proper procedure, and finally throwing out after them the container with Ken's wireless set; the large, covered hole in the floor of the fuselage through which they would drop; and the two lights above them, the red that told them to climb down to the hole and sit with their legs dangling into space, and the green that told them it was time to jump. As they looked around inside the belly of the bomber, it slowly taxied into position on Tempsford's runway and the engines roared as they came to full power. The pilot, Flight Lieutenant J. Downes of 138 Squadron, held the brakes as the aircraft tried to lurch forward, but finally let the Halifax loose. Ken and Frank were jolted as the tires pounded along the tarmac, and then suddenly the jarring stopped as the wheels cleared the pavement. The aircraft quickly climbed to about six hundred feet, then levelled off; they would fly low to avoid German radar, ascending briefly as they crossed the French coast so the navigator could pinpoint his position. Months of intensive training had led up to this moment. They were on their way.

On the fifteenth of June 1943, Gilbert Norman received a wireless signal from England telling Physician to expect two agents that night in the

Sologne. He immediately contacted Pierre Culioli and Yvonne Rudelatt, and asked them to arrange a reception party. Early on the morning of the sixteenth, a Halifax roared over a field at Châtillon-sur-Cher, not far from the town of Blois, and soon two parachutes popped out of the gloom. More than a month later, on 20 July 1943, a signal with Ken Macalister's call sign flashed across the board at SOE's wireless station. Archdeacon was operational—or was it?

NINE

THE COLLAPSE

Late on the evening of 12 June 1943, just three nights before Frank and Ken flew to France, Pierre Culioli was waiting in a field in the Sologne with his reception team. He was far from happy to be there. A few days earlier, he had asked Henri Déricourt, who controlled air operations for Physician, to inform London that the Germans had stepped up their presence in the district. But to his amazement, instead of being advised to lie low, he was told to prepare a drop zone for an incoming agent. Culioli checked the men working the signal lamps and lit another cigarette—real tobacco, courtesy of SOE, not one of those ghastly concoctions that could be traced back to the men who haunted the Paris metro and used long sticks to collect butts from between the tracks. As the distant throb of engines sounded in the distance, he stubbed out his cigarette and tucked it into his pocket: at least the aircraft is on time, he grumbled to himself. Soon, a single parachute wafted down and Culioli ran over to collect the new arrival, dispose of the parachute, and clear the area. But when he saw who it was, he got a shock: it was Francis Suttill, returning from a few weeks' rest in England. Normally, Suttill would have arrived on a Lysander arranged by Déricourt, but he had specifically asked to be dropped in the Sologne to Culioli, who had welcomed him back to France the previous November. He refused to discuss the reason for his decision.

Culioli immediately sensed that Suttill was no longer the optimistic, confident man who had left for England a month earlier. He was haggard and edgy, and had lost the easy confidence that gave him such charisma.

No one could question his accomplishments—he had gone a long way to building Physician into a major force in northern France—but the pressure was getting to him. Suttill was torn between a desire to expand the circuit to assist with the impending invasion, and the realization that the larger it grew, the more vulnerable Physician was to infiltration by the Germans. He had quarrelled with some of the officers at Baker Street, accusing them of jeopardizing his work and expressing doubts that Physician could be kept alive until the invasion occurred. His great resistance empire already living on borrowed time, Suttill would need every ounce of his perseverance to hold Physician together.

Perhaps Physician's greatest weakness was that F Section had asked so much of it, and that its inner circle had been dead set on delivering even more. In their single-minded determination to succeed, Suttill and his subordinates ignored basic security precautions that had been drilled into them at SOE training schools and fell into traps that they should have avoided, some coincidental and some laid by their enemies. And in the German security forces, they faced a well-armed foe that was getting better at its job with every passing week, a classic case of professional policemen chasing amateur agents. Then, at the critical time, Physician's luck started to run out, something that made every situation much more dangerous. Suttill could not have been more justified in his pessimism.

•

In November 1942, André Girard, the dreamy mastermind behind the Carte circuit, had sent a courier from Marseilles to Paris with the names and descriptions of some two hundred people who might be recruited for resistance work. Thanks to Girard's passion for record-keeping, each potential résistant was the subject of an exhaustive report containing sixty-one paragraphs of detailed personal information, including addresses, telephone numbers, descriptions, and habits, all written *en clair* (uncoded). This was bad enough, but the courier fell asleep on the train and awoke to discover that his briefcase was missing, taken by Abwehr agents who were shadowing him. Probably not knowing that these documents had been captured (for Girard was hardly one to admit it when one of his grand schemes went wrong), Suttill used some of the people on the Carte list when setting up Physician in late 1942. It was entirely possible that from its earliest days Physician was contaminated.

But this, in itself, was not necessarily fatal. SOE protocol said that circuits and subcircuits should be self-contained, with minimal contact between organizers, as a way to reduce the damage caused by contaminated or captured agents; only a few intermediaries, or cut-outs, would know the details of other resistance groups. But as Physician grew to comprise nearly sixty circuits and subcircuits and over a thousand full-time agents and lower-level operatives, this fundamental precaution was all too often ignored. Sadly, it was ignored at the very top of the organization. The inner circle of Suttill, Norman, Borrel, and Agazarian spent far too much time together, passing many evenings playing poker in public places, often speaking too much English and spending too much money; they became creatures of habit, and too many people knew where they were likely to be found on any given night. When he first met Suttill in a Paris apartment, Ben Cowburn warned him that there were too many agents in one place. Suttill agreed, but said there was nothing he could do about it. "The small world of resistance rallied to a strong personality," Cowburn later wrote, "to one who never refused help and assistance." Perhaps, as one of his operatives mused, Suttill lacked the necessary ruthlessness: he was "magnificent, strong, young, courageous, decisive, a kind of Ivanhoe; but he should have been a cavalry officer, not a spy."[1] Despite the fact that common sense, not to mention everything they had learned in F Section's schools, should have told them to avoid each other as much as possible, circuit heads in the Paris area were drawn together by the enormous pressure of their work. They were careless, yes, but one can understand why. They congregated out of a basic human need, as Michael Foot put it, "for companionship with people who could share with them the secret of their identity and their mission. They made an intelligible, pathetic error."[2]

Suttill's other error was in associating with too many recognizable people. With the exception of the Communist cells that he supported, most of his close contacts were drawn from the landed classes and the intelligentsia, people who were known in Paris and spent much of their time there. Other circuits recruited from all social strata, but Physician's top layers were resolutely upper class. One of Suttill's safe locations was l'École nationale d'agriculture at Grignon, where Dr. Alfred Balachowski, the noted entomologist and senior researcher at l'Institut Pasteur, organized the resistance operation. Visitors to Grignon included the filmmaker and writer Jean Cocteau, Octave Simon, head of a Physician subcircuit but better known as the up-and-coming sculptor whose work had so impressed the crowds at the 1937 Exposition Universelle, and the Irish playwright Samuel Beckett. Such luminaries didn't move around occupied France unnoticed.

Another of Physician's weaknesses was not of its own doing. F Section was perpetually short of WT operators—not enough of them were trained in the first place (later, F Section would realize this problem and train all agents to operate WT sets), and they were easier to capture once they reached the field. So, the few operators in France found themselves having to work for many more circuits than they should have, something that also broke the cardinal rule of maintaining separation between circuits. Charles Grover-Williams was parachuted into France in May 1942 without a wireless operator; he was told that one would be sent to him soon, but it wasn't until March 1943 that Roland Dowlen, an Englishman who had worked for the Royal Bank of Canada since 1923 at its Paris and London branches, arrived to transmit for him and another organizer. Gustave Bieler's circuit had to wait more than six months for a WT operator. If any of these circuits were to function, they had no choice but to rely on the only WT operators available, Gilbert Norman and Jack Agazarian. The shortage became so dire that Agazarian was in contact with as many as twenty-four different subcircuit heads, all of whom had to use his services for communication with London.

But it wasn't just the wireless operators; there were too many other points of contact between the subcircuits under the Physician umbrella. In September 1942, the same aircraft that brought Andrée Borrel to France dropped Lise de Baissac to establish a circuit around Poitiers. (In the few days they spent together, the two women discovered a coincidence: before the war, de Baissac had bought her bread every day from the Paris boulangerie where Borrel worked.) However, Lise spent much of her time acting as a liaison between Physician, her younger brother Claude's circuit Scientist, and Henri Déricourt, upon whom Suttill in Paris and Claude de Baissac in Bordeaux relied for air operations. Furthermore, Claude de Baissac had a group of agents in Paris, and it occurred to him that they would be more useful to Suttill, to whom he directed them. But Suttill sent them back to de Baissac, preferring to use his own people. It seemed a small matter, but it established yet another link between Physician and Scientist. Even circuits that were far removed from Physician seemed to be drawn in. Ben Cowburn, the chief of Tinker, which operated around Troyes, should have had nothing to do with Physician—except that when Cowburn was dropped south of Blois in April 1943, he was received by Culioli and Rudelatt.

And then there were the two Tambour sisters, Germaine and Madeleine, whose rented house at 38 avenue Suffren in Paris became a boîte-aux-lettres and rendezvous for Physician. This was normal practice for SOE, but the Tambours weren't the best candidates for such an important role. Madeleine had been André Girard's secretary before the war (in fact, the sisters' names were among those on the information sheets taken from the courier) and, although she was keen to help, she was inclined to be skittish and was terrified of confrontation. Germaine was completely uninvolved at first, but insisted on doing everything her sister did. The avenue Suffren was Andrée Borrel's first stop when she arrived in Paris, and thereafter it became something of a mecca for incoming agents. It was unusual for a boîte-aux-lettres to have contact with so many agents; nearly a dozen of them knew and used the address. This was a serious security breach, and when the sisters were arrested in April 1943 (actually, only Madeleine was arrested, but Germaine wouldn't be left on her own and insisted on being taken into custody too), Suttill realized that the consequences could be disastrous. He even took the extreme step of offering one million francs (which he would personally deliver) for their release, a deal that, needless to say, never came off. But he didn't close the boîte-aux-lettres until the owner of the house was arrested as well.

The case of the Tambour sisters was a straightforward matter of a boîte-aux-lettres gone wrong; Henri Déricourt was something else entirely. When he came to the attention of SOE in 1942, he appeared to be the answer to F Section's problems: a civilian pilot before the war, a training and test pilot with the French air force, and a man with experience flying the kind of aircraft that were used in SOE's air operations, he seemed to possess almost unique qualifications for organizing the air movements for Physician and its connected circuits. He took up his duties in January 1943 and lived with his wife, openly and under his own name, at 58 rue Pergolèse in Paris. His neighbour at number 56 was none other than Abwehr agent Hugo Bleicher.

This, of course, is no evidence of duplicity, but however much he impressed the leaders of Physician at first (although he was never able to ingratiate himself with the formidable Andrée Borrel, who distrusted Déricourt from their very first meeting), it wasn't long before there were rumblings of concern about his reliability. When in London on leave, both Henri Frager and Jack Agazarian expressed concern about Déricourt, and even Suttill told the brains trust in Baker Street that he feared Physician had been infiltrated, although he didn't mention Déricourt specifically. One of the reasons he requested more agents from F Section was so that he could shift operatives around within Physician, to isolate people who might have been contaminated. Eventually, Déricourt was brought back to London, partly to discuss the accusations against him and partly because a commander of 161 Squadron, after a Lysander struck a tree when Déricourt's men laid the signal lights incorrectly, thought he had become careless and needed a refresher course in organizing Lysander pickups. Déricourt took the course, but, more important, he allayed the concerns of everyone in

Baker Street and was duly despatched back to France. Just where Déricourt's loyalties actually lay remains a subject of debate and, sixty years after the events, it is difficult to venture beyond Michael Foot's sage observation that Déricourt's "only unswerving loyalty was to himself."[3] But in serving himself, he almost certainly passed F Section secrets to the Paris SD.

Still, Déricourt was just one of the many weak links in Physician. Although Suttill could have had no idea, the network was being infiltrated elsewhere; it had become so large that when the Germans started to nibble away at the edges, those in the centre scarcely realized what was happening. The fact that the bitter power struggle between the German security forces, the Abwehr and the SD, was reaching its peak should have played into Physician's hands; instead, Suttill and his network were caught right in the middle. Part of the dispute stemmed from mutual dislike. The SD doubted the Abwehr's commitment to National Socialism (for that reason, Hitler had ordered that all security suspects captured by the Abwehr be turned over to the SD, an order that the older intelligence service did its best to evade), while the Abwehr saw its rivals as little more than extremist thugs. And the two agencies did approach their work differently. The Abwehr operated in a more traditional, and perhaps more respectable, manner, relying on agents to infiltrate resistance organizations and destroy them from within, a tactic that was extremely effective but took time, patience, and expertise. The members of the Paris SD, on the other hand, preferred a much blunter approach. Rather than the fine scalpel of the Abwehr, they wielded the sledgehammer, letting it be known that there was a vast amount of money available for information and using members of the Bony-LaFont gang, a notorious pack of thugs led by a violent criminal and crooked inspector of the Paris Sûreté, to do their legwork. Some of the information that came in was useless, but enough of it paid off that it was worth the expense; in the end, it turned out to be a quicker and cheaper way to get the same job done.

In the battle against Physician, the Abwehr drew first blood. After taking the Carte courier's briefcase in November 1942, the Abwehr sat on the information for the rest of the winter, content to see where it might lead. In March 1943, it finally decided to arrest the courier and some of the people whose names were in his case. The courier was the first to fall for Hugo Bleicher's claims to be anti-Nazi, and he led the Abwehr agent to Roger Bardet, Henri Frager's deputy; once Bardet was turned and Frager's Donkeyman compromised, some historians have argued, Physician's fate was sealed. Bardet led Bleicher to Peter Churchill; on 16 April 1943, the day after Churchill parachuted back into France after a rest stay in England, he was arrested. This outraged the SD officers, who felt they had been bested, and their anger grew when Abwehr agents arrested the Tambour sisters later that month, finally bringing them close to the heart of Physician.

But what the SD really wanted was to duplicate the success of the Abwehr in the Netherlands. Beginning in November 1941, German agents there began to infiltrate resistance and intelligence circuits, and eventually captured wireless sets and codes. They decided to turn the sets against their owners: posing as Allied agents, they would pretend that operations in the Netherlands were proceeding as planned, and request further drops of arms and agents. On 27 March 1942, an Allied aircraft parachuted the first shipment of arms to waiting Abwehr agents, and for almost two years, the Abwehr posed as SOE's presence in the Netherlands in an operation it called Nordpol-Spiel (North Pole Game). Over that period, the Germans operated eleven radio posts and thirty drop zones, to which SOE obligingly sent more than fifty agents and many tons of supplies (including more than 33,000 pounds of explosives, 3,000 Sten guns, 500,000 rounds of ammunition, and a king's ransom in various currencies), all greeted by German reception teams. The game might have continued had two of the captured agents not escaped from prison in the Netherlands and reached Switzerland to reveal the truth.

The SD took credit for the success in the Netherlands, referring to Nordpol as England-Spiel and claiming to Berlin that SD brains had been responsible, but it desperately wanted to work the same game in France. In February 1942, a group of F Section agents were captured in Brittany and the SD tried to work the wireless set to establish a dummy network. But the operator refused to reveal his security checks, and Baker Street was immediately aware of the breach. A year later, the SD arrested another operator but he, too, refused to divulge his checks and the SD got nothing out of every effort to work the set.

The Abwehr and SD *Funkspielen* (radio games) came together in the summer of 1943, while Suttill was in England. SOE's Dutch section in Baker Street had requested the return of a particular agent in the Netherlands, instructing one of the Abwehr's fake radio posts to send the man to Paris to be shuttled out by Lysander. This left the Abwehr in a bind: the agent had been in prison for months, so it had no alternative but to find an imposter. Hermann Giskes, the Abwehr officer running Nordpol, chose two of his subordinates, Karl Boden and Richard Christmann, to go to Paris and establish contact with F Section agents there. There are a number of versions of what transpired, but the most likely scenario has Boden and Christmann being directed (without too much difficulty) to an acquaintance of Déricourt. They asked the man where they might find Gilbert (Déricourt's code name), but the man misunderstood and told the two agents that Gilbert Norman, alias Gilbert Aubin, was probably playing cards in the Square Clignancourt. Boden and Christmann easily found Norman, Borrel, Jack and Francine Agazarian, and two other Physician operatives playing poker in a café near Sacré Coeur. Norman was not at all put off by the unexpected visitors, and told them to come back in a few days to confirm the arrangements. The Abwehr, perhaps without even knowing it, had cracked Physician's inner circle.

On 9 June 1943, Jack Agazarian returned to the café to meet Boden and Christmann and inform them of the flight plans. But Giskes couldn't allow the flight to take place, or Nordpol would be ruined. Instead, he came up with a brilliant ruse. While Agazarian was chatting with the two Germans, the police arrived for what appeared to be a routine paper check. But it was far from routine. The police were there on Giskes's orders, and they "arrested" Boden on the spot. An apparently shaken Christmann quickly left the café and took a roundabout route to Abwehr headquarters. At once,

Giskes had solved both of his problems: he no longer had to explain why the "SOE agent" wouldn't be flying back to England, and he had convinced Agazarian of the genuineness of his operatives. But when Suttill heard of the incident after returning from England, he was furious. His relations with Agazarian had always been frosty, and Suttill was already concerned about his willingness to send messages for anyone who asked. Now he accused Agazarian of endangering Physician by carelessly meeting with people whose identities no one could verify. On the night of 16 June 1943, on Suttill's orders, Agazarian was put on a Lysander for England. Gilbert Norman, who was equally at fault, was next in line for a rest. But the damage, whatever its extent, had already been done.

Finally, there was the curious incident early on the morning of 14 June 1943. It was a very clear night with excellent visibility, and a Halifax bomber was scheduled to drop ten canisters of arms and supplies onto a field near the village of Neuvy. The drop zone was as good as they came: a large, sloping field with woods at the top, a bog at the bottom, and haystacks dotted around to provide cover for the reception party. The Halifax arrived right on time, but then something went very wrong. At least one of the canisters exploded in a shower of fireworks, setting a haystack alight and scattering the team sent to collect the supplies; those who stuck around gathered up the canisters, concealed them as best they could, and made themselves scarce. A few German soldiers eventually arrived and made a cursory search of the area but found nothing, even though the canisters had been hidden very hastily. The next morning, the farmer who owned the field had no choice but to report the incident to the local police. It remains unclear what happened in the immediate wake of the Neuvy mishap. Some of Culioli's agents who had been part of the reception committee insisted that all drops in the area had to stop until things calmed down; someone else, perhaps even Suttill himself, ordered that the drops continue, to build up Physician's armoury even more. Whatever the case, Pierre Culioli took it upon himself to have Norman ask London to suspend all drops until further notice. But the message apparently never went, and when Culioli received orders to prepare for the arrival of Frank Pickersgill and Ken Macalister, he had no choice but to go ahead.

Sixty years later, it is easy to pick out the mistakes that were made and see where everyone connected to Physician—from Baker Street to Paris— had gone wrong. In hindsight, Physician seems to have been predestined to fail. But the situation wasn't so clear in the spring of 1943. Without question, Francis Suttill had many reasons to be concerned on the fifteenth of June 1943. During his month in London, he had learned that his sprawling network had to be held together indefinitely, until the promised invasion occurred, and had found little sympathy in Baker Street for his fears that Physician had been infiltrated. Then he returned to Paris, only to discover that an appalling security breach had occurred in his absence. Finally, with the Tambours still in prison (and no one in Physician having much confidence that they could stand up under interrogation), he was ordered to receive two more agents into an area that, the night before, had been the scene of a mishap that should have drawn every German security official for fifty miles around. What was worse, Suttill knew from his time in London that the new arrivals were Canadian; he doubted that they could pass as Frenchmen, and assumed they would have to be hidden somewhere out of the way. But many of his fears were based on supposition rather than hard evidence, and Suttill knew from experience that if he was to close up shop every time things appeared to get hot, Physician might as well not exist at all. So, instead of protesting, he merely asked Culioli to meet the new arrivals and escort them to Paris, where they would rendezvous with Suttill at a café near the Gare d'Austerlitz to be taken to Armel Guerne's apartment in the Montparnasse district.

•

Above the village of Châtillon-sur-Cher on the night of 15 June 1943, Frank and Ken sat in the fuselage of the Halifax and watched as the despatcher hooked their parachutes to the static line. Seconds later, the red light blinked on, the despatcher pulled the cover off the chute in the floor, and the two Canadians sat down, their pant legs whipped by the wind that rushed past the aircraft. They felt the bomber descend and level off at about five hundred feet, low enough that they were unlikely to be spotted as they floated down. Then the green light flashed. The despatcher gave them each a hearty slap on the back and Ken and Frank were gone. They were still swinging under their silk canopies when they hit something solid—the trees. There were a few tense moments as résistants from Roger Couffrant's Romorantin group worked to untangle them from the branches, and when Ken hit the ground, he twisted his left ankle badly. For the next few days he would walk with a noticeable limp, just the kind of distinguishing feature that made one stand out in a crowd.

Culioli had arranged temporary accommodation for the two Canadians at La Garde, a large but isolated estate seven miles outside Romorantin. With its five hundred acres of woods and a pond for boating, it was the perfect place for Ken and Frank to acclimatize themselves to being in occupied France. La Garde was owned by Antoine Charmaison, a pharmacist and the mayor of Romorantin, and his son Jean, and Ken and Frank found their hosts to be as congenial as their surroundings. The newcomers ate and slept in the Charmaison cottage, but spent the rest of the time out of doors. They had the run of the estate—they could wander the forest paths, sunbathe in the meadow, or row around the pond. Antoine's only request was that they stay close to cover at all times; German reconnaissance aircraft were constantly flying over at low altitude, and Ken and Frank were instructed to hide whenever they heard one approaching. Charmaison also arranged a signal system so that the Canadians could see from a distance if there was any danger around the cottage. The war seemed far away, however, as Ken and Frank spent hours chatting with the Charmaisons about every subject under the sun. One afternoon, the four sat under the canopy of an old oak and talked about art and science, literature and philosophy—anything from Plato's cave to the ways of blowing up a locomotive or sneaking itching powder into enemy uniforms. For once, Ken was the more talkative of the two; Frank was content to listen and think about what lay ahead.

The sojourn at La Garde was short, and early on the morning of Saturday the nineteenth of June, Pierre Culioli arrived to take Ken and Frank to their next safe house. He had hidden his car off the main road, and came to the Charmaison cottage through the woods; after hasty goodbyes, he led the Canadians back the way he had come. Jean Charmaison called out in English, "Good luck!" but Ken and Frank had already disappeared into the woods. Years later Charmaison would recall—was it anything more than hindsight?—that the words had stuck in his throat and that a feeling of foreboding had been hanging over the cottage ever since the two Canadians arrived. He couldn't explain why, but Jean Charmaison feared that all the luck in the world wouldn't be enough for them.

If Culioli felt the same way, he certainly didn't show it and, with the assurance of a local, he swiftly backtracked through the bush to his car. In less than an hour, they had arrived at Culioli and Rudelatt's latest hideout, an even more isolated forester's hut at Veilleins. Already ensconced in the hut was another recent arrival, Pierre Raynaud, who had parachuted in on the night of the seventeenth of June to become a sabotage instructor for Francis Cammaerts's circuit. Raynaud was a soldier who had escaped from France in 1942, only to be found by F Section, trained, and sent back in. He was convinced that the Germans had been watching his drop zone (Culioli thought it was more likely that boar hunters were skulking in the underbrush), and he was still a little edgy.

Frank and Ken were brought to Veilleins and on Sunday the twentieth, all five went to a safe château nearby to decide how to get the three agents to Paris. The most obvious way was to take the train from Blois on Monday morning, but Raynaud insisted on starting immediately; he left that afternoon for Paris, met up with Cammaerts on the twenty-second of June, and settled down to train saboteurs. While Culioli and Rudelatt were getting him started on his journey, the two Canadians stayed at the safe house and enjoyed a fancy tea put on by the château's very English nanny, whom the occupiers had left at liberty on the assumption that someone so aged must be harmless.

They had a delightful afternoon, but Rudelatt returned in a state of high agitation. She refused to say exactly what had happened, but insisted that everything was about to blow up; she had to get back to London immediately to confer with Buckmaster. What had she heard, and from whom? Or did she simply have the feeling that something was wrong? In fact, Ludwig Bauer, the SD chief in Blois, had been warned that Suttill might be arriving in the Sologne that night, or that he might already be there. The Paris SD office had instructed him to put his forces on the alert, so that Suttill could be tailed. Instead, Bauer decided upon a show of force and arranged for an immense security operation in the area on Monday; checkpoints were put up throughout the Sologne, staffed by as many as three thousand Germans, from the Luftwaffe to the field police to the SD. One command post was set up in the house of a local chatelaine. She was understandably alarmed to find a party of policemen at her door, but they reassured her. "We're not coming for you," one of them said. "We're looking for someone else." Physician's house of cards was about to collapse.

A series of arms drops had been scheduled for the night of the twentieth of June and, given everything else that had happened, they should probably have been cancelled. But they went ahead anyway, and Roger Couffrant's group dutifully went out to collect some of the canisters and take them to Veilleins to be hidden. But just outside of the village of Dhuizon, they came upon one of the new checkpoints. It's difficult to explain away a truckload of machine guns and explosives at 4 a.m.; all Couffrant could do was admit to being the ringleader and claim that the others were his dim-witted school friends who had agreed to help him deliver some packages to a contact waiting at the Romorantin railway station. The Germans immediately sent a security team there, where they were tied up for hours in a futile ambush for the non-existent contact.

Around seven o'clock on the morning of the twenty-first, Culioli, Rudelatt, Pickersgill, and Macalister left the hideout in Veilleins in a Citroën sedan, bound for the railway station at Beaugency, where they would catch the Paris train. It almost seemed as if Charmaison's apprehension had infected the group. Rudelatt was still agitated by whatever she had learned the previous day, and Culioli seemed distracted. Frank whistled tunelessly, putting up an unconvincing air of nonchalance. Only Ken, a mask behind his dark glasses, was silent, impassive, and apparently unconcerned. Perhaps this air of uncertainty contributed to the fact that Culioli's sense of security, usually so sound, deserted him. He was exhausted, having been up for most of the night dealing with four separate drops, and should have waited for Couffrant to arrive with the canisters, to make sure that everything had gone without incident; had he done so, he would soon have learned of the arrests and could easily have spirited the two Canadians away in the other direction. But the trains in and out of the Sologne weren't much better than the roads, and they had to leave early if Ken and Frank were to make their connections. Culioli did, however, take the precaution of hiding his Colt revolver in a bush beside the road as they left Veilleins. In the trunk of the car were the supplies that Ken had brought, a wireless transceiver, six crystals, and all the necessary codes, and four messages for Physician members brought in by Raynaud, all written en clair. Everything was packed into a small parcel labelled for a fictitious POW.

There were no problems at the first checkpoint, on the outskirts of Dhuizon, but then Culioli noticed that the road ahead was lined with German soldiers. Turning around would immediately arouse suspicion: they had no choice but to drive on and hope for the best. It was a vain hope. A security official who stopped the car told Ken and Frank to get out, and pointed them toward the mairie; a heavily armed soldier got in, and directed Culioli to park beside the mairie. Inside, the council chamber was full of people (including some of Roger Couffrant's party) waiting to have their identity papers checked, but the new arrivals were dealt with immediately. A policeman examined Rudelatt's papers and then Culioli's, asking him why they were out so early. Culioli replied that he was a civil servant with the finance department, and that he had recently started to work in the area and was keen to make a good impression. Dhuizon's mayor, who was wandering around with a glum expression on his face, told the policeman that he had indeed seen Culioli around recently (which was patently false). Then one officer asked about the parcel, which a guard had retrieved from the trunk of the car. Culioli replied nonchalantly that it was simply a food parcel for a POW friend, an answer that apparently convinced the police official. He quickly wrote out a pass for the couple, and waved them away.

Culioli and Rudelatt immediately retreated to the Citroën to decide what to do. They could certainly save themselves if they drove off right away but that would leave Ken and Frank in the mairie with no way of getting to Paris; furthermore, the Germans would wonder why they were so keen to leave Dhuizon that they deserted their passengers. On the other hand, Culioli had no great faith in Ken's French, and felt certain that he wouldn't get through a rigorous interrogation; if the Germans discovered his identity, Culioli and Rudelatt would immediately be arrested as well. After a hurried discussion, they decided on a plausible middle course: they would park the Citroën a few yards away from the mairie and leave the motor running while they waited for Ken and Frank to reappear.

Minutes later, the front door of the building banged open and a German soldier looked around the square. Spotting the Citroën, he shouted "Revenez!" The game was up. Culioli dropped the clutch, stomped on the accelerator, and sped out of Dhuizon. He probably should have pulled off onto one of the many forest tracks that criss-crossed the region and tried to lose his pursuers in the woods, but he stuck to the roads, counting on the head start and the nimble Citroën to outrun the three large sedans that were soon pursuing him. Culioli careened the car through Neuvy, but found the road to Bracieux blocked by a wood and barbed-wire barricade that had been thrown up as a checkpoint. Before he could smash through it, gunfire from the guards splintered the windshield: one bullet went through Culioli's hat, and another struck Rudelatt in the head. She slumped down across the front seat and, assuming she was dead, Culioli decided that he should kill himself as well, so he floored the accelerator again and headed straight for a stout brick house beside the road. But instead of a head-on collision that would have catapulted Culioli through the windshield to his death, the car glanced off the wall and landed in a field. Rudelatt, apparently lifeless, was left in the ditch, while Culioli was dragged from the wrecked vehicle, beaten up by his pursuers, and driven back to the mairie in Dhuizon. There, he found Frank and Ken in shackles; sitting on the table in front of them was Ken's moneybelt and the "POW parcel." The police official had opened the small box to find the wireless set, the crystals, the codes, and the four notes, one "Pour Prosper," two "Pour Archambaud" (Gilbert Norman), and the fourth "Pour Marie Louise" (the wife of Claude de Baissac).

What had gone wrong inside the mairie? The conventional wisdom has long been that either Frank or Ken was let down by his French, and that the police immediately realized they weren't who they claimed to be. There is likely some truth in this. After all, both of them admitted more than once that their command of French wasn't as good as it should have been (strangely, William Moran, Frank's friend from St. Denis, recalled that he never spoke French in the internment camp—Moran would speak to him in French, and Frank would reply in English), and other agents they encountered remarked on their less-than-convincing language skills. Forest Yeo-Thomas of RF Section, who ran into the two Canadians later in the war, assumed at first that they were not agents at all, but soldiers who had somehow escaped capture after Canadian troops raided the French coastal resort town of Dieppe in August 1942. Peter Lee, who was in charge of security at the SOE training schools while Pickersgill and Macalister were being prepared for the field, said after the war that Ken's French "was so villainous that I did not think he would have a chance of getting away with it if he was caught."[4] One of the reasons why Raynaud had elected to go off on his own was that he was worried about getting dragged down by Macalister's poor French. Even Jeannine Macalister didn't have a lot of faith in her husband's fluency, especially after he had been living in England for three years. "My husband spoke correct French which he improved during his frequent visits to France," she later wrote, "but he could in no way be taken for French. His accent and grammatical mistakes were sufficient even for a not very good ear to realise he was of foreign origin."[5]

But many F Section agents lacked perfect fluency in the language, and SOE was used to finding ways to cover up such things. Agents could be given a background in Brittany, because few Germans were well versed in the oddities of the Breton accent. Other operatives whose excellent French still had a hint of English could pass themselves off as Belgians. John Starr's brother, a very successful agent in the south of France, travelled as a retired Belgian mining engineer, an identity intended to cover, as Michael Foot put it, "the inimitable eccentricities of his accent, which was certainly not French."[6] In any case, occupied Europe was teeming with transient workers, refugees, and travellers, so a strange accent was not necessarily something to be remarked upon.

Even if Frank and Ken's French had been impeccable, it seems unlikely that they would have escaped the dragnet. Given what Gestapo members already knew about the Physician network, they certainly had their eyes open for "persons of interest." And with the events in the Sologne over the previous week, the security services were bound to be intrigued by two young men travelling together, particularly since they knew of the frequent parachute drops in the area. But most damning would have been the moneybelt around Ken's waist, which might have contained as much as one million francs, too much to be explained away by the standard answer, that one was involved in the black market. Cash for financing resistance operations was often tucked into the containers, but it was standard practice to send agents with a good supply of money to keep them going until regular supply drops could begin. In April 1942, one agent had brought in three million francs stashed under his clothing. Most of the banknotes came from prewar stocks at the Bank of England, something that often cost agents dearly. Three agents who were arrested in August 1942 might have talked their way out of custody, but the franc notes they carried were crisp and unused and, what's worse, carried consecutive serial numbers. As soon as their turn came up for questioning in the mairie, Ken and Frank would certainly have been subjected to a body search, and even a cursory one would have revealed the thick wads of French banknotes in Ken's belt. Once those came to light, nothing could have saved them.

•

While the interrogations were going on in Dhuizon, Francis Suttill was sitting patiently at a café in the forecourt of the Gare d'Austerlitz, waiting for Ken, Frank, Culioli, and Rudelatt. Coincidentally, sitting a few tables away was Pierre Raynaud; he and Suttill didn't know each other, so Raynaud was waiting for Culioli to make the introductions. Suttill had had a busy few days since returning from England, and had just finished a three-day tour of Physician subcircuits outside of Paris. He had already had one meeting that morning, with Henri Déricourt about flying out a circuit organizer and an Allied airman on the run, and now he had to make arrangements for the two Canadians, who were to spend the night at Armel and Pérégrine Guerne's flat before heading north to the Ardennes.

Suttill wasn't overly worried when the group from Blois failed to arrive; he had heard nothing of the trouble in Dhuizon, and standing orders were that a missed rendezvous should be kept the next day, and then the next, until information to the contrary was received. So he left the Gare d'Austerlitz and had lunch with Borrel, Norman, Professor Balachowski and his wife, and a few other résistants before joining a Physician team to receive a drop near Grignon that night. It was an exhausting operation. Despite their best efforts, the résistants had lost track of the number of containers that came down—some claimed to have seen one, others said they hadn't seen any, while Suttill himself was sure he had seen two. What was worse, the agent who was dropped was nowhere to be found. Suttill, who had other business to attend to, left Armel Guerne in charge of cleaning up the mess. They searched fruitlessly for hours in the darkness and were about to give up when Gilbert Norman arrived. He had been transmitting from the gardener's house at Grignon that morning, and had received a message confirming that one agent and a specific number of containers had indeed been dropped. Guerne's men were sent back into the forest and around 10 a.m. they found a parachute, folded neatly under a tree—but no agent. Not far away, they found his suitcases, and two hours later they finally happened upon the last container, containing two WT sets. By this time, Suttill had returned with Borrel to supervise the removal of everything to Grignon, where it would be hidden until it could be dispersed. Because he had been up all night, Suttill sent someone else to the Gare d'Austerlitz on the twenty-second to keep the rendezvous with the group from Blois. The agent waited for over an hour past the appointed time, but when the four didn't show up again, he informed Suttill. Still, it wasn't unusual for agents to be a few days late for a rendezvous, so Suttill wasn't bothered by the missed meeting.

But he didn't know that days earlier, the chain of events that would finally bring down his empire had been set in motion. On the night of 16 June 1943, four agents arrived in the Lysander that would take Jack Agazarian back to England. Unaware that Suttill had already returned to France, Josef Kieffer had been expecting him to arrive on that Lysander and had sent a gang of Bony-LaFont thugs to await his arrival and tail him. As it happened, they had to make do with tailing the new arrivals, and even then one of them easily gave his pursuers the slip. Annoyed that his prey had slipped through his fingers, Kieffer soon learned about the gold mine that had been found in the trunk of Culioli's car: everything that Ken had carried, the four notes brought in by Pierre Raynaud, and, from Culioli's briefcase, the addresses of Norman, Borrel, and a boîte-aux-lettres. Finally, the SD decided that it was time to swoop down on Physician.

•

On the evening of the twenty-second of June, Gilbert Norman and Andrée Borrel dined with Armel and Pérégrine Guerne. It was a pleasant evening, with France Antelme dropping in briefly to discuss the debacle at Grignon. They agreed that Norman would ask London for a list of the missing agent's contact addresses, in the hopes that he might have reached one of them, and that Antelme would send a car to Grignon on the twenty-ninth to collect the two new WT sets. But the party broke up around 11 p.m. because Norman and Borrel had a long night's work ahead of them. The Germans had instituted a new variety of identity cards—with profile photographs instead of full face, and rivets holding the photographs to the card instead of staples—and they had to put together replacements for everyone in Physician's inner circle. They split up when they left the flat, with Norman going by bicycle and Borrel taking the metro to the rue de la Pompe station, and met again at Norman's new lodgings in the apartment of two old friends, who lived near the Porte de la Muette in the sixteenth arrondissement. Norman, perhaps humming his favourite tune, Maurice Chevalier's "Every Little Breeze Seems to Whisper Louise" (which also served as one of his code poems), dropped a stack of identity cards on his desk and the two got right down to work. Just after midnight, the doorbell rang and a well-dressed young man asked if he could speak to Gilbert; before anyone could answer, the visitor had slipped inside and trained his pistol on Norman and Borrel. Borrel, who was never far from her own weapon, didn't even have a chance to draw it. The following morning, two SD men went to Borrel's flat and took away one of her WT sets; the concierge couldn't help noticing that they seemed to know exactly where to find it.

After leaving the Guernes' apartment, France Antelme had gone home for another important rendezvous—Francis Suttill was to collect one million francs in cash for distribution to resistance groups. The two men chatted briefly and Suttill was soon on his way, for he was travelling to Gisors the following evening to meet with the head of a Physician subcircuit in the area. He spent the night there, but was back in Paris the next morning, the twenty-fourth of June, for a 9 a.m. meeting at the Gare St. Lazare with another resistance leader. They spoke for about thirty minutes, and then Suttill left to return to his new lodgings, a hotel at 18 rue de Mazagran, near the Porte St. Denis. He arrived there sometime between 10 and 11 a.m., but the SD had arrived much earlier; Suttill opened the door to find his modest room filled with policemen. Perhaps he had been tailed over the previous few days, but more likely he had fallen victim to the cache of identity cards in Gilbert Norman's apartment, for only Norman and Borrel knew of the Porte St. Denis hotel; Suttill's identity card, with his photograph and rue de Mazagran address, may well have been in the pile on Norman's desk.*

On the twenty-fifth of June, Baker Street received a letter from Suttill, written on the nineteenth of June and brought out by Lysander. It blasted F Section for sending new agents in with instructions to use the Tambours' now closed boîte-aux-lettres and for breaking the cardinal rule that circuits should have no contact with each other. Suttill wrote that he was cancelling all boîtes-aux-lettres and passwords immediately, but that he feared Physician's security had been irreparably breached. The same day, SOE received a priority message that Suttill, Norman, and Borrel were missing.

---

*Coincidentally, on the same day that Ken and Frank were arrested, a much greater disaster struck F Section when Jean Moulin, the charismatic leader of the Gaullist resistance movement, and most of his senior colleagues were arrested in a northern suburb of Lyons. Moulin remained silent through brutal torture, but the arrests left the Gaullist resistance leaderless, arguably a more significant blow than the loss of Physician. Visitors to France will know that the young resistance leader hasn't been forgotten but is commemorated in countless boulevards Jean Moulin across the country.

TEN

THE RADIO GAME

As the Paris SD was preparing to scoop up the leaders of Physician, German officials in Blois, in the Sologne, were crowing over their success. The head of the local SD, a puffed-up fellow named Ludwig Bauer, fancied himself a French country gentleman and dressed the way he thought such a man should—in tailored riding breeches, knee socks, and a checked jacket. To go along with his ridiculous appearance, he was also a martinet and a bully, and he ordered his men to take Ken Macalister and Frank Pickersgill to his headquarters in Blois, in a large house on a hill overlooking the railway station. There, Bauer himself took pleasure in inflicting a savage beating on both of them. The Canadians refused to reveal anything, and insisted that they had been parachuted in early that morning. A Frenchwoman working in Bauer's office later admitted that Frank said nothing more than "I know the fate in store for us. I demand that you notify my family of the circumstances of my arrest, sentence, and execution."[1]

Elsewhere in Blois, the Germans were caring for their other new prisoners. Yvonne Rudelatt, remarkably, had survived the bullet to her head and was transported to St. Nicholas Hospital; Culioli, whose wounds were slight, was treated at a Luftwaffe clinic before being returned to the SD. To Bauer's men, he spun a farcical tale about being recruited for resistance work by a craggy old Breton sailor he met in a bar, and claimed that the sailor had introduced him to Prosper and Archambaud, names that Culioli knew he could reveal because they were on the notes that Ken carried. He also gave the locations of two drop zones that hadn't been used for months and a system of recognition codes that had long since been replaced. Whether the SD believed him is a mystery; Culioli never had time to find out because on the twenty-fourth of June, he, Ken, and Frank were dispatched to Paris, to the notorious Fresnes prison.

When it was completed in 1898, Fresnes was hailed as a new model for prison architecture and was copied around the world, at penitentiaries such as Riker's Island in New York. In 1940, the SD took over Fresnes to use as its main high-security prison in France. When the party from Blois arrived, it held over three thousand inmates, some in large communal cells, others in single cells measuring six by fifteen feet. The windows were covered with opaque glass or iron bars, and the beds, tables, and chairs were all secured to the floor. The only other feature of interest was a small slot in each door. Three times a day, a prison trusty wheeled a rickety metal cart along the corridors and pushed through each slot a small tray of what passed for food. Meals, even though the food was disgusting, were one of the few diversions available to the prisoners. On weekdays they could pass their time listening to the sounds of the neighbourhood around them, but on weekends even the streets went quiet. When there was a Sunday afternoon soccer match at nearby Fresnes stadium, they could follow the game by the roar of the crowd. For the rest of the weekend, there was only the incessant noise of prisoners trying to communicate with one another by shouting messages from cell to cell. Frank killed some time by carving his name into the wall of cell 159: "Pickersgill canadian army officer 26–6-43," and later, "7–7-43. Trial and condemnation 8–7-43." But there would be far too many hours to pass that way; for months, Fresnes would serve as the temporary home of Macalister, Pickersgill, and Culioli when they weren't at avenue Foch for interrogation.

Sitting behind the massive desk in his avenue Foch office, Josef Kieffer was taking stock of everything that had been captured since the twentieth of June: Ken's wireless set, complete with codes and transmission schedules; the four notes that Raynaud had brought in; Gilbert Norman's wireless set, with the new crystals that were in Ken's package; and a note, probably also from Ken's package, listing en clair all of the arms drops scheduled for the next few months. By any measure, it was a gold mine. But what to do with it? The biggest prizes were obviously the wireless sets, codes, and crystals, which almost gave the SD enough to play the kind of radio game that the Abwehr had been running so successfully in the Netherlands. SD leaders also knew that they were close to breaking open the resistance movement in all of northern France. But to achieve both of those goals, they needed a few more pieces of the puzzle: they needed to be able to work the WT sets to send messages back to London, and they needed a way to root out each of the subcircuits that Physician controlled. The only way forward was to break Suttill and his inner circle.

Kieffer surveyed his new prisoners, trying to decide where to begin. He concluded that Roger Couffrant's Romorantin group were merely foot soldiers and not worth spending any time on. Culioli, he deduced wrongly, was also a bit player and could be dealt with later. The real catches were Suttill, Norman, Macalister, Pickersgill, and Borrel. Kieffer may well have thought that Andrée Borrel, being a woman, would be easiest to crack. If that was his assumption, he was dead wrong. According to her interrogators, she uttered not a single sentence, maintaining, in Michael Foot's words, "a silence so disdainful that the Germans did not attempt to break it."[2] By her demeanour, she made it perfectly clear that she regarded her captors as something to be scraped from her shoe after a walk in the park. Even Boemelburg and Kieffer were impressed, both later testifying that she struck everyone with her strength of character and that she was the toughest prisoner they had ever dealt with. After that, Andrée Borrel was kept well away from the other Physician prisoners, lest she inspire them with her determined resistance.

Having given up on Borrel, Kieffer's men turned their attentions to Suttill, Norman, Macalister, and Pickersgill. They were subjected to appalling abuse, from savage beatings that broke one of Suttill's arms to near-drownings in a tub of icy water. Anyone who passed out had cognac forced down his throat to revive him, and the process continued. But after four days of torture, the SD was no farther ahead than when it began questioning Borrel. The sledgehammer methods having failed, the SD turned to the more refined tactics favoured by the Abwehr. Realizing that Ken and Frank, as new arrivals, probably didn't know very much, it focused on the two men who it knew were at the top of Physician, Francis Suttill and Gilbert Norman. The physical abuse was over, at least for now; the psychological warfare was about to begin. Within a matter of days, the SD had everything it needed to begin its radio game, and to dismantle dozens of Physician circuits and subcircuits that had taken months to assemble. It had all been ridiculously easy.

But how? Suttill and Norman had both received stellar evaluations on security awareness from SOE instructors, and neither was the kind of man to be easily duped. Physical abuse had no effect on their will to resist, nor would they have been moved when the SD started pampering them with *pain de fantaisie,* butter, cheese, and coffee for breakfast; meat and vegetables for lunch; and soup, cold sausage, bread, and coffee for dinner—the same food, in fact, that was served to Kieffer and his staff. What, then, broke them down? The question has fascinated students of SOE for decades, producing a series of conspiracy theses of varying degrees of plausibility.* But if we avoid what cannot be verified and focus on the evidence, the chain of events is fairly straightforward.

The Germans had learned much about the workings of SOE in London from the success of Nordpol, but they also had a much more potent weapon to use against Suttill and Norman: hundreds of pages of operational messages and personal letters sent by agents in the field to England via Lysander. Although it was never proven in court, the SD could have gained access to this material through one person only, Henri Déricourt, who was in charge of all correspondence that went by air and who probably took everything to the SD to be photographed before send-

*See appendix.

ing it on to England. Kieffer and Goetz admitted after the war that most of what they knew about Physician was provided by Déricourt. And they used that material to devastating effect.

SD interrogators began by showing their prisoners copies of documents that should have gone straight to London. Kieffer presented Suttill with all sorts of correspondence, from personal letters to details of the "Messages Personnels" that had been broadcast over the BBC since January 1943, as well as charts they had made of SOE's activities. One was a map of France that showed F Section's circuits, subcircuits, and personnel, complete with photographs of everyone from Nicholas Bodington to France Antelme. Another covered SOE facilities in Britain and included dozens of names, from Maurice Buckmaster right down to some of the sergeants who taught physical training at the Stately 'Omes. Suttill was impressed—other agents who saw the charts were astonished to discover that the SD knew more about The Firm than they did—but what really shook him was a copy of a letter he had sent home to his wife. The SD used the same tactics on Gilbert Norman, presenting him with folders full of copies of supposedly secret communications, but there was a much greater sense of urgency with him. The Germans realized that if Physician's main communications set went off the air for a few weeks, it would certainly arouse suspicion in London. Determined to lose no time in trying to work Norman's set, Kieffer pressed him to give up the proper security checks to accompany his radio transmissions. True to his training, Norman revealed only his bluff check, saying nothing about his true check. The double-security check system was the ultimate safeguard, and Norman was confident that if the Germans used only his bluff check, F Section would immediately realize that he had been captured.

On 29 June 1943, SOE's wireless station received a message from Norman that dealt merely with routine matters. The wireless section reported that the transmission was oddly hesitant but technically normal, except for one thing: the message included only his bluff check, and not his true check. That should have told Baker Street that Norman was not in fact transmitting himself. But, despite the fact that he had sent 143 messages, all of them impeccably coded and with both his bluff and true checks exactly where they were supposed to be, someone at F Section decided that he had suddenly become careless. Instead of closing off all contact with Norman and declaring the circuit lost, someone simply composed a message chastising him for forgetting to use his true check and advising him to do better next time. That one message was as good as a death sentence for dozens of agents and résistants.

Josef Goetz had gone home on leave to see his newborn son the day before the Blois arrests, but was now back in Paris in response to an emergency summons from Kieffer. He was surprised when the rebuke came in from London, but Gilbert Norman was crushed when Kieffer showed it to him. In his mind, it could mean only one thing: that the SD's claims of having a mole in Baker Street, something that captured agents had always dismissed as bluster, were in fact true, and that Physician's cover, and the cover of every other F Section agent transmitting from France, had been blown. Goetz and Kieffer later testified that it was this realization, mistaken though it was, that finally broke Norman's will.

The reply to Goetz's first transmission as Gilbert Norman confirmed for the SD agents that they now had a viable radio game, so they elected to turn their attentions temporarily to cleaning up Physician's subcircuits. They could return to the tried-and-true methods of pre-dawn raids, sending out the Bony-LaFont thugs to round up anyone who was implicated, and then sifting through the suspects to sort out the résistant from the merely unlucky. Or, given the success they had had against Suttill and Norman, they could try something a little more refined. So they proposed a deal: in exchange for the locations of arms dumps and the names of local operatives, anyone taken into custody would be treated as a prisoner of war. Kieffer even offered to provide a written guarantee, on official SD letterhead direct from Berlin.

It has long been assumed that both Suttill and Norman were privy to the pact and that, whoever was approached first, they both ultimately accepted the terms. However, it seems unlikely that Francis Suttill played an active role. Even though Kieffer told many of his captives that Suttill agreed to cooperate after concluding that the SD already knew everything about Physician's operations, there is no evidence that Suttill approved the deal or even knew of it. None of the other imprisoned agents saw Suttill after the pact was concluded, despite the fact that parading around a cooperative Prosper would have done incalculable damage to the morale of resistance groups. In any case, with an arm broken by SD interrogators, he was hardly an effective advertisement for the trustworthiness of the Germans. Furthermore, he was promptly transferred to Berlin, which suggests that the SD saw some risk in keeping him in Paris. Did it fear that Suttill would somehow make contact with his fellow prisoners and encourage them to hold firm?

Instead, all evidence suggests that Gilbert Norman was the active party in negotiating the deal. As an F Section report later concluded, it was Norman who was used for confronting arrested agents: "To each of them he told the same story, that it was useless to hold out as the Germans knew everything about the organisation already, & that he and PROSPER had made a pact with the Germans to reveal the whereabouts of the arms dumps, etc, so as to save the lives of the resistance groups." The Germans had no wish to harm anyone, especially the agents from Britain, Kieffer told his captives; their main concern was to recover all the arms and ammunition before they could be distributed to local résistants, whom he referred to as nothing more than Communist bandits. According to Pierre Culioli, Goetz first brought him the terms of the deal, saying, "Nous savons tout. Nous avons quelqu'un à Londres au siège central de votre service. Depuis plusieurs mois nous savons tout ce que fait votre organisation—par la radio et par les messages Lysander." ("We know everything. We have someone in your headquarters in London. For several months we have known everything your organization was doing—by radio and by the messages coming by Lysander.")[3] Culioli immediately asked to see Suttill for advice, but was told that was impossible; instead, Gilbert Norman was brought in and counselled Culioli to accept the pact as the only way to save the lives of their helpers. Deeply disturbed by what he was hearing, Culioli hesitated; finally, Goetz left him with a pencil and a sheet of paper, and told him to think about it. Remembering the thick sheaf of Physician messages, reports, and sabotage plans going back four or five months—along with the addresses of some key resistance organizers and a Michelin map of the Sologne showing sixteen drop zones, which Goetz had brought to prove F Section had a traitor in its midst—Culioli felt he had no choice but to agree. He wrote down the names and addresses of four of his subcircuit heads, and gave the hiding places of some ninety containers, about half of what his subcircuit Adolphe had received over the past few months. But it wasn't enough. Soon, a note arrived from Gilbert Norman saying that Culioli had established six radio posts but that the SD had found only five—could he please say where the sixth was? Later, Culioli learned that Norman had also revealed the names of Culioli's two brothers-in-law, who had been part of the reception team that had welcomed Norman to France the previous November, the location of two of Culioli's hideouts, and details of some sabotage activity that his teams had carried out.

At the same time, parties of SD agents, sometimes with Gilbert Norman in tow, were visiting resistance cells with news of the deal that had been struck. They didn't really need him, but realized that his presence would have a devastating effect on the morale of résistants—one circuit member recalled after the war, "I do not think I have known a more painful moment in my life than when Gilbert Norman came toward me and said with the most beautiful poise: 'You can tell them everything. They are stronger than we are.'"[4] Norman even took three plainclothes policemen to collect a radio set he had left with the parents of Andrée Borrel's brother-in-law. The elderly couple, believing that Norman had convinced the Germans to work for the Allies, gave them the radio (which hadn't yet been properly hidden) and offered cigarettes and drinks. The visitors left in good spirits, but the SD returned the next day, arrested the brother-in-law, and dispatched him to a concentration camp. Usually, the visits went smoothly, the local résistants accepting the word of Norman and the SD that they would be treated fairly, but on a few occasions operatives smelled a rat. George Darling, head of the subcircuit at Gisors, received a message (ostensibly from Suttill) asking him to assemble his men at a given time and place for a meeting. But instead of the Physician chief, Darling's headquarters was visited by a few rogue Frenchmen and an SD official brandishing a copy of the letter from Berlin. Quickly whispering to his men that it was a trap, Darling feigned cooperation and took the security official to a few arms dumps, but as soon as he saw his chance, he hopped on his motorcycle and sped off down a lane. Darling didn't get far before being brought down by German bullets; he died in hospital within hours. Five of his men were killed that day too.

But something must be said in mitigation of Gilbert Norman's conduct. Having been presented with piles of reproduced documents and then seeing the double-check security system collapse before his eyes, he must have believed himself in an impossible position; anyone in his shoes might well have accepted that the SD had a mole in Baker Street. Furthermore, Physician was now crippled and leaderless and, given what the Germans obviously knew about the organization, it seemed only a matter of time before its members would be picked up. He couldn't be sure that Kieffer would actually keep his word, but the deal at least offered the possibility, however slim, that some lives might be saved in exchange for the arms and ammunition. There is also evidence that Norman did what he could to minimize the damage. One of the places he revealed to his interrogators was an insane asylum that had once been used for transmitting. The warden carefully led the policemen on the most roundabout path through the building, and in each ward they were confronted by shrieking, babbling inmates who pawed and spat at them. For its trouble, the SD took away nothing more than a handful of old, useless radio crystals. And although he appeared to be cooperating fully with the SD, those who knew him best weren't convinced. Culioli refused to believe the worst about Norman— "Ce qui demeure certain c'est qu'Archambaud a fait souvent une lumière trop vive sur certains details sans importance" ("It still seems certain that

Archambauld told everything about certain unimportant details")*—and Andrée Borrel too was confused by Norman's behaviour. She was able to smuggle notes out of Fresnes to her sister, one of which said simply, "C'est Gilbert qui nous a tous vendu" ("It was Gilbert who sold us all out"). But a few days later came another note, this one saying, "Gilbert nous protège" ("Gilbert is protecting us").[5] Even at the heart of the debacle, it was hard to tell who was on what side.

•

But one thing is certain: the circuits connected to Physician were beginning to fall. On 1 July, Armel and Pérégrine Guerne were lunching with another resistance leader at Chez Tutulle, a restaurant previously frequented by Suttill, Norman, and Borrel that was not far from the building where Bleicher and Déricourt lived. The organizer of a Physician subcircuit was on his way to meet them, but when he approached the restaurant and saw unmarked trucks blocking both ends of the narrow street, he quickly ducked into a café and ordered a cognac. Half an hour later, he saw the Guernes and their friend led out in handcuffs. The same day, the Gestapo descended upon Grignon and arrested the institute's director, the gardener from whose house Norman had transmitted, and a few students; the Balachowskis were taken into custody a day later.

Chestnut circuit hung on longer, largely because of its size; it consisted only of the two racing drivers, Robert Benoist and Charles Grover-Williams, as well as their families and WT operator Roland Dowlen. They holed up at one of the Benoist family estates, at Auffargies; France Antelme hid there as well, until a desperate recall message from London put him on

---

*Interestingly, one of Armel Guerne's operatives, who was arrested shortly after Norman, recalled a strikingly similar conversation at avenue Foch, when Norman told him, "Ils [the SD] savent presque tout sur nous. Inutile de nier. Je vous donne l'ordre de faire de la lumière." ("They know almost everything about us. It's useless to deny anything. I order you to shed some light.") Norman then winked, and the man took from his words ("faire de la lumière" rather than "faire toute la lumière") that Norman knew exactly what he was doing, and that he had told the Germans as little as he could to keep them satisfied.

a Lysander in mid-July 1943. But on the last day of the month, a German RDF unit tracked Dowlen's wireless signal and quickly took him into custody. Two days later, SD agents arrested Robert Benoist's brother Maurice, who willingly took them to the villa at Auffargies, where they picked up Grover-Williams, his wife, a few other members of the family, and dozens of containers of arms that had been hidden around the estate. Angry that Robert Benoist wasn't there, the SD men instead arrested his parents in an effort to flush him out. Benoist remained at large until the fourth of August, when he was plucked off a Paris sidewalk and stuffed into a German police car. But the canny Benoist didn't miss a trick. Crammed between two SD officials in the back seat, he waited until the car rounded a sharp curve, and then quickly reached over and jerked open the door. Bracing his feet on the floor, he pushed hard on the hapless guard and centrifugal force propelled them both out of the car. Benoist landed on his former captor and, before the car had squealed to a stop, he melted into the crowds on the street. Two weeks later he was in a Hudson on his way back to England.

Butler, a successful circuit around LeMans, had slightly better luck, because Jean Bougennac, Marcel Rousset, a Mauritian who ran a wholesale fruit business before joining F Section, and the other leaders had little interest in the delights of Paris and preferred to stay in the comparative safety of their own territory in the Sarthe. But in September 1943, on one of their rare trips to the French capital, Bougennac and Rousset were arrested while having lunch. Michael Trotobas, running his circuit in Lille, had seemed invulnerable. He deliberately chose to recruit people who understood the need for discretion: as Suttill reported during his May sojourn in London, Trotobas moved "in a very tough circuit of *maquereaux* [pimps] & race horse gangs," not the sort of people who made friends easily.[6] But Trotobas won them over and they became passionately loyal to him. Even so, he too had been touched by Physician. Trotobas's WT operator had never been able to establish reliable contact with Britain because of a faulty radio set, so he had to rely on Suttill's transmitters; indeed, Trotobas was supposed to meet with Suttill in Paris the day after Suttill's arrest to discuss communications problems. Ultimately, this connection may have cost Trotobas his life. In November 1943, acting on a tip, German police raided his flat and in the ensuing gunfight, Trotobas, his girlfriend, and a policeman were killed. However, his agents were so loyal to him that there were almost no weak links in his network; there were few arrests, and the circuit was quickly back at work sabotaging railway targets. Even today, Trotobas's name is spoken with reverence by the elders in Lille's gritty working-class districts, where he is honoured by a street named rue le Capitaine Michel.

Sadly, all too many of Physician's agents and operatives shared Trotobas's fate. One by one, other circuits fell. The numbers are sketchy, but perhaps as many as fifteen hundred arrests were made in the wake of Suttill's capture. And despite the assurances of the SD, most of the men captured were ultimately executed, although many of their family members (who were usually arrested too) came home from the concentration camps. The only groups that were untouched were the Communist cells in Paris's sprawling working-class areas. They kept to themselves, accepting arms and money from Suttill but wanting nothing to do with the agents who came from Britain. In contrast to the lunchtime rendezvous and afternoon card games that Physician's inner circle favoured, the Communist cells operated very differently, as one courier later recalled: "They were very mysterious. I never knew who they were. Their man would walk up to this house, neither so slowly nor so fast as to attract suspicion, knock, step aside, hand me a packet and receive one from me without a word, and depart. I several times offered coffee or a cognac, but it was always refused, as was any conversation."[7] The Communist résistants had long suspected F Section's people of not taking seriously enough the need for security. Perhaps they were right.

•

As the arrests were taking place, agents were slowly being moved from Fresnes as they outlived their usefulness. Suttill had long since been sent to Berlin, while Ken Macalister and Frank Pickersgill were moved to a house on the avenue Kléber (just down the street, ironically, from the Boulangerie

Pujo, where Andrée Borrel sold bread in happier days) that had been converted into a Gestapo prison; Pierre Culioli was put in the cell beneath them. Later, Macalister, Pickersgill, and Culioli were sent to a special Gestapo prison at 3-bis Place des États-Unis. They didn't know it, but the radio game was about to be taken to another level without them.

Despite the initial success, Goetz soon found that working Gilbert Norman's set wasn't as easy as it sounded. For one thing, it was an exhausting job. He was responsible only for composing and coding the messages (a platoon of wireless technicians did the actual transmissions), but that was the most difficult part of the process. Before the summer was out, the chain-smoking Goetz was spending fourteen hours a day, seven days a week in his office, poring over message drafts and codes to ensure that each transmission said exactly what he wanted it to. He didn't know, however, that F Section was suspicious. When France Antelme returned to London by Lysander in July 1943, he confirmed the arrests of Suttill, Borrel, and Rudelatt but knew nothing definitive of Norman. Buckmaster was reluctant to write him off and decided to send someone to Paris to find out exactly what was happening. A message was duly dispatched to Norman, advising him that F Section was sending two agents to France and asking him to arrange a rendezvous for them in Paris. A response came back using a switch code, a fairly simple cipher that could easily be memorized and need not be recorded on paper. It was unusual for Norman to use such a code, but F Section accepted the rendezvous address. On 22 July 1943, F Section official Nicholas Bodington and WT operator Jack Agazarian were ferried to France in a Hudson to see what was going on with Physician.

In the meantime, the men and women of F Section were still trying to understand what was happening in and around Paris. They had plenty of radio traffic to examine, but they also had France Antelme. Together, they frantically attempted to piece together the events of late June and early July. The first concern was the wireless communications that had been coming in from Gilbert Norman since the twenty-ninth of June. That first message had seemed oddly hesitant ("quite possibly the work of a flustered man doing his first transmission under protest," concluded one report[8]) and had omitted the true security check, but since then, Norman's messages had been, in terms of their coding and transmission, entirely normal. At Antelme's first debriefing, on 5 August, they considered three possibilities: that Norman was free and transmitting normally; that he had been arrested on or after the twenty-fourth of June and was transmitting under duress; or that he had been captured and someone else was operating his WT set. Collectively, the brains in F Section examined each of these scenarios from every possible viewpoint. Buckmaster and Antelme dismissed out of hand the possibility that Norman was transmitting under duress; "Archambaud is not the type," they concluded, and insisted that he would have killed himself rather than transmit for the Germans. On the other hand, if a German operator was transmitting as Gilbert Norman, the most likely villain of the piece was Armel Guerne. Norman had received top marks for his security precautions while at Beaulieu and had never been known to commit a breach of security while in the field, but Guerne knew all eleven of the safe locations from which Norman transmitted. It was quite possible that Guerne had returned to one of those locations, found some coding materials, and passed them on to the SD. But Antelme, although he didn't care for Guerne personally, found this difficult to believe. The two had spent much time together in the last two weeks of June, and Guerne had never shown any signs of unease or guilt; Antelme observed that if he was a traitor, he was also an incredibly good actor. Furthermore, Guerne was well connected in Physician and could easily have turned in dozens of agents; at that moment, many of the men and women he could have betrayed (at one million francs each) were still at large, and would remain free for the rest of the war. After two days of exhausting discussions, F Section and Antelme were scarcely any farther ahead. In the absence of convincing evidence, Antelme refused to pass judgment on Guerne. Buckmaster's conclusion was that "we have absolutely no convincing evidence against his [Norman's] being free."[9]

But Antelme's mind was hounded by one thing: the content of Norman's wireless messages. He was still uncomfortable with the message of the twenty-ninth of June, and didn't subscribe to Buckmaster's view that the hesitancy should be put down to nerves. On the contrary, Antelme recalled that he had watched Norman transmit many times in the past and that he had never been anything but absolutely confident in his transmissions; Norman would often carry on a conversation at the same time as he tapped away on his key, and his messages had always been letter perfect, no matter what the circumstances. Antelme was also bothered by the sequence of Norman's messages, "quite unimportant messages being given priority, and the important ones, such as the whereabouts of PROSPER, etc, glossed over." None of his messages said anything about Guerne, Déricourt, Culioli, or any of the agents with whom he worked closely and who should have been waiting for instructions. Norman's messages, which had always been so rational, had become inexplicably confusing. Antelme suggested sending Norman a specific question that only he could answer, and was asked to come up with something. However, it appears that Buckmaster had finally been swayed. At the bottom of Antelme's debriefing report of the seventh of August, he pencilled in a note: "I am coming more & more to the conclusion that BUTCHER [Norman] is a goner." Then at the top, for emphasis, he added: "For working purposes we must assume BUTCHER to be in enemy hands and take all consequential steps."[10]

Sadly, F Section had already sent Bodington and Agazarian into the trap. Agazarian should really have stayed in London, for he must have been considered contaminated. However, there were literally no other WT operators available so Agazarian agreed to make the flight. Once they reached Paris, Bodington decided to send Agazarian to a rendezvous on the rue de Rome that Norman's message had specified; of course, it was actually Goetz who had set up the meeting, and Jack Agazarian was arrested as soon as he arrived at the restaurant on 30 July 1943. At the next available opportunity, Bodington was flown back to England and reported that the whole Physician circuit was lost. In the certainty that either Norman or someone posing as him had given F Section the address that had led to Agazarian's arrest (and in the probability that Norman, rather than Suttill, had sent the SD to George Darling's headquarters at Gisors; after all, concluded F Section, Suttill had just spent a night there—if he had wanted to meet Darling's men, he would have arranged it then), wireless contact with "Gilbert Norman" was finally broken off and his last message, received on 18 August 1943, was ignored. Of Archdeacon, however, Bodington had nothing to report.

•

When Ken Macalister's set fell into the SD's hands, Goetz realized that he had been presented with a unique opportunity. Not only did the SD have the transceiver itself, but it had the frequency crystals, transmission schedules, codes, and security checks.* They also knew, and not necessarily from Ken or Frank, the territory that Archdeacon was to cover. Finally, they had a virgin set; there was no back traffic from Ken to London that could be used to check the authenticity of future messages or to detect changes in the characteristics of transmissions. Goetz realized that he could repeat Nordpol; he could establish and operate Archdeacon, and SOE would be none the wiser.

So on 20 July 1943 Goetz sent the first message from Ken's WT. It said, "Saw Archambaud and received set from him," and reported that a Physician courier in Paris, a Madame Rose, was being pursued by the Gestapo. No one in Baker Street knew Madame Rose but it was not unusual for Ken to have received a second set—some operators had half a dozen sets hidden in various places—and all indications were that Archdeacon was getting down to work. It was, but with a different Bertrand at the helm: SD official Josef Placke, a former salesman who had joined the security service in 1939. Because the résistants around Sedan had never met Frank or Ken, it was easy for the SD to send in its own man to establish the circuit. Placke, as

---

*The documents do not reveal if Ken had mistakenly committed his codes to paper or if he gave them up under interrogation. Given the way the radio game operated, it is more likely that he revealed his bluff check, as he had been trained to do, and the SD was able to work the wireless set without the true check.

Frank Pickersgill, began to appear in the villages of the Ardennes promising to start a resistance movement. He did everything that the real Bertrand would have done. He interviewed potential helpers and attentively listened to their suggestions for drop zones, then spent days cycling around back roads and farm lanes inspecting fields. He organized his people into reception teams and, with the knowledge gleaned from observing previous air operations, showed them how to set signal lights for an approaching aircraft. He was able to secure the use of a few trucks, and told his workers that he personally would take care of hiding the arms and ammunition that would be dropped to them (no one remarked on the fact that the drivers didn't say much, probably because their first language was German, and that no one was allowed to see the weapons caches, which were actually SD warehouses). Placke also took custody of the downed airmen that local farmers occasionally brought to him, never imagining that he was sending them on to prison camps.

Usually Placke worked alone, but occasionally he was accompanied by a Frenchman named Pierre Cartaud, who had been with a resistance circuit known as Capri until he was arrested in May 1942, after which he agreed to work for the SD under the name Albert von Kapri. The other key figure was Goetz, who wrote and coded the updates on Bertrand's progress, notifying Baker Street of the locations and code names of drop zones that had been established and sending the addresses of safe houses that Archdeacon would use. Placke, Goetz, and Cartaud even organized a few minor acts of sabotage, carefully timed so that the damage could be repaired promptly and with a minimum of disruption. In its first month, Archdeacon was a conspicuous success, achieving everything that F Section had asked of it and more.

Clearly, it was time for the circuit to start receiving more resources, beginning with a demolitions instructor. In September 1943, F Section sent a request to Ken's set that one of the safe addresses be readied. A sabotage expert would soon be sent to Archdeacon, and would rendezvous with Frank at the safe house. The reply came in the next transmission period: the new arrival should go to a café called Au Vrai Gars du Pas de Calais, at 35 rue St. Quentin near the Gare de l'Est in Paris, and ask for the owner, who would put him in touch with Frank. On the twenty-first of September, a sabotage expert named François Michel* climbed out of a Hudson at an Archdeacon landing field. His instructions were to have Frank introduce him, through a cut-out (whose identity was known to the SD), to a small group of factory owners (whom Placke knew only by rumour) willing to help with Archdeacon's demolitions training. The entire scheme, cooked up by Kieffer and Placke and unwittingly aided by F Section, went off to perfection. Michel made his way to the café, but found only a squad of SD officials there who took him into custody. Then, Placke assumed Michel's identity and called on the cut-out who, with no reason to be suspicious, arranged a meeting with some of the factory owners. Within days, they too were in Nazi prisons.

The success emboldened Kieffer, whose plans for Archdeacon became more ambitious. When the SD learned of a small independent resistance cell operating out of a church hall in the rue Championnet in Paris, it decided that Bertrand might be used to destroy the group completely, rather than the SD just picking up a few of its leaders. So Placke, as Frank Pickersgill, made contact with a member of the group (led by John Gay, whose father, a Scotsman and long-time resident of Paris, had coincidentally been interned in St. Denis with Frank) and asked them to mount an attack on a German transport facility in Paris. Gay's group was able to make radio contact with London, and Baker Street confirmed that Bertrand was who he claimed to be—a Canadian officer directing resistance operations. But when Gay sent a large party of résistants to the garage, an even larger party of Germans was waiting for them. Dozens were arrested, and few survived the war.

In November 1943, Goetz used Ken's set to organize another movement of agents. A Hudson flew to a landing zone known as Achille to pick up a large group that included Francis Cammaerts and François Mitterrand (the

*Michel served under the name Frank Mitchell.

222

head of the National Movement of Prisoners of War and a future French president) and leave behind five agents. But the operation was carried out under the watchful eyes of Kieffer's men, who immediately split up to tail the new arrivals. Two of them dropped their shadows with little difficulty, but the other three were less careful; they all boarded the same train to Paris and were arrested at the Gare Montparnasse. One new agent, André Maugenet, who was on his way to join wireless operator John Young and courier Diana Rowden, of John Starr's Acrobat circuit, crumbled under questioning. He told Kieffer of his planned rendezvous with Young and Rowden near Clairvaux, and the SD sent an impersonator in his stead, armed with a letter from Young's wife that Maugenet had brought from England. Young had no reason to doubt the new man's credentials, at least until the SD arrived to arrest him and Rowden. Henri Déricourt later admitted that the SD had paid him four million francs for his role in the double-cross.

Through it all, Goetz carefully kept to the transmission schedule that F Section had laid out for Ken. There was no inkling at all in Baker Street that Archdeacon was anything but a conspicuous success—despite Antelme's warning that no one he had spoken to in France had the slightest knowledge of Archdeacon's status and that it would be prudent to assume that it had been lost. On the contrary, it is a sign of F Section's complete faith in the new circuit that, as its agents were puzzling over the status of Gilbert Norman, they proposed sending a message to Ken Macalister to ask when he had last seen Archambaud.

Macalister's set was operational, but the SD was desperate to expand the radio game. Goetz tried to work Dowlen's set, but Dowlen refused to reveal his security checks and Goetz gave up after six messages to Baker Street brought only silence. Then, they captured Marcel Rousset and his set in September. At first, Rousset denied his identity but then Norman, who had trained with him, and Dowlen confirmed that he was an agent. Norman also maintained that they had all been betrayed by Déricourt, and that he and Suttill had decided to cooperate with the SD to save as many lives as possible. Hung out to dry, Rousset could only admit the truth, but he did all he could to ensure that F Section knew of his fate. He agreed to help the SD transmit messages to London on his set, but he told the Germans that he always put his security checks after the date (when in reality he had always put them at the end of the message) and that he always transmitted in English for Jean Bougennac and in French for Gustave Bieler (when in fact the reverse was true). He was sure that F Section would see through this ruse immediately, and was stunned when his captors informed him that the only response from F Section was to inquire why he had changed languages. Rousset's set, from which Goetz sent his first message on 26 September 1943, turned out to be just as useful a tool as Ken's. Into the waiting hands of the SD, F Section dropped dozens of containers of weapons, cash, and, more important, four agents, all of whom went straight into German prisons.

But neither Norman's nor Rousset's set brought the SD any closer to its last significant prey in Paris, Noor Inayat Khan, who, after Agazarian's arrest, was F Section's only WT operator in the French capital. She was terribly vulnerable—the SD was fully aware that she was the only operator in the city, and could focus all of its RDF capability on finding her—but she still refused Buckmaster's suggestion to return to England. On her shoulders would fall the responsibility for rebuilding F Section's empire in northern France.

•

Born in Moscow to an Indian father and an American mother, Noor was a descendant of the legendary Tiger of Mysore, who had rebelled against British rule in India in the eighteenth century. She was raised in France but, as a successful author of children's stories, she seemed hardly suited for clandestine work. Still, after the family escaped to England in 1940, she joined the Women's Auxiliary Air Force, where someone eventually drew her to the attention of SOE. Just two weeks before Frank was interviewed, Noor was summoned to the same shabby room in the Hotel Victoria. She signed on with The Firm and went through Wanborough in course 27X, about a month after Ken and Frank. A number of her handlers at F Section's training schools argued strenuously against sending her to France. She was too distinctive physically—"twice seen, never forgotten," said one officer of her, an unfortunate trait in a business where the best face was the one that was eminently forgettable—but, more important, they judged that she lacked sufficient security sense, and was too unstable and temperamental to make a successful agent. One biographer described her as "vague, timid and unworldly."[11] But the conducting officers had been wrong before (one of F Section's most successful agents, Francis Cammaerts, had been rated poorly at Beaulieu) and, in any case, Buckmaster had no one else to send.

On the night of 16 June 1943, just as Physician was about to crumble, the same Lysander that took Jack Agazarian and his wife, Francine, back to England left Noor at a drop zone that had been given the code name Indigestion. When Noor got settled, she committed some serious breaches of basic security—more than once, she left her code book lying open in very public places—but she quickly proved that her strengths far outweighed her weaknesses. Gilbert Norman (who had attended the same school as Noor, although she was two years behind him) had given her access to a wireless set (hers hadn't arrived from England yet) that was hidden in a greenhouse at the Grignon agricultural school. It was there that she first met Suttill, and from there she sent her first messages, under Norman's watchful eye. Just days after her arrival, when the first big series of arrests occurred and the Grignon academy was raided, Noor went to ground, not returning to the air until September. She then reported to England that there were apparently two Physician subcircuits still intact in Paris: the Giraudist cell l'OCM (l'Organisation civile et militaire), which joined Claude de Baissac's Scientist; and a circuit run by Émile Garry out of his apartment in the sixteenth arrondissement. Garry wasn't an F Section trainee, but a local recruit; he had started as a courier for Philippe de Vomécourt until France Antelme sent him to Suttill as a potential circuit organizer. Suttill liked what he saw of Garry, and put him in charge of a circuit that he dubbed Cinema, because Garry bore a marked resemblance to the American film star Gary Cooper (F Section didn't care for the name of the circuit, and insisted that it be called Phono instead). Noor had been dispatched to France to be Garry's WT operator but after the collapse of Physician, she became the transmitter for anyone who remained at large. Noor proved to be much wilier than Beaulieu had given her credit for. She found as many as five different safe locations in Paris from which to transmit, and never used the same location for two consecutive transmissions. She constantly changed her appearance, always altering her clothing and colouring her hair so often that it went brittle and straw-like from all the chemical dyes she used. Josef Kieffer later said that her security precautions made it very difficult to locate her.

It is all the more ironic, then, that F Section sent her into the trap. Noor had made contact with a small group of anti-German industrialists led by Maurice Déspret, the director of a steel works at Hirson, right in the heart of Archdeacon's territory. SOE was keen to arrange a meeting between Déspret and Frank Pickersgill, so the two of them could establish a new radio post in Hirson. The SD was equally determined to infiltrate Déspret's group, which thus far it knew about only by rumour. When Goetz received a signal from London instructing Pickersgill to meet with Noor and Déspret, he could hardly believe his luck. The meeting was to take place in the basement of the Café Colisée on the Champs d'Elysées. Using the cloakroom attendant as a go-between, Noor would meet with Frank and Ken and make arrangements for them to rendezvous with Déspret. The only problem for Kieffer was that he had to find a Frank and a Ken. Frank was easy—Placke had been impersonating him for weeks—and to pose as Ken, Kieffer found Harl Holdorf, an SS-Hauptscharführer in the Gestapo office who had once worked as a steward for an American shipping line. The meeting went exactly according to plan. Noor gave "Frank" and "Ken" the names of Déspret and his associates, and the three parted company on the assumption that they would soon meet again. Placke and Holdorf promptly went back to avenue Foch and filed their report, and Déspret and two of his colleagues were arrested.

Noor cleverly slipped away, leaving Kieffer with new respect for her skills. But he couldn't leave her at large; she was too dangerous. Before Kieffer could set a trap, however, he had an interesting visitor: Émile Garry's sister Renée, who handed over Noor's new address for the paltry sum of £500 (not only was Renée a traitor, but she was quite dim—the Gestapo would have paid ten times that amount, and probably much more, for Noor's whereabouts). Even so, she was maddeningly difficult to catch. The first time SD agents tried to arrest her, Noor gave them the slip, but on 13 October 1943, a Frenchman working for the Gestapo took her into custody. Four days later, Émile Garry and his wife were arrested by Pierre Cartaud in their flat. Phono, almost the last viable remnant of Physician, had been brought down.

For the next ten days, Noor missed every scheduled transmission time, something that was duly noted in Baker Street. But F Section did not find this in itself especially worrying, because Noor had advised them that she would be going off the air for a while. When transmissions began again, the tone seemed different and one of SOE's coding and transmission experts was convinced that Noor was not operating the set. Buckmaster, however, wasn't so sure. Vera Atkins was also suspicious, and arranged for a series of personal questions, about things that only she would know, to be transmitted to Noor. When Goetz presented the message to Noor, she naturally refused to say anything, but Goetz had learned enough in his interrogations of her that he could make educated guesses. This evidently satisfied Baker Street, for containers (including one with a half a million francs in cash) soon started arriving in response to Goetz's requests.

By now, the SD had three WT sets in operation, Ken's, Rousset's, and Noor's. All were working so well that there was little need to take up prison space in Paris with SOE agents who seemed to be of no further use. And some of their captives were being troublesome. On 27 October 1943, Marcel Rousset was taken to the prison at 3-bis Place des États-Unis and soon discovered who was in the cells around him. He watched through a small hole in his cell wall to see Émile Garry being put into a cell two doors down, and tapped out messages on his wall in Morse code to learn that François Michel was beside Garry. When Michel was taken away, Frank Pickersgill moved in and Ken Macalister was put in the cell across the hall; in the seven months they were there, Rousset never saw Ken leave his cell. In snatches of conversation, Pickersgill told Rousset where he had been for the last few weeks. During an interrogation one day in late September, Frank had spotted a wine bottle on the table in the room; in a flash, he snatched it up, smashed the end of it on the table, and slashed the jagged edge across the neck of the nearest guard. He dashed out into the hall, still brandishing the bottle, which he used on another guard who got in his way (both guards died from their wounds). There was only one way out so, despite the fact that he was on the second floor, Frank hurled himself through the casement windows and landed on the pavement below. Picking himself up and clutching the elbow he had broken in the fall, he ran toward the avenue d'Iéna, only to be brought down by a hail of bullets. The Germans whisked him off, more dead than alive, to l'Hôpital de la Pitié to be treated for the broken elbow and two bullet wounds. He pulled through but his biggest concern, as he told Rousset, was that he may have revealed something while under anaesthetic.

Culioli, too, was determined to continue the fight. Growing increasingly concerned for the fate of his helpers, he vowed to escape from Fresnes. He told Goetz that there were five more containers hidden east of Blois, and offered to show him the exact location. Once outside of the prison, Culioli would wait for the first opportunity to make a break for it. But he was too closely guarded throughout the entire journey. All he got was a very nice dinner, courtesy of Goetz, and confirmation of how much the SD knew: after a few glasses of wine, Goetz smugly told him the current addresses of three of the most important resistance leaders, Lise de Baissac, France Antelme, and Ben Cowburn. Culioli could barely conceal his shock. Later, Goetz couldn't help but crow about his successes, saying that Norman was transmitting willingly for the SD and that Placke was working Archdeacon. An alarmed Culioli tried to get a warning out. He hid a message in a parcel of dirty laundry—the Germans allowed prisoners to send their laundry out to family or friends, because they could save a few francs on each prisoner whose clothes they didn't have to wash—asking for food and instructing the contact to pass on a warning about any transmissions that came from Archdeacon. Culioli knew that the message got through because he received his food, but he never learned if his warning had gone anywhere. Frank tried the same ruse. When two British commandos were brought into the prison in early 1944, he asked one of them who was bound for a POW camp to send a coded message home informing the War Office of their capture. He couldn't have known that Nazi policy was to execute all commandos, and that the message was unlikely to reach the outside world.

•

Culioli's message wasn't the only warning sign; there were other indications that all was not what it seemed with Archdeacon. Just before Christmas 1943, agents in the field began sending special messages to their families. One of them came from Ken Macalister. Buckmaster, who saw Kay Moore occasionally and often told her how pleased he was with Ken and Frank's work in France, was still completely convinced that Archdeacon was operational, and asked Kay to compose a personal message for the pair, to accompany the Christmas cake and some other treats that were being parachuted to Archdeacon. She thought it best to keep the message short and simple, but Mary Mundle insisted that it be something personal. It didn't take long for the three women, who had found the flat far too quiet after the departure of their rambunctious house guests, to come up with the perfect message: "The tea samovar is still bubbling at 54A." They waited for Ken to send back an amusing retort from Frank, but Buckmaster said nothing about a reply to Kay when their paths crossed. Eventually, she asked if any message had come back, and was told that it had read simply "Thank you for your personal message" instead of something personal or playful. Kay's spirits sank. Her first instinct was that Frank was simply too busy to compose anything witty, which was bad enough, but then it dawned on her that the message simply couldn't have come from either Ken or Frank. She was convinced that he had been caught. And yet she never told Buckmaster of her fears. Moore, after all, was a very junior member of the staff at Baker Street—who was she to be giving advice to the head of F Section? And so a generic letter was dispatched to Jack Pickersgill: "We have pleasure in informing you that we have good news of your brother, Lieutenant Frank Pickersgill, and that he is very well."[12]

Shortly afterwards, when Jack Pickersgill was in London with Prime Minister Mackenzie King for a meeting of Commonwealth leaders, he pulled a few strings and had a personal message sent to Frank: "Jack says mother is well." But then Kay Moore got a curious telephone call from someone in F Section. Did Frank have an Uncle Jack, because a reply came back saying simply, "Thank Uncle Jack for his message." She admitted that she didn't know for certain if there was another Jack in the Pickersgill family, but said that Frank would never have assumed that the message came from anyone but his brother. Later that day, Kay got another call from F Section and was asked the same question, to which she gave the same reply. The following day, an even more senior officer in Baker Street telephoned, and Kay told her story again. The evidence was mounting, if only someone would put the pieces together, that Ken and Frank were no longer at liberty. Instead, the message was altered to avoid alarming the Pickersgill family, and sent on to Jack: "All the best to Jack. Thanks for personal message from mother. Please send her all my love and tell her I hope to be back soon."[13]

Only from one source was Goetz's Archdeacon in imminent danger. An agent named René Dumont-Guillemet had been assigned to track down German operatives who had penetrated F Section's network. Shortly after being parachuted into France in February 1944, he learned from his sources in Belgium of a Canadian officer who was promising all manner of help to résistants in the Ardennes. It sounded a little too good to be true and, upon investigation, Dumont-Guillemet discovered that the Canadian was in fact Josef Placke. He immediately put in train plans to eliminate the imposter and even managed to locate the address of Placke's mistress. However, although he came close on more than one occasion, Dumont-Guillemet was never able to get near enough to Placke to kill him. Archdeacon remained safe and sound within the SD fold.

And so the radio game continued, and Goetz's workload grew correspondingly. On one night, he later recalled, the BBC broadcast thirty "Messages Personnels" to the resistance in France; twenty-seven of them were meant for circuits that Goetz was running. Over four nights in January 1944, a Special Duties aircraft dropped nearly two dozen containers and one agent, Paul Tessier (sent in response to a request from Placke), to three different Archdeacon drop zones; all the supplies went directly into the hands of the SD, and Tessier soon joined the other prisoners in 3-bis Place des États-Unis. Then, on the fifteenth of January, the Germans finally ran down Gustave Bieler, whose circuit Musician had been operating successfully in St. Quentin for so long. Kieffer let no time pass before turning the set against its owners; Placke got straight to work, and convinced SOE that the messages coming in from St. Quentin were written by Frank Pickersgill. Musician joined the growing list of circuits that were operated by the SD. The following month, the SD's haul was even richer. In February 1944, the RAF flew at least seven operations to northern France and delivered dozens of containers of arms, supplies, and money to Archdeacon, Butler, and Phono drop zones. More important, Goetz used Noor's and Ken's WT sets to arrange the dispatch of eleven agents to various fake Phono and Musician drop zones. The biggest prize was France Antelme himself, who was arrested with two other agents after being parachuted east of Chartres.

At the end of February, a small boat landed two men at a deserted cove on the Breton coast. One was the redoubtable Henri Frager, who went off on his own to resume control of Donkeyman. The other was Ange Defendini, a tough Corsican "fired by an overwhelming desire for vengeance against the enemy," as his conducting officer put it; he was headed for the Meuse region to establish a circuit called Priest. Defendini's orders were to proceed to a safe house that had been arranged for Archdeacon, at 33 rue Raspail in

St. Quentin, to meet his wireless operator. But the safe house was manned by the SD, and Defendini was immediately arrested. A week later, Goetz transmitted a message on Ken's set saying that Defendini had arrived safely and was in contact with Pickersgill. Another aircraft flew to the drop zone Archdeacon 6 with Adolphe Rabinovitch, who was to organize his own circuit, and Canadian Roméo Sabourin, who was to be Ange Defendini's WT operator. Sabourin, a student in Montreal before he enlisted in the Fusiliers de Mont-Royal of the Canadian Army, was young—just twenty years old when he started F Section training in 1943—and he hadn't made a great initial impression at secret agent school. His first conducting officer judged him to be "very immature, irresponsible and vain" but Sabourin, fired by the same desire to help France that motivated Ken and Frank, worked hard to impress his instructors and in the end F Section decided that, if Sabourin wasn't likely to "set the Seine on fire," he would at least make a capable WT operator.[14] But he never got the chance to prove himself. As Rabinovitch and Sabourin looked for the résistants who had flashed the recognition signal from Archdeacon 6, they heard German voices in the bushes. Both immediately opened fire and in the ensuing gun battle, two Germans were killed and both agents wounded.

But the evidence was starting to mount in Baker Street that something was up, and when one of the recently captured WT sets came on the air on 27 March 1944, F Section responded with a message to verify its authenticity. The operator was supposed to reply "Merry Xmas" but when a response came back that said "Happy New Year," SOE concluded that he had been captured. It was the same with another captured set; the operator told his captors to put the security checks in the wrong places and never responded to the verification message, so F Section immediately decided that he too had been captured; they did, however, keep up the pretense until 11 May 1944, in the hopes of learning something from the SD. Then, when neither Sabourin nor Rabinovitch sent back the customary messages to indicate that they had arrived safely, F Section assumed that they too had been lost, although Baker Street maintained the radio link until late May on the off chance that it might prove useful. Even so, the drops continued in response to Placke's demands; on the night of 11 April 1944, a Halifax dropped twelve containers of arms, ammunitions, and supplies to the German-controlled drop zone Archdeacon 2.

A note in Ken Macalister's SOE file records that, on 2 March 1944, there were "rumours re arrest of his Organiser." The origin of those rumours isn't specified, but it may have been Gerry Morel, F Section's operations officer. He had become convinced that Noor's set was being worked by the Germans and that any agents who had been sent in response to her requests had fallen directly into captivity. And despite Buckmaster's continued faith in Archdeacon, Morel suspected that it too was fake, and had been for some time. Adding to Morel's concerns was the fact that Archdeacon occupied such a strategic location in Allied invasion planning. If it had been compromised, the area might be full of Germans posing as résistants who could cause havoc when the landings occurred. To convince Buckmaster that Archdeacon should be written off, Morel proposed a test: a conversation with Frank Pickersgill using an S-phone.

The S-phone was a kind of walkie-talkie that had been introduced in the summer of 1943. It offered clear, secure communication between a set on the ground and one in an aircraft overhead; if the aircraft was at two thousand feet, it was good for up to ten miles, but the range could be increased to fifteen miles if the aircraft climbed to five thousand feet. Its great disadvantage, and the reason it was not used more frequently, was that the aircraft had to circle for communication to take place; this could attract either enemy fighter planes or security forces, who were always drawn to the sound of an aircraft circling. But for Morel, the risks of using the S-phone were far outweighed by the risks of allowing Archdeacon to operate in a climate of such uncertainty. So in early May 1944, F Section transmitted a message to Ken's set, summoning Frank to a field northeast of Châlons-sur-Marne on the night of the eighth of May to speak to Morel.

For Josef Kieffer, the message spelled disaster because he had no idea where Frank Pickersgill was. On 18 April 1944, the SD had done some house-cleaning at Place des États-Unis. Nineteen prisoners, including Macalister, Pickersgill, Norman, Rousset, Dowlen, Agazarian, Antelme, and Bougennac, were loaded onto a bus; on the way to the railway station at Vaire-sur-Marne, they stopped at Fresnes to pick up a group of prisoners that included John Young and some women who had no connection with the resistance, and then they boarded an eastbound train. Chained together but permitted to talk, the men found that the hours passed agonizingly slowly as the train chugged through Maastricht, Düsseldorf, Leipzig, and Dresden. The Germans off-loaded the women at Breslau and a few hours later, the train reached its destination, Rawitsch in German-occupied Poland, south of Posen, the site of one of the Nazis' lesser-known but no less evil concentration camps.

Each man was stripped naked and led to a cell, to find inside a set of grimy convict clothing. During the day, they spent endless hours making rope; at night, they lay handcuffed on bare iron bedframes. There would be no contact between them, save during the half-hour they spent in the exercise yard, and no medical attention, which some of them desperately needed. One agent had several wounds in his neck, into which a German doctor had clumsily inserted a drainage tube. Norman was desperately thin and hardly recognizable. A few months earlier, he had taken advantage of a guard's inattention and dashed out the front door of the avenue Foch building. He was steps away from hopping onto a streetcar when he was brought down by a bullet in the leg. The wound had never been properly treated, and had become a festering hole. Norman wasn't alone in believing that few of the nineteen would ever leave Rawitsch alive.

Kieffer, for one, fervently hoped they would, for he desperately needed Frank Pickersgill to continue his radio game. Still, he was a little surprised, after putting through a call to the concentration camp, to learn that Pickersgill was indeed alive. His relief was short-lived: Frank refused to cooperate and would have nothing to do with the S-phone conversation. But Kieffer had one more chance. Sitting in a Paris jail cell was the enigmatic John Starr. He had started his second tour of duty on the Continent in May 1943 with his WT operator John Young, but was arrested and eventually landed in SD headquarters at avenue Foch. There, Kieffer took a liking to him because of his artistic talents and asked him to redraw the SD's rather sloppy map of SOE circuits in France. The result so pleased Kieffer that Starr soon enjoyed special privileges, privileges that seemed to suggest he had turned.

In fact, he was trying to work a game against his captors. He was able to engineer the escape from avenue Foch of himself, Noor, and another agent (their freedom lasted only a few minutes, but merely getting out of the building alive was an accomplishment), and still Kieffer trusted him enough to ask him to pose as Frank Pickersgill for the S-phone conversation. Once again sensing a chance to foil his captors, he was noncommittal, telling them day after day that he would think about it. Kieffer must have imagined that he would eventually agree, because he made no other arrangements; then, just as they were about to leave for Châlons-sur-Marne, Starr announced that he wasn't going to cooperate. As he knew full well, he had placed Kieffer in an impossible position: it was too late to find another native English-speaker for the charade, so Kieffer had no choice but to use the people he had on hand.

Accordingly, Placke and Cartaud were taken to the rendezvous; Placke, after all, had lived in Canada for a few years, and Kieffer blithely assumed that he must speak English with a Canadian accent. At the appointed time, the Halifax droned overhead and Cartaud established the connection, speaking to Morel in French. He then put Placke on the S-phone to say a few words in English. Morel said nothing. He had no idea who the French-speaker was, but he was certain that "Frank Pickersgill" was German. There was no longer any doubt in his mind that Archdeacon was lost. But the very same night, two aircraft dropped twenty-three containers and twelve packages to the German-controlled drop zones Musician 7, Archdeacon 8, and Archdeacon 14. One of those containers held half a million francs, bringing F Section's donations to the SD via Archdeacon to over 2.2 million francs (nearly 500,000 dollars in current values) since Ken and Frank had been captured the previous June.

Incredibly, Buckmaster remained unconvinced. Maintaining that Pickersgill's voice could have been distorted by atmospheric conditions, he had another message, addressed to Frank, transmitted to Ken's set: "Disappointed not to hear your voice on the S-phone." This drew an even more curious reply: "Send Kay Moore over in the plane and she will recognize my voice."[15] Most of Archdeacon's message traffic has not survived so it is impossible to determine if Kay's name had come up in earlier transmissions or whether it was simply part of the vast fund of knowledge that the SD had about F Section and its personnel. But it was evidence enough for Buckmaster, who ordered that drops to Archdeacon should continue. Still, he did agree to another test, not only of Macalister's set but of Rousset's as well: messages would be sent to Frank and Rousset containing specific questions of a personal nature that only they could answer. Again, Kieffer made a panicked call to Rawitsch, and a little after midnight on 18 May 1944, Macalister, Pickersgill, Rousset, Bougennac, and another agent were dragged from their cells to a waiting car and driven to Gestapo headquarters in Berlin. They assumed they had been taken there for execution and were all heartily surprised when, twenty-four hours later, they were taken to Tempelhof airport and flown to Paris. Frank and Bougennac were driven directly to avenue Foch, while the other three were left to cool their heels at Place des États-Unis. One at a time, they were all offered comfortable accommodations in exchange for cooperation; Ken and Frank were even plied with considerable quantities of alcohol, but to no avail. Having experienced the SD's hospitality already, all five of them refused. F Section's questions to Archdeacon went unanswered. The fake Butler survived a little longer, receiving drops at three separate zones on 28 May 1944 (another German-controlled circuit, Delegate, received four drops on the same night), but Archdeacon was finally declared dead. The radio game was over.

There was one final exchange of messages. On 6 June 1944, as Canadian, British, and American troops fought their way up the Normandy beaches, the set that had supposedly been operated by Marcel Rousset for the past nine months sent a message thanking SOE for sending such generous quantities of arms and ammunition and "the many tips you have given us regarding your plans and intentions." It was signed "Geheime Staatspolizei." Shortly after, a message came in with Ken's call sign. It also thanked SOE for the weapons and said "certain of the agents had had to be shot" but that others had been willing to do what their captors had asked of them. It too was signed "Geheime Staatspolizei."[16] A few days earlier, a letter from the War Office had dropped through the door at the Macalisters' home in Guelph. Celestine quickly scooped it up and tore it open, then tossed it on the hall table in disgust. It was just another one of *those* letters, she murmured: "We have pleasure in informing you that we continue to receive good news of your son and that he is in the best of health."

ELEVEN

NACHT UND NEBEL

Paris, August 1944. The French capital had been transformed by four years of occupation. Concrete pillboxes now dotted the sidewalks and boulevards, replacing the eighteenth- and nineteenth-century statues that the Germans had melted down to make munitions. Sentry boxes and armed guards were everywhere, for the Nazis had requisitioned hundreds of buildings as offices and residences. The streets were ruled by bicycles and evil-smelling *gazogènes,* vehicles that had been converted to burn wood or charcoal instead of gasoline. And Parisians were getting thinner on a weekly ration that included two eggs, three ounces of cooking oil, and two ounces of margarine. The meat ration was so meagre, went the joke, that it could be wrapped in a metro ticket—as long as it hadn't been punched by the conductor, in which case the meat would fall through the hole. After all, only a few people (like resistance leaders and SD officers) could afford the black market dinner for four that cost nearly three times what an office worker earned in a month. But at least the end was in sight. American and Free French troops were less than fifty miles away. Paris would soon be delivered from its tormentors.

There were two facts, however, of which most Parisians remained blissfully unaware. General Dwight Eisenhower, supreme commander of the Allied forces in western Europe, had made a difficult decision. The invading armies had been badly held up in Normandy—the Canadian and British armies were still bogged down in the hedgerow country south of the invasion beaches, while it had taken American units until the end of

July to break through the German defences and sweep toward Paris from the west—and Eisenhower felt he couldn't risk more delays. Fearing the French capital would become another Stalingrad that would chew up his armies and stall his advance for weeks, he had elected to advance on either side of the city, cut it off from the rear, and wait until its defenders gave up. In a tactical sense, the plan was very wise; the second fact made it all the more so.

Unbeknownst to Eisenhower, Adolf Hitler had vowed to make the Allies pay dearly for Paris, the last great occupied city still in his hands. Every arrondissement, every block, every house would be bitterly defended, regardless of the damage to the city. He had even ordered to the city the largest artillery piece then in existence, a massive mortar nicknamed Karl that could throw a two-and-a-half-ton shell nearly three miles; half a dozen rounds from Karl would bring down even the sturdiest office tower. And when Paris did fall, the Allies would find nothing of value there, for the Nazis had devised elaborate plans to turn the city into a wasteland. The four aqueducts that brought in 97 per cent of the city's water would be demolished, along with the entire electrical grid and the city's gasworks. All of the more than forty bridges across the Seine would be brought down, and Paris's most important factories reduced to rubble. The city's central telephone exchange would be blown up and dozens of architectural gems— from the Palais du Luxembourg to the Quai d'Orsay—were mined, to be exploded before the city was abandoned. Paris, Hitler demanded, should be made uninhabitable for a generation.

There were a few other details to be taken care of. The Nazis couldn't do much about the 25,000-strong Communist underground army, much of it armed with weapons supplied by Francis Suttill, that was ready to take to the streets at a moment's notice. But the Nazi prisons in Paris were filled with nearly seven thousand Allied agents, local résistants, and security sus- pects. Many of them were simply common troublemakers—a brick through a German office window here, a tire on a Wehrmacht truck slashed there— or people who were in the wrong place at the wrong time, swept up in one of the many *rafles* (raids) that the Nazis mounted in Paris. But there were also hundreds of important resistance organizers, circuit heads, wireless operators, and demolition instructors, local recruits as well as F Section and RF Section operatives. Most of them were at Fresnes and Place des États-Unis, and had been subject to lengthy sessions of interrogation and torture at avenue Foch. The rabble-rousers could safely be left behind, but a different fate awaited the more dangerous prisoners. They could not be allowed to fall into Allied hands—they had seen too much. As German army engineers laid explosive charges to prepare for the obliteration of Paris, the SD got ready to ship its important captives to Germany. The security service had a name for such prisoners—*Nacht und Nebel* (night and fog), so called because they were meant to disappear without a trace. They no longer had any rights, or even any legal existence; they still lived, but in the Nazi administrative system they had ceased to exist. None of them knew where they were going or why but most could guess, even without seeing their SD files—which had been stamped *Rückkehr Unerwünscht* (return not required).

Early on the morning of the eighth of August, the prisoners in Fresnes heard the usual sound of the coffee trolley, its squeaky wheels clattering along the corridor. But today it wasn't dispensing the usual cup of nauseating coffee; on the cart was a box of red cards, and the soldier pushing it stopped at the occasional cell and stuck a card on the door. Later, a trio of guards came to the marked cells, hauled out the inmates, and sent them down to the prison yard. There, they were loaded onto three waiting buses, two for male prisoners and one for female. They were driven to the Gare de l'Est to join another group of unfortunates, some of whom had come by bus, some by the black sedans preferred by the Gestapo, some in the trucks that the Abwehr favoured. They were all resistance agents, many of whom had been held at a German camp near Compiègne. On the platform, they were strip-searched and hustled into a special railway carriage that had been modified for the transportation of dangerous criminals (the rest of the train was packed with wounded German soldiers). One compartment of the carriage was reserved for the women. The others, each of which would normally seat eight passengers, had been stripped of everything but the hard, wooden benches, and iron grilles had been fastened over the windows. Into two such compartments were packed thirty-seven prisoners.

Most of them were casualties of the fall of Physician: Ken Macalister, Frank Pickersgill, and Pierre Culioli; Ange Defendini and Roméo Sabourin, the intended principals of Priest, both of whom had fallen victim to the fake Archdeacon; Henri Frager, who had run Donkeyman for so long without suspecting it had been infiltrated until Bleicher himself arrested him in July 1944; the racing driver Robert Benoist, who had returned to France in October 1943, only to be arrested on the way to visit his dying mother not long after D-Day; Harry Peulevé, the WT operator who had recovered from the injuries sustained in his first parachute drop, returned to France in September 1943, and been captured six months later after being denounced by a neighbour who thought he was a black marketeer (Peulevé had attempted to escape from Fresnes, but had been shot in the leg while trying to scale a wall; refused medical treatment, he had to dig the bullet fragments out with a spoon); Maurice Southgate, one of the most successful resistance leaders in France—"the uncrowned king of five large départements,"[1] Buckmaster called him, with a legendary circuit called Stationer and over six thousand armed men under his direct control—arrested in May 1944 after spending three months' leave in England; Jean Bougennac of Butler; Pierre Mulsant, a lumber merchant who had been Ben Cowburn's second-in-command at Troyes, as well as Cowburn's WT operator Johnny Barrett; Émile Garry of Phono; and Belgian Julien Detal, who was drawn in by the SD's operation of Marcel Rousset's wireless set.

One member of the group, Forest Yeo-Thomas, has left the fullest account of their sufferings. Yeo-Thomas was from an English family that had lived in Dieppe, on the north coast of France, since the 1850s, when his grandparents had left Wales to escape family disapproval of their marriage. Forest was born in England but spent most of his life in France, including a stint with the U.S. Army during the First World War while he was still a teenager; by 1932, he had risen through the business world to become general manager of the Paris high fashion house Molyneux. Yeo-Thomas was a rarity among English-born agents: his French was letter-perfect, without a hint of an accent, and his use of slang and idiomatic expressions was faultless. That was his strongest card. His weakest was that, after he was recruited by RF Section, he became fond of dreaming up hare-brained and completely unworkable plans, like commandeering the Molyneux yacht and sailing it from the south of France to Gibraltar or kidnapping the commander-in-chief of the German navy, Karl Dönitz, and spiriting him away to England.

Fortunately, the cooler heads of RF Section prevailed, and Yeo-Thomas was given more useful missions, such as trying to pick up the pieces of the Gaullist resistance movement after the loss of Jean Moulin. After his second operation in France, Yeo-Thomas was put behind a desk and told to interview potential candidates for Jedburgh missions. But Yeo-Thomas wasn't cut out for administrative work and he was sent back into France for a third mission, only to be arrested at the Passy metro station in March 1944 after being betrayed by one of his operatives. He had been held near Compiègne but found a number of old friends in the group from Fresnes, including Johnny Barrett, with whom he had served in 1940. In talking to Ken and Frank, he also discovered that they shared a mutual friend in Kay Moore, who also worked with RF Section.

Yeo-Thomas, Frager, and Southgate, as the senior officers in the group, quickly took control of the situation; Frenchman Stephane Hessel, an RF Section recruit who spoke the best German, was deputized as liaison with their guards. The first thing to do was establish a rotation system so that the men, who were handcuffed in pairs, could take turns sleeping. Four men would sleep on the floor at a time, while all of the others squeezed onto the benches; every two hours they would swap places, giving another four men a chance to sleep. It wasn't much of a solution, but it prevented chaos in the cramped compartments. Yeo-Thomas, Frager, and Southgate also tried to arrange a pooling of food, but some of the prisoners who had been given Red Cross food parcels were unwilling to be generous and refused to part with their treasures. Hessel had more luck with the guards, convincing them to allow pairs of prisoners to go to the toilet when necessary. On one of those trips, Yeo-Thomas stole a glance into the third compartment and saw that it held some two dozen women prisoners.

Progress was slow as the train shunted from track to track through the suburbs of Paris, and conditions in the carriage were grim. It was a blazing hot August day, and the temperature inside the unventilated compartments quickly became unbearable. While Hessel tried to persuade the guards to give them some water, Frank Pickersgill kept up a non-stop banter of corny jokes in an effort to lighten the mood. At first, his efforts were met with glum silence or curses, but gradually a few of the men started to enter into the spirit of things. A little of the gloom lifted, at least for a short while. The reward for his efforts was a small cardboard box of malt syrup that Yeo-Thomas had been saving for an emergency. Now it was clear that Frank and Ken, whose physical condition was among the worst because of the months of abuse they had endured, could really use the extra nutrition. But after his two hours on the floor, Frank put his hand in his pocket to discover that he had rolled over while sleeping and crushed the box. His hand was covered with the gooey liquid, and the attempt to clean it off only succeeded in smearing it all over Ken and those sitting near them. Frank then tried to lick the syrup off his hands but the result was a face covered with sticky brown liquid. Despite Hessel's pleas, the guards refused to allow any of the prisoners to wash.

By the afternoon of the ninth of August, they had been on the train for nearly thirty-six hours, but had travelled less than a hundred miles. By now, the appalling heat, frayed nerves, lack of water, cramped conditions, and overpowering stench of dirty bodies had pushed the men into a sullen silence. Even Frank had run out of jokes. Then, yells from the guards shook the men out of their stupor. An instant later they heard aircraft engines— the Allied air forces ruled the skies over France and would shoot at anything that moved—and then the world erupted in violence. Cannon shells slammed into the carriages and the ground around them as the guards returned fire with light and heavy machine guns. Explosions could be heard up ahead of them and, between the blasts, the screams of terrified civilians. Amidst the panic, a couple of the women from the third compartment crawled back to bring water to the men.

Then it was all over. The prisoners, who had flung themselves to the floor in search of cover, tried to disentangle themselves from each other. The only sounds now were the shouts of the guards collecting the bodies (seventeen German soldiers had been killed in the attack) and tending to the wounded. And then—nothing. They waited for the train to start again but as the hours passed it became clear that either the engine or the track had been damaged by the Allied aircraft. In time, two requisitioned farm trucks pulled up beside the carriage and the prisoners were herded out of the compartments, the men into one truck and the women into another. The policeman in charge of their guards announced that if any one of them tried to escape, the entire group would be shot. That was enough to dissuade Harry Peulevé and Johnny Barrett, who were busily hatching a getaway plan, from making a break for it.

The nearest SD office was in Châlons-sur-Marne, so the trucks headed off in that directions to get instructions. The convoy eventually pulled into the courtyard of an old château, and the policeman rushed away to find out what to do with his charges. The prisoners waited for hours—the only liberty they enjoyed was being allowed to wash themselves in the courtyard's fountain, no mean feat for men handcuffed in pairs—and finally were packed in the trucks again and driven away. Some of the men had spent the idle hours writing notes to their families on scraps of paper, which they then tossed to civilians as the trucks pulled out of Châlons. It was nearly midnight when they arrived in Verdun and the streets were deserted; the only sounds came from heavy boots on the cobblestones and raucous singing in a German mess somewhere in the town. Their accommodation for the night was a stable in the old army barracks. Six or eight men were put into each stall and were warned, on pain of death, not to cross the twine that separated them from the women in the opposite stalls. But string and threats weren't enough to deter a few of the inmates from creeping out of the stalls and starting whispered conversations across the corridor. One of the women, WT operator Lilian Rolfe, had worked in the Canadian Legation in Rio de Janeiro before the war.

In the morning, the guards removed the handcuffs and gave the captives a few minutes to get cleaned up. Battered tin mugs of coffee were passed around—it was called coffee but it was actually made from scorched grains or acorns—and then they were rechained and herded back into the trucks. Their journey eastward continued, but hours later the atmosphere changed. Since their departure from Fresnes, their spirits had been buoyed by the French civilians who risked a beating, or worse, to shout a word of encouragement or flash two fingers in a victory sign. But as soon as they crossed into Germany, they were well and truly among the enemy.

The rude introduction came when the trucks drew up outside Neue Bremm, a small concentration camp in Saarbrücken that held prisoners awaiting transfer to the death camps farther east. As the prisoners jumped to the ground, German guards greeted them with a rain of punches, kicks, and rifle butts. By the time they were shoved into the nearest building to be registered, half of the men (the women had continued on to Ravensbrück concentration camp) were bloody and dazed. The formalities completed, they were chained together in groups of four or five and forced, under the blows of the guards, to shuffle and stumble across the compound to the latrine. Attempting to relieve oneself while chained to three or four other men was both challenging and humiliating, but there was worse to come. They were led toward a small, tin-roofed hut about nine by eight feet; there were narrow benches around three sides, and an oil drum in the corner to use as a toilet. In this tiny, suffocating space, the thirty-seven men would spend the next three days.

Again, the senior officers had to come up with a system that gave everyone an equal opportunity to stretch out on the floor. Finally, they decided that eight men could lie down at once, with four facing each way. Twenty-four men would sit on the benches, trying to keep their feet off the men on the floor, and the rest would lean against the other wall of the hut. Every few hours, they would change positions. It wasn't very comfortable, but there was no other way to arrange things equitably. They remained hand-cuffed in pairs and locked in the hut for most of the day and night; the only time they were let out was to wash and collect their rations. Neither was as pleasant as it sounded. To wash, they were led to a round pool filled with murky water; it was supposed to be used to fight fires in the com-pound, but the guards got more use out of it for drowning prisoners for sport. The water level was so low that one had to lean far over the side to reach it, and the guards took great pleasure in knocking a delicately bal-anced prisoner into the pool, to be hauled out by the man to whom he was handcuffed. Mealtime was equally disappointing. Breakfast consisted of a few half-cooked chunks of beetroot floating in a container of boiled water, a lump of bread whose main ingredients were dark grain and sawdust, and a cup of cold water. Lunch and dinner was the same, only without the soup. It was disgusting fare, but no one was in a position to be picky.

On the fourth day, the men were rousted from the hut to line up before an officer from the Paris SD and a troop of bored-looking field policemen. They were directed to a number of prison vans, and locked in pairs in their iron cubicles. Compared with the tiny hut, the cubicles for two were posi-tively spacious. Then they noticed that bags containing their few pathetic possessions, things that had been considered lost once they left Fresnes, had been put into the vans. Maybe things were starting to look up. The men were locked in and driven to the Saarbrücken railway station, where two cattle cars, one for the prisoners and one for the guards and the baggage, awaited them. For the first time in days they had space to stretch out, and they were also pleasantly surprised to discover that the cattle-car door was left open when the train chugged out of the station.

The combination of fresh air and improved circumstances enlivened some of the men, and they soon began to discuss their probable fate. Some of them deduced, from the presence of the field policemen, that they were being taken to a prisoner-of-war camp and that the worst was over. The realists among them were convinced that their death warrants had been signed long ago and that their only chance of survival was to escape. Frank and Ken agreed, but were in such poor physical condition that they wouldn't be able to make a break even if a golden opportunity presented itself, and would have to stay behind to face the certainty of brutal reprisals. Frank and Yeo-Thomas debated the issue for ages; in the end Pickersgill's concerns remained, but he told Yeo-Thomas that he and Ken would still offer any help they could. Meanwhile, a local résistant named Yves Loison had been hunched over his handcuffs, trying to open the lock with a hairpin and a few bits of metal, and swearing disgustedly each time he failed. But then he heard a slight click and the manacle fell open. He quickly released the men around him and, in hushed voices, they hatched a plan. There were only three guards riding on their wagon. When darkness fell, they would remove their handcuffs, kill the guards using either their own weapons or their bare hands (dim memories of the teachings of the Heavenly Twins came to mind), and jump off the carriage, trying to get as far away from the track as possible before the train stopped and the rest of the guards took up the pursuit. The optimists, however, remained convinced that they were headed to a comfortable prison camp and threatened to alert the guards if any escape was attempted. There was no choice but to shelve the plan.

The anger of the would-be escapers was soothed a little when, in the early evening and before the planned escape time, they were transferred from the goods wagon into a proper passenger carriage. For the first time, they could sit comfortably on the benches, look out the windows, and chat freely with each other. A few of the prisoners began talking to their escorts, and the mood improved sufficiently for Yeo-Thomas to inquire if they were going to a POW camp. The field police officer told them that their destination was a special camp for officers where they would enjoy concerts, a cinema and theatre, a well-stocked library, and perhaps even the company of women. It was, he smiled knowingly, a kind of holiday camp. Buchenwald, he called it—Beech Wood. Perhaps, thought a few of the more optimistic souls, it wouldn't be too bad after all.

•

Most prisoners reached Buchenwald after a five-mile hike up the Ettersberg from Weimar station, but the group from Paris was spared this trek. Instead, their carriage was shunted into the camp on a specially built rail line that SS chief Heinrich Himmler himself had ordered. It had cost the lives of hundreds of slave labourers and was a triumph of bad engineering—after countless closures to repair rock slides and collapses under the roadbed, it was ready for use in the summer of 1944. Just before midnight on the sixteenth of August 1944, the thirty-seven resistance men filed out of the carriage and onto the platform. They had been dropped directly into the bowels of hell.

Since its first 930 inmates arrived in July 1937, Buchenwald had grown into one of the largest concentration camps in Germany, with some 130 satellite compounds and work camps in addition to the main site. Created to hold enemies of the Nazi state, by 1942 it had been transformed into an enormous slave labour camp, its prisoners working in a number of factories within the camp itself, including the Gustloff Armament Works (which manufactured rifle barrels, pistols, motor vehicles, and gun carriages) and the German Armament Works (DAW), where they made cartridge cases, anti-tank shells, and aircraft parts. The inmates were also farmed out to dozens of industries in the surrounding area, including a BMW engine factory, eight different Junkers aircraft plants, and other operations that made everything from hand grenades to parts for the V_1 and V_2 rockets.

For the SS officers who staffed the camp, Buchenwald was a plum assignment. To entertain them, there was a casino, a brothel, a falconry, and a zoo (where the monkeys, bears, deer, foxes, and boars feasted on meat, honey, marmalade, milk, and white bread, things that never reached the prisoners' tables). A steam bath, complete with a masseuse, was available, along with wine and spirits in limitless quantities, enough for the commandant's wife to bathe regularly in a tubful of Madeira. And to ensure that they were surrounded by only the finest trinkets, any sculptors, woodcarvers, gold and silversmiths, bookbinders, and painters were plucked from the prison population and sent to a special workshop, where they crafted objets d'art for their captors.

There was no baccarat, Madeira, or fine porcelain for the prisoners. Their captors may have been well fed and entertained, but it would be difficult to imagine a more despicable collection of characters. They ran the gamut from sadists to sexual deviants to common thugs, but they were united by a fervent desire to make their prisoners' lives as miserable (and often as short) as possible. The inmates were divided into various classes, identified by coloured triangles on their clothing: red for political prisoners, green for criminals, purple for Jehovah's Witnesses, black for "anti-socials," pink for homosexuals, yellow for Jews. There were other identifying marks as well. Foreigners had the first initial of their nationality printed on their triangle, while a repeat offender had a coloured stripe above his triangle. What the Nazis called "race defilers," people who had violated the Nuremberg race laws that isolated Jews by restricting their political and marriage rights, wore a black triangle superimposed over their first patch.

Despite these distinctions, the brutality was shared out equally, leniency being shown only to those who could or would make themselves useful to their captors. The rest were starved, beaten, subjected to horrifying medical experiments, sexually abused, and summarily executed on a whim. Some who were singled out for special punishment were consigned to the stone quarry, which seems to have existed in large part so the guards could gain pleasure from watching prisoners being crushed by large boulders. But among the miscreants who staffed the camp, some were feared and hated even by their own. After the war, American soldiers found graffiti scrawled on the wall of an SS guard barracks: *Gott erschuf in seinem Zorn den Hauptsturmführer Weissenborn* (God in his wrath created SS Captain Weissenborn). One of the camp's deputy commandants, Weissenborn enjoyed a kind of notoriety for keeping the skull of a murdered prisoner on his writing desk. For the cruel, the vicious, the sadistic, Buchenwald was a pleasure ground.

This was the world into which the thirty-seven agents were transported, to join over 82,000 others in a battle for their very lives. The struggle began as soon as they left the train and were marched along the Caracho Way, named by the prisoners after their slang word for "double time." For the newcomers, the experience was surreal. Despite the hour, the August heat was still oppressive. A few bare light bulbs cast dismal shadows around the perimeter wire; the stars and moon should have made for a bright summer night sky, but an almost unnatural gloom lay over the camp. Just as stifling was the silence. The guards' rifle butts kept the prisoners quiet, so the only sounds were the occasional wail of a dog and the faint buzz of the electrified fence. It seemed as if they had entered the city of the dead.

The Caracho Way took them out of the administrative section of the camp and toward the prisoners' compound. At its entrance, the main gate was decorated with two phrases that summarized the philosophy of Buchenwald: the inscription painted on the stucco above the gate, *Recht oder unrecht—mein Vaterland* (My country, right or wrong); and in the iron latticework of the gate itself, *Jedem das Seine* (To each his due). The men were taken first to a large hall where their new escorts, prisoners from the camp population known as kapos, told them to put their belongings on a table and sleep on the tiled floor. They had just settled down when, after a flurry of conversation between the escorts, they were ordered to stand, remove all of their clothing, and fold it into neat piles on the table. The thirty-seven men stood in the hall, naked and filthy, for half an hour until another change of plans was announced: they were to dress again and go to sleep. The newcomers didn't know it at the time, but the kapos were trying to determine what to do with them: were they going to be executed right away, or should they go to the trouble of registering them as camp prisoners? When Stephane Hessel asked one of the kapos why they couldn't make up their minds, he was told that the safest course was just to obey orders. "You have no friends here," said the kapo. There was no malice in his voice; in fact, there was no emotion at all. Hessel thought it was the voice of a man who was beyond the capacity to feel.

They were ordered to strip a second time, and led to the delousing station. It may have given them the wrong idea of what they should expect.

As Harry Peulevé recalled, "The delousing station impressed us. We passed through a hall where we were made to empty our pockets, the contents of which were put into little bags. We then stripped and our clothes were put on clothes hangers and enclosed in large paper bags; we were given a metal disc as a receipt. From here we went into a long room full of white-coated barbers, each of whom had electric clippers with which he shaved us completely from head to foot. After the clippers we were doused in disinfectant which burned horribly, each given a handful of soft soap and passed into an enormous white tiled room with hundreds of sprinklers in the ceiling. The hot water was turned on and we had a good shower."[2]

Next they were issued with new clothing, the blue-and-white-striped concentration camp uniform, as well as any other assorted pieces of clothing that they could pick up. They were given loose clogs that made them stumble and trip, red triangles to sew on their shirts and pants, and a fabric strip on which was printed an identification number. Ken had been known by many names over his life—the British Army called him John, the instructors in SOE's Stately 'Omes referred to him as 27-OB14, and to F Section he was Jean Charles Maulnier, Valentin, or Plumber—but his final alias was Prisoner Number 9636. Frank, who had been "Peek-air-jill" to his French friends before the war, British Internee 1135 in St. Denis, 27V-3 while at secret agent school, and François Marie Picard or Bertrand to F Section, became Prisoner Number 9992. It was during this process that they got their first surprise. An inmate who looked no different from the other sorry specimens shuffling around the camp began speaking to them in English, warning them that they had landed in one of the worst concentration camps in Germany, where the treatment and death rate were more frightening than anything they could imagine. They soon learned that this was Maurice Pertschuk,* an F Section agent who told them of other SOE members in the camp: Christopher Burney, the last man sent to the ill-fated Carte network, was there after spending nearly a year in solitary

---

*Pertschuk served under the name Martin Perkins.

confinement in Fresnes prison. He was living in Block 14 with Pertschuk and Alfred and Henry Newton, who knew both Maurice Southgate and Johnny Barrett from the SOE training schools. They had spent the pre-war years touring France as travelling acrobats under the stage name the Boorne Brothers, and were first dropped to work as sabotage instructors for Philippe de Vomécourt; they were eventually arrested while trying to set up their own circuit in the Haute Loire. Elsewhere in the camp was Dr. Alfred Balachowski, the scientist who worked at the Grignon agricultural academy near Paris, the site of a Physician radio post.

The new arrivals didn't join them, but instead were sent to Block 17, a separate hut surrounded by barbed wire. They were supposed to be in isolation but it wasn't difficult for them to get out into the main compound, where they enjoyed a kind of celebrity status. They had been issued with better clothing than usual, received better rations (to the extent that some of them, after months of harsh treatment, actually began to put on weight), and found that Block 17 was the most comfortable barracks in the camp—akin to having the best cabin on the *Titanic*. While most of the huts had sleeping shelves stacked four or even five high, each of which had to accommodate four prisoners, those in the special block slept two to a bunk, sharing a thin, vile-smelling blanket and a mattress of coarse fabric stuffed with mouldy straw. Their hut commander, or *Ältester*, was a kindly fellow named Otto Storch, a Communist who had been an inmate of Buchenwald since the very beginning. He acted as liaison with the camp staff, passing on orders and regulations and counting the prisoners every day. The men of Block 17 were thus spared the daily agony of roll call on the gravel parade ground, when the guards painstakingly counted every inmate, the living and the dead (the corpses of prisoners who had died overnight had to be dragged out to roll call and propped up by their erstwhile hutmates so they could be counted), a process that could take four or five hours, while the prisoners stood in lines in the blazing sun or bitter wind. Occasionally, the ordeal proved to be too much and an emaciated body would fall out of line and slump to the ground lifeless, another victim of Buchenwald's brutality.

For the new inmates, the existence was bearable, if bleak. Storch asked only that they turn out for exercises every morning, while Yeo-Thomas demanded that they wash and shave each day, to maintain a semblance of military decorum. Other than that, the days were their own. Henry Newton, who had worked himself into a position of some influence in the compound, visited them with a gift of onions and garlic. Robert Benoist was very depressed because he thought his brother Maurice had turned on the family (in fact, he had—despite Maurice's attempts to shift the blame onto others for telling the SD about the family estate, there is compelling evidence that Maurice was a willing accomplice in the arrest of most of his family), while Henri Frager talked endlessly about how they had all been betrayed by Henri Déricourt, who he said had been in league with the SD all along; the year before, on a visit to London, Frager had told his superiors that if they didn't get rid of Déricourt, he would do it himself. Frank preferred to focus on the future, telling Pierre Culioli that he was thinking about a career in documentary film after the war.

The resistance group soon learned that they weren't the only newcomers. Not long after they arrived, virtually the entire Copenhagen police force had marched, in perfect order, into the camp after the Nazis decided that they were doing far more to undermine the occupation of Denmark than assist it. Then, on the twentieth of August, came a group of 168 Allied airmen. They too had been at Fresnes, and almost all of them had been arrested in the company of resistance members trying to help them evade capture. They had left Paris on the fourteenth of August and pulled into Buchenwald after five days crammed into boxcars. Some of them had spent months in solitary confinement.

The airmen proved to be valuable allies, for the realists in the SOE group remained convinced that their only hope of survival lay in escape. They enlisted the help of some of the flyers and set about making a reconnaissance of the camp. It immediately became clear that breaking out of Buchenwald was a daunting task. The electrified perimeter wire and guards who had no compunction about shooting prisoners on a whim meant that the only option was a charge on the main gate. That meant enlisting as many potential escapers as possible—because it was a foregone conclusion that dozens of men would be killed in the attempt—and finding some source of weapons. Here, the resistance men came up against the internal dynamics of Buchenwald. For years, the camp had seen a bitter struggle for control between the criminals and the political prisoners, most of whom were Communists. At stake were all the perks that went along with running the compound on a day-to-day basis—better food, control of who was sent to which work camps, access to the German staff, light duties in the cookhouse or the hospital. The battle waxed and waned, and at the moment the Communists were in the ascendant, despite the fact that Ernst Thälmann, the leader of the German Communist Party and a prisoner since 1933, was executed at Buchenwald just two days after the SOE group arrived. And rumour had it that they had a secret arsenal hidden somewhere in the camp—but they weren't about to share it with the SOE officers, most of whom they regarded as loathsome capitalists. If there was to be an escape, they had to find a way to win over the Communists.

The resistance group had been in Buchenwald for only a week, but once the escape reconnaissance was completed, the days degenerated into a tedious sameness. The twenty-fourth of August was no different—a wan sun broke over the camp, the inmates were pushed and shoved into lines for counting, and the slave labourers were marched off to the factories for the day. The other prisoners, the resistance group, the airmen, and the odd collection of people in a special compound known as the Spruce Grove were left to their own devices, to do what they could to make time pass as quickly as possible. Hundreds of miles to the west, 129 aircraft from the Eighth Army Air Force droned across northern Europe, the sun flashing off the polished silver surfaces of the Flying Fortress heavy bombers. In their bellies were over three hundred tons of bombs, both high explosives and incendiaries. There was little conversation between their crews as they scanned the sky around them for German fighters.

In Buchenwald, the prisoners had finished another disgusting lunch and trailed out into the compound to spend the afternoon in the sun. A few of the airmen were sunning themselves beside their hut when the whine of air-raid sirens broke the stillness of the afternoon. This was nothing new—bomber streams frequently passed over the camp—and the POWs watched idly as the Fortresses approached at about 25,000 feet. Then one of them spotted a puff of smoke from the lead aircraft overhead, and an American flyer said nervously that it was the signal to the bomb-aimers to release their loads. It was 12:18 p.m.

Minutes later they heard the sound of explosions as the bombs plastered the airfield in Weimar. The prisoners exchanged relieved glances until one of them spotted a much larger force approaching from the same direction. By now, the German anti-aircraft guns were in action and black smudges appeared in the bomber stream as flak shells exploded. One struck a Fortress, blowing it to pieces and scattering the fragments through the sky like so many silver leaves. And then came another puff of white smoke, this time while the bombers were still off to the west. There could be no doubt about the target this time.

Within minutes, high-explosive bombs began hitting the Gustloff workshops and garage areas, as well as the SS offices in the southeast corner of the camp. There was a short pause, and then another wave of bombers hit the SS camp and the Gustloff and radio factories with incendiaries. As the bombs fell, the smoke got thicker and thicker, until the whole camp was covered with a choking blanket of smoke that blotted out the sun.

Most of the inmates had taken cover to avoid being hit by stray bombs, but the prisoners of Block 17 had a different attitude. Convinced they would soon die one way or another, they stood outside their barracks to watch the explosions rocking the southern part of the camp. The smoke obscured much of the target area, so they couldn't appreciate the chaos that had overtaken the camp. The slave labourers were forbidden from leaving their workshops during the raid, but some of them took the opportunity to try to make their escape. The Ukrainian SS guards immediately opened fire on the fleeing prisoners, but some of the German SS men were caught in the crossfire and a brief gun battle between the two groups of guards erupted. Angry shouts, terrified screams, and bomb blasts filled the air as the resistance prisoners watched with barely concealed glee. And then, propaganda leaflets detailing how well the Allies treated German POWs fluttered into the compound and the last bombers droned away from Buchenwald. Exactly thirty minutes had passed since the prisoners had spotted the first puff of white smoke.

Gradually, the inmates' ears stopped ringing, and then they picked up a new sound: burning buildings. The last few loads had consisted of incendiary bombs, and fires were taking hold in the factories and administrative compounds. Desperate for help, the camp staff demanded that the fitter airmen assist in the firefighting effort, despite the fact that they had no shoes. Nor was there any water, so all they could do was pull down a few buildings and drag away the wood in hopes of stopping the fire from spreading. As they were doing so, a couple of the airmen came across the camp museum, and saw the lampshades and book covers made from tattooed human skin that Georges Vanier would later see. For their efforts, they received the thanks of the camp commandant, a spineless despot named Hermann Pister, and then a harangue that they would be made to pay for the damage that their comrades had caused.

Gradually, the scope of that damage became evident. In the DAW compound, thirteen of the factory buildings were completely destroyed and two more burned out. In the immense Gustloff works, only two buildings remained undamaged; inside them were dozens of now useless machines that the slave labourers had sabotaged in the confusion. Four buildings of the radio factory were destroyed, as well as all of the administrative buildings up to the main gate. The SS barracks were only slightly damaged, but the garage and storage areas were almost completely flattened. The boiler building, the washhouse, the laundry—all were reduced to ashes.

Bombs also struck the Spruce Grove, killing twenty members of Romania's Iron Guard, a fascist movement that had fallen afoul of its own extremism, and severely wounding Princess Mafalda of Savoy, the daughter of the king of Italy. Her legs shredded by high explosive, she was taken to the camp brothel, where one of the Nazis' sex slaves tried to comfort her. The camp medical officer immediately decided that her legs should be amputated, even though there was no anaesthetic; to no one's surprise, she died within minutes of shock and blood loss. At that moment, she ceased being a member of the Royal House of Italy and became just one more corpse, her naked body tossed on a pile with the other dead. In all, the Germans admitted that nearly 150 of their guards and SS transport staff were dead or missing, along with dozens of their family members who lived in the camp (Pister's wife and daughter were among the casualties); over 300 prisoners died, and nearly 1,500 more were wounded. Perversely, the Nazis seemed most outraged by the fact that their pride and joy, the Goethe Oak, had been reduced to a charred trunk.

After the excitement of the air raid, the day-to-day battle for survival seemed even more tedious than ever. One man had a tiny chess set that he had carried with him ever since leaving England, and it provided hours of diversion; Frank even took it upon himself to teach chess to those men who had never played it before. He and Ken also scoured the camp for small scraps of cardboard, which they and the other inmates turned into miniature playing cards. Thanks to such simple pleasures, the days passed a little less slowly.

On the ninth of September, Otto Storch was called to the administrative office just after lunch and returned to Block 17 with a list of prisoners designated for "special handling," a list that Pister had just received from the SD's headquarters in Berlin. At 3:30 that afternoon, Storch told the SOE group, sixteen prisoners were to present themselves at Signpost 3, near the camp gate: Desmond Hubble, a friend of Yeo-Thomas's from RF Section who had been on one of the first Jedburgh teams and was captured in the Ardennes; Gerard Keun,* the English-born son of a Dutch Sephardic Jew, he had come from the French Foreign Legion and French naval intelligence to work for

*Keun served under the name Gerard Kane.

SIS in the field (rumour had it that his very successful resistance group had got the plans for the Atlantic Wall, the German defences along the western coast of Europe, from none other than Abwehr chief Wilhelm Canaris); prisoners of war turned secret agents Élisée Allard and Pierre Geelen, and Corsican Marcel Leccia, who were arrested in April 1944 when they were turned in by an acquaintance; James Mayer, one of three Mauritian brothers who served in F Section; Charles Rechenmann, an engineer from Alsace who had worked under Ben Cowburn; Arthur Steele, a musician and a victim of an SD trap in Marseilles; and the casualties of the fall of Physician, Ange Defendini, Julien Detal, Robert Benoist, Jean Bougennac, Émile Garry, Roméo Sabourin, Ken Macalister, and Frank Pickersgill. Storch wouldn't say where they were going and most of them professed to believe that they were to be interrogated. Only Marcel Leccia would say out loud what the others must have been thinking—that they would soon be executed. He even gave Storch his ring to pass on to his fiancée.

At the appointed time, the sixteen marched in perfect order to the main gate, where an SS-Unterscharführer called their names, tied their hands, and read out their death sentences. Prisoner Franz Eichhorn, who had stayed alive in Buchenwald by becoming the commandant's personal barber, and another inmate had walked them to Signpost 3. They urged the men to put up a fight and perhaps take a few of the guards with them, but one of the agents (likely Rechenmann, who was the most fluent German-speaker of the group) said that they were already dead and didn't want others to suffer reprisals because of their resistance. He had only one request of the guards: that they suffer the honourable death of soldiers, by firing squad. With that, the group was escorted to the *Zellenbau* (cellblock). After they had left, Yeo-Thomas, Peulevé, and Hessel pressed Storch for information, but the Ältester remained evasive. Finally, he said quietly, "I do not think that you will ever see your comrades again." They were considered terrorists, he said, and there was no doubt that they would be executed. The three decided to tell Southgate and Frager but no one else until there was some confirmation. The following day a Polish prisoner reported that the sixteen were still alive but under sentence of death; someone even claimed to have seen a few of them on the small exercise yard beside the Zellenbau. But on the eleventh, the scientist Alfred Balachowski, whose fate had been bound up with those of the Physician agents for nearly two years, brought the terrible truth.

After leaving their block, the sixteen men were put in cells, two men to a cell. Each measured just over three feet wide and not quite seven feet long, with a cement slab for sleeping. Small windows looked out onto the parade ground, but they were of no use to the inmates. Sitting down or looking out was forbidden; every prisoner in the Zellenbau had to remain standing at attention, facing the peephole in the door, between the hours of 5 a.m. and 8 p.m. Except for a few minutes on the exercise yard and the occasional savage beating by their guards, they were left alone. Then, at around five o'clock in the afternoon of the tenth, they were removed from their cells, brutally beaten again, and marched past the main gate to the crematorium, a modern facility with a large courtyard surrounded by a high fence. Ken and Frank, who had been together almost every day for the last eighteen months, remained together. The guards pushed them all down the stairs to the basement, to a long cement room known as the *Leichenkeller* (corpse cellar). As the sixteen men looked at the dozens of hooks sunk into the walls seven or eight feet off the ground, they realized that Rechenmann's last request had been ignored. Waiting for them was the block's executioner, SS-Scharführer Walter Warnstädt, and the kapos who worked in the crematorium. Warnstädt ordered that the prisoners' hands be bound, not in the shape of a cross but with the wrists parallel to one another, because it caused more pain. One by one, each man had a noose of thick wire slipped over his head, and was then hauled up and suspended from a hook. Death came agonizingly slowly—it was nearly twenty minutes before the last man gave a final twitch and went limp. The bodies were heaved down, piled on the electric lift, and sent upstairs to the coke-fired crematorium. Then, as on a thousand other days in Buchenwald, oily smoke stained the bright blue sky over the Ettersberg as the wind caught flecks of ash and carried them toward France.

TWELVE

REMEMBERING

Jack Pickersgill was exhausted by the time he reached the St. Francis Hotel in San Francisco in April 1945. With Russian armies closing in on the heartland of the Third Reich from the east, and British, Canadian, and American armies from the west, the war in Europe was all but over. Along with Prime Minister Mackenzie King and Louis St. Laurent and Lester Pearson, two future prime ministers, Jack was part of the Canadian delegation to the international conference that would draft the charter of the United Nations and start building the new world from the ruins of the old. But he didn't feel much like rescuing the world after spending four days on the train from Ottawa to California. He hadn't slept well on the journey, his mind running over the concentration camp horror stories that were reaching the daily newspapers, and he was looking forward to a few hours of sleep before getting down to business. It seemed as if he had just dozed off when a soft rap on the door awoke him. It was Hume Wrong, another member of the delegation, with a telegram from Georges Vanier in Paris: "Have just heard from an unimpeachable source that Frank Pickersgill was executed."[1]

By his own admission, Jack had almost given up hope that Frank would survive the war. The wireless messages sent early in 1944 had been the only news he had (Jack didn't yet know that they were actually written and sent by the SD) until September 1944, when official notification came through that Frank had been captured; it was just two days before the first executions at Buchenwald. In February 1945, Allied officials scouring Fresnes prison for clues as to the whereabouts of captured agents and airmen had found Frank's inscriptions in his cell, dated June and July 1943, and relayed the information to London and Ottawa. The more Jack learned about the crimes of the Nazi regime, the more convinced he became that Frank would be one of its victims. Still, Vanier's news left him stunned.

His first thoughts were for his mother, and he immediately got on the telephone to make sure that she didn't receive the standard military telegram. Instead, he arranged for Tom Pickersgill, who was in Vancouver working with the Ministry of Labour, to travel to Port Rowan and tell Sara himself. The details of Frank's death were held back—the authorities knew full well that he had been hanged but SOE advised that "it would be unkind to pass on this distressing news to the next-of-kin"—but that did little to cushion the blow. Jack later wrote that Sara was stoical but "that some of the light had gone out of her life forever."[2]

We know nothing of how the Macalisters reacted to the news of Ken's death, but they must have been just as shattered. Alexander maintained a brave face, keeping his correspondence as cheerful as could be under the circumstances. He referred to Ken as "our boy" and allowed himself to show little outward sentiment. "He was such a fine fellow," he wrote in one of the few comments that betrayed the emotion within him.[3] In Oxford, C.K. Allen, who had been a kind of surrogate father to Ken for years, was deeply affected by the news, even more deeply than he had imagined he would be. Perhaps more than anyone, he knew what Ken might have achieved had he lived, and he grieved for the world as much as for himself. "A brave man, and all the braver because war was not naturally his game," he wrote to the warden of New College, "and he was certainly not the 'insensitive, fearless' type." Nor did time reduce the magnitude of the loss. The following year, he reflected that Ken "was one of the most brilliant Rhodes Scholars we have had from Canada for many years, and his loss is especially regretted by everybody who knew his calibre."[4] This from a man who, for decades, had watched some of the world's best and brightest minds come through his Oxford office.

•

With the Third Reich in its death throes and the war in Europe drawing to a close, the Nazis' concentration camps started to give up their terrifying secrets. For SOE, the greatest concern was uncovering the fate of its agents who were missing. F Section had sent some 470 agents to France, 118 of whom were unaccounted for. Many of them were known to have been captured, but dozens had simply vanished. There were rumours of executions and hazy reports of sightings, but very little that could be confirmed. What had happened to them?

Buckmaster's office already knew something of the truth behind the fall of Physician from one of its agents whose WT set had been worked by the SD. In May 1944, Marcel Rousset had been brought back to Paris with Ken Macalister and Frank Pickersgill to provide information that would allow the SD to keep playing the radio game. Not only had Rousset refused to cooperate with the Nazis, but in June, while he was sweeping the floors at the Place des États-Unis prison, he noticed that there was only one guard watching him. In a flash, he clubbed the guard unconscious, dashed out into the street, and disappeared into the crowds before his captors realized he was missing. He went into hiding until the city was liberated in August, when he reappeared to supply some of the information that F Section had been trying to piece together since the previous year.

But Rousset could fill in the details only until June 1944; he knew nothing of the eventual fate of his comrades. However, just before noon on 13 April 1945, SOE received a message from Bernard Guillot, a locally recruited résistant who had been in Ken and Frank's group when it left Paris in August 1944. Guillot had escaped from German custody and arrived in Paris just days earlier, to report to French authorities what he knew about the executions at Buchenwald. Then came another report, this time from Alfred Balachowski, that corroborated everything Guillot had said, and added more specific details about the executions.

Balachowski reported that the SOE group in Buchenwald had refused to believe the news of the September executions at first, and only accepted it when the personal effects of the dead were returned to Block 17. Strangely, a few took it as a good sign: if the Nazis were going to execute the entire party, they reasoned, they would have killed everyone at the same time. But most of them were certain of the fate that awaited them, and they hatched a desperate plan. With the help of Balachowski and Eugen Kogon, an Austrian journalist who had been an inmate since Buchenwald's first year in operation, Forest Yeo-Thomas made an offer to Dr. Erwin Ding-Schuler, commander of the SS Typhus and Virus Research Division, housed in Blocks 46 (the isolation block for typhus patients) and 50 (where research on typhus vaccines went on). In return for a promise to testify on his behalf in future war crimes trials, Ding-Schuler would help to save as many of the resistance prisoners as possible. Ding-Schuler may have been a sadist, but he wasn't stupid—he realized that it was only a matter of time before the Third Reich crumbled and he was called upon to answer for his crimes. When that happened, someone like Yeo-Thomas might be the only person who could save him from the gallows.

Ding-Schuler agreed that a number of prisoners would sneak into the research block, where the kapo would inject them with something to produce a high fever. They would then return to their own block and, the next day, report sick to the hospital; while they were there, the same kapo would visit, apparently by chance, and diagnose their symptoms as typhus. They would then be taken to Block 46, and their identities switched with real typhus patients who were on the verge of death. When one of the genuine patients died, Ding-Schuler would simply enter an agent's name on the death certificate and report it to his superiors. The agent would then be free to rejoin the general camp population under a new name. The plan was the first good news he had had in weeks, and Yeo-Thomas was overjoyed. He compiled a list of the prisoners to be saved, beginning with the most junior and ending with himself. Then Ding-Schuler came back with a condition: he could free only three prisoners, and Yeo-Thomas must be one of them, so that he would be around to sing the doctor's praises after the war. Yeo-Thomas was devastated but Ding-Schuler was adamant, insisting that involving any more might ruin the whole plan. Yeo-Thomas was left in the unenviable position of having to choose the men who would go with him to the typhus block. Balachowski suggested that one be French and one British and, after an agonizing night, Yeo-Thomas picked Harry Peulevé and Stephane Hessel. Both were bachelors and tried to convince Yeo-Thomas to choose two married men instead, but he refused to reconsider.

But before the three could be injected, the wheels began to turn. On the first of October, Pierre Culioli and Bernard Guillot were summoned to the main gate. Storch said they were being sent to a work camp, but Yeo-Thomas and Frager thought it unlikely. Four days later, the Ältester returned from the administrative compound with a list of thirteen men, including Yves Loison, the local résistant who had undone their handcuffs on the train from Paris, Henri Frager of Donkeyman, Ben Cowburn's second-in-command Pierre Mulsant and his WT operator Johnny Barrett, and Harry Peulevé, who were to present themselves at the gate at 6 a.m. the following morning. They certainly weren't being sent to a work camp, and Frager and Storch urgently discussed their options. Frager asked if Storch had access to poison so that the condemned men could commit suicide rather than give the Germans the satisfaction of killing them, but Storch said there was nothing readily available to do the job. He suggested that the thirteen men overpower their guards and try to make their way out of the compound; they would certainly die in the end, but at least they would take some of the enemy with them. Frager thought about it, but decided that it might bring reprisals down on the other prisoners in Block 17 and he had no wish to make others share their fate. In the end they concluded that there was no way out. The next morning, with Storch and another prisoner to provide support, they marched to the gate in perfect order. SS-Oberscharführer Hermann Hofschulte, notorious because of his fondness for whipping inmates, called their names, tied their hands, and took them to the detention block. Hours later, they were taken in two vans to the SS rifle range and shot. Some of the survivors believed that the courage shown by the first group to die had so impressed the SS that this group was given a more honourable execution.

But only twelve men had gone to the Zellenbau that day; Harry Peulevé had already been transferred to the typhus block with a raging fever. Yeo-Thomas and Hessel were there too, and the plan surprised everyone by working perfectly. The three genuine patients died, the identity switches were made, and Yeo-Thomas, Hessel, and Peulevé were released with new names as soon as their symptoms passed. When they returned to the compound, they learned from Balachowski that three more of local résistants from their group had gone to their deaths.

Miraculously, the others survived. When American troops liberated Buchenwald on 11 April 1945, they found in the charnel house not only Balachowski, but Christopher Burney, the Newton brothers, and Maurice Southgate, who had somehow escaped the attention of the executioners. Culioli turned up shortly as well; he and Guillot had indeed been sent to a work camp. On 14 April 1945, Harry Peulevé walked into a U.S. Army position near Magdeburg; sent to a Junkers aircraft factory in November 1944, he had escaped his captors and walked to freedom. Stephane Hessel appeared a few days later after spending the previous few months at another Junkers plant. Then Yeo-Thomas surfaced, having escaped from captivity in the dying days of the war.

But most of the news that came back was bad. F Section lost about a quarter of all the agents it sent to France, but the death toll for those who were in any way connected to Physician was much higher. In addition to the thirty-one agents who had been executed in Buchenwald in September and October 1944, almost everyone else who fell into enemy hands over the course of the long Physician debacle was dead. Andrée Borrel, Noor Inayat Khan, and six other women had left Paris on 16 May 1944 to be sent to the civilian prison at Karlsruhe. From there, local Gestapo chief Josef Gmeiner sent them on to concentration camps.* Borrel was in a group of four

---

*Gmeiner was hanged in 1948, but not for his part in the deaths of the SOE agents. He was executed by the British for the murder of Flying Officer Dennis Cochran, who, like Ken Macalister's University of Toronto friend Gordon Kidder, had been recaptured after the Great Escape of March 1944.

women who were given injections of phenol and shoved into a furnace at Natzweiler concentration camp on 6 July 1944; Noor and three other agents were shot at Dachau in August 1944. This marked the beginning of a flurry of executions as the Nazis started murdering dozens of resistance members in the wake of Paris's fall. Gilbert Norman was executed at Mauthausen on 6 September 1944 and three days later, Gustave Bieler was shot by firing squad at Flossenbürg; this was a rare honour, but Bieler's fortitude had so impressed his captors that, in a twisted display of respect, his executioners arranged an SS honour guard to escort him to his death. France Antelme, who had tried to unravel the Physician mystery before returning to France, only to be arrested, was killed at Gross Rosen concentration camp, probably on the same day that Ken Macalister, Frank Pickersgill, and the first group of SOE agents in Buchenwald died. In the spring of 1945, as their regime collapsed, the Nazis liquidated as many of the remaining resistance prisoners as they could. Jack Agazarian was murdered at Flossenbürg in March 1945, just a few weeks before the end of the war; with him died Roland Dowlen, the former Royal Bank clerk who was Robert Benoist's wireless operator. Ironically, one other major player met his end at Flossenbürg around the same time: Abwehr chief Wilhelm Canaris, whose organization had played a major role in bringing down Physician. The old admiral had finally fallen afoul of his Nazi enemies. Maurice Pertschuk had been taken to his death, alone, on 29 March 1945, just two weeks before Buchenwald was liberated. Francis Suttill, who the Nazis still believed might be of possible use as a hostage, was sent to Sachsenhausen concentration camp, where he was held in solitary confinement for all but fifteen minutes of exercise a day. He was kept alive until 21 March 1945, when he was hanged along with Charles Grover-Williams, the racing driver turned agent. Yvonne Rudelatt survived the horrors of Bergen-Belsen, but only by a few days; shortly after British troops liberated the camp, she went to an anonymous death from disease and exhaustion, her fellow inmates and her liberators never knowing her real identity. Less is known about the fate of the local recruits, but the statistics are likely just as grim. From the Charmaisons' Physician subcircuit in the Sologne, for example, only four of the forty-four captured résistants returned from Germany.

The radio game proved to be particularly deadly for F Section agents. Marcel Rousset's WT set had been used to lure in four agents, while Noor Inayat Khan's had drawn in another four; all eight had been executed in Nazi prisons. Ken Macalister's set had been the most active, with Placke using it to trick F Section into sending fifteen agents, including François Michel, André Maugenet, Paul Tessier, France Antelme, Ange Defendini, Roméo Sabourin, and Adolphe Rabinovitch, directly into the hands of the SD. To this list must be added Diana Rowden and John Young, who were arrested by an SD officer posing as Maugenet. Only one of the agents, Paul Tessier, survived captivity (he escaped from Place des États-Unis, only to die in the liberation of Paris's suburbs); the others, twenty-four in all, were put to death in Hitler's concentration camps.

The few who returned went through intensive debriefings by their superiors in SOE, but more painful to deal with were the queries from family members and friends who were desperate for any scrap of information that they could get. Georges Vanier wrote to Alfred Newton asking for anything he could tell them about Ken, Frank, and Roméo Sabourin, but Newton was far too ill to reply and asked Vera Atkins to respond on his behalf. Christopher Burney was in better health and, though he had little to offer, asked Atkins to pass on his condolences to the Macalisters and the Pickersgills. The letter was brief, but eloquent and deeply moving: "I saw them constantly right up to their execution and . . . they behaved wonderfully well. I also heard from a prisoner who worked in the crematorium that they died as bravely as I should have hoped to do had my turn come. I cannot say more. Sympathy from someone unknown would cut little ice with the families, though they most certainly have mine." To C.K. Allen, he wrote an equally powerful note: "The tragedy of that day (in which seventeen of our group were hung together) is such that I cannot find the means of redecorating it in heroic colours, and I must chafe at my impotence to comfort those who really suffered from it."[5]

Along with the grieving came the recriminations and the scapegoating. The fall of Physician had been a major disaster that had cost hundreds of lives—it must have been someone's fault; someone should shoulder the blame. The obvious culprits were the members of the German security services who had been involved in the radio game, but postwar investigations proved that they had nothing to do with the physical abuse. Placke, Goetz, and Vogt were all cleared by the British and French of any involvement in war crimes. Josef Kieffer might have faced trial for the torture at avenue Foch, but before that could be pursued he was convicted and hanged for his role in the execution of a group of British commandos in 1944. A U.S. war crimes tribunal sentenced twenty-two members of the Buchenwald staff to death in 1947, but camp commandant Hermann Pister cheated the hangman by dying of a heart attack while awaiting trial. Dr. Ding-Schuler didn't wait to see if Yeo-Thomas's testimony would save his life; he committed suicide while in Allied custody.

And it was easy to find fault with Gilbert Norman's conduct after he was arrested. While admitting that "nothing has ever been proved for or against him," F Section was left with the conclusion that "BUTCHER was either a traitor or broke down under examination." "We do not doubt that his mistakes were committed in good faith," wrote Vera Atkins in 1945, "but his attitude for the first months after capture is open to criticism."[6] But in the effort to determine where Norman went wrong, attention turned back on F Section, to the blunders that allowed the SD to play the radio game with such success, at the cost of so many lives. For ignoring all of the warnings that came in from Gilbert Norman, Marcel Rousset, and a handful of other WT operators, the senior officers of F Section should bear much of the blame. When Rousset surfaced shortly after the liberation of Paris, he took Vera Atkins to the Gestapo prison at Place des États-Unis to show her the blood on the walls; he was furious that SOE had been so stupid as to ignore every hint that he had tried to give, including the wireless security precautions that the training schools had impressed upon their students. Atkins could only reply that she recalled receiving a series of strange messages from Rousset, but that nothing had been done about them. Maurice Southgate was just as outraged. He held nothing back in his debriefing, slamming F Section for ignoring the system of checks that it had created and demanding that those in Baker Street who were responsible for the blunder face court martial for causing the deaths of so many agents.

In the end, at least five people were investigated in connection with the fall of Physician. John Starr, who survived Sachsenhausen and Mauthausen and returned to France after the war to live, came under scrutiny by French magistrates for his conduct at avenue Foch in 1943, but in the end they decided not to pursue charges. Renée Garry was brought to trial for denouncing Noor Inayat Khan, but was acquitted when another resistance member testified that Noor was already under surveillance by the SD, in the guise of Macalister and Pickersgill, so Garry's information was meaningless. Maurice Benoist was tried for turning in his family to the SD, but also escaped with an acquittal. In 1947, Pierre Culioli was brought to trial for betraying Physician and sending so many agents to their deaths. It was a tawdry trial, with much of the evidence coming from the Frenchwoman who had worked for Ludwig Bauer in the Blois SD office. Sentenced to twenty years' hard labour for collaboration herself, she was determined to take someone down with her, and almost succeeded in torpedoing Culioli. He was found guilty of "acts prejudicial to the Resistance," but was simultaneously given amnesty by the government. Culioli was outraged, as much by the verdict as by the baseless accusations that had been made against him: he demanded that he be either acquitted or shot, and eventually he was acquitted of all charges. In 1948, Henri Déricourt was acquitted by a French court (curiously, the defence had called as witnesses Gerry Morel, Georges Bégués, and Ben Cowburn, while the prosecution called Hugo Bleicher, Josef Goetz, and Roger Bardet), perhaps because of the timely intervention of Nicholas Bodington on his behalf. Déricourt apparently died in an air crash in Laos in 1962, although some argue that he faked his own death and went to live in comfortable obscurity somewhere.

In England, the depressing banalities that follow any death were under-way. In her office in Baker Street, Vera Atkins cleaned out her cupboards of the personal possessions that agents had entrusted to her before leaving for France. She carefully packaged them all up and mailed them to grieving families around the world. In Rhodes House, C.K. Allen quickly got over the shock at learning that he had been named Ken's executor and set to the task of closing out his estate so that the probate could be registered and the legacy sent to Jeannine. He methodically contacted every flat that Ken had ever rented, located a long-forgotten bank account containing some £700, and slowly gathered together the small remains of Ken's life: his uni-form badges, a cheque book, a diary, an address book, a couple of suitcases and kit bags, a cigarette box, a travel clock, some keys, an academic gown, some shirts and sweaters, a scarf, a navy blue overcoat, and some old letters, pathetically little from such a full life. Among the last things he tracked down were a dozen letters that Jeannine had tried to send to Ken through the International Committee of the Red Cross; they were dated between May 1943 and May 1944. When he was sure he had collected everything, he carefully packaged it up and sent it to Jeannine.

But he was frustrated at a lack of help from Alison Grant, who he believed knew the whereabouts of the rest of Ken's possessions. He had written to eight other friends of Ken's, Allen wrote to Alison in September 1945, and every one of them had responded quickly and helpfully; this was his third letter to Alison, with no reply at all. He implored her to respond, because Jeannine could not receive the proceeds from Ken's estate until everything was found. Still there was no reply. Why Alison declined to answer Allen's letters is unclear; perhaps she was overwhelmed by the pros-pect of sorting out all the belongings of Ken's and Frank's that had been left in the Walton Street flat. When Ken and Frank had left for France, the three women were faced with the task of cleaning up after them. "You can't imagine how badly they left their stuff," Kay wrote to Sara Pickersgill. "Bunged in any old fashion, dirty clothes with clean, boots with white things and so on."[7] They had sorted everything out, washed it, and wrapped it up with mothballs to await their return. But with Kay and Mary having left London, it was left to Alison to dispose of everything. Eventually, she decided to give most of Frank's clothing to a couple of Frenchmen from F Section who had just been freed from the concentration camps and who had nothing but the clothes on their backs. To Canadian Military Headquarters in London she turned over the few things that remained: a .38-calibre revolver, a Sam Brown belt and cross strap, a pair of brown boots, a pair of brown Oxford shoes, two pipes and cleaning rods, some personal papers, a few photographs, fifteen French books, some brass buttons, a paper knife, a change purse, uniform rank badges, a shoehorn, two leather straps, and a wallet. Again, it seemed so little for one who had done so much.

When Frank's estate was being settled, Jack wrote to his French friends to tell them that Frank had left them money in his will. They weren't interested. "Je ne veux absolument pas des deux mille francs dont vous me parlez," wrote Jean Pouillon. "Il me serait insupportable que la dernière chose que je reçoive de Pick soit de l'argent." ("I want nothing to do with the two thousand francs that you mentioned. It would be unbearable to me if the last thing I received from Pick was money.")[8] George Ford, Frank's old friend from Winnipeg, accepted the forty-dollar bequest, but only on the condition that he use it to type Frank's letters for publication. He and Jack Pickersgill had agreed to publish them as a memorial to Frank, and they both canvassed friends and relatives in Canada, England, France, and the United States for material. *The Pickersgill Letters* was published in a limited print run in 1948, with all the proceeds going to a scholarship fund at the University of Manitoba. In 1978, in response to growing public interest in the story, Jack got in touch with Frank's many friends again, discovered some new material, and arranged for its publication under the title *The Making of a Secret Agent*.

Ken's University of Toronto classmate Douglas LePan, who had gone on to become a university professor and one of Canada's finest poets, spent years working on his own tribute, an epic poem called *Macalister, or Dying in the Dark* (1995). It is a powerful piece based on intensive research into the events of Ken's life and the circumstances of his death. At the end, after Ken and Frank have been hanged and their bodies cremated, the poet ponders what remains:

> So what is left? I ask of the dawn wind
> as morning rises blue and bruised, like a boxer.
> What is left? I ask of the silence at the heart of the whirlwind,
> ask of high heaven, with its ragged, indifferent clouds.
> Ash, ash in the wind, in my mouth, in my nostrils.
> Ash, with the ribbons of death streaming around it.
> A proud sad archangel turning in the wind.
> A song, a song strangling in sobs.

In Guelph, at the reunion of the Guelph Collegiate–Vocational Institute class of 1933, Ken's school chum George Penfold and some of Ken's other old friends decided to do something in memory of their classmate. George tried to track down anyone who had known Ken, and the response was overwhelming. Offers of assistance and cheques poured in from across Canada— from fellow students, former teachers (including John Diefenbaker, on behalf of his late wife, Ken's former teacher Olive Freeman), and even people like Alison Grant, who hadn't known Ken in Guelph. When George got everything sorted out, the committee arranged to have a park dedicated in Ken's honour in 1981, and there was more than enough money to endow a scholarship in his name at GCVI. They couldn't have known of C.K. Allen's request to his student, that once he became a success Ken should provide the means for other young people to follow in his footsteps. Without knowing it, Ken's friends had honoured that request.

While working on the memorial project, George Penfold had despaired of finding any of Ken's relatives, but in the late 1970s he got a break: he tracked down Jeannine Macalister in Paris. She was delighted by the initiative and welcomed the chance to write about her first and only love. In 1946, after months of trying to sort out the paperwork and permissions, Jeannine had come to Canada to visit Ken's parents. It was a difficult encounter. The journey had been a challenge and constraints on shipping had forced her to travel via Marseilles and New York. She wasn't prepared for the bitter Canadian winter, for which she had neither the wardrobe nor the constitution. Her English wasn't good, and the Macalisters spoke no French. And Celestine appeared to be at once obsessed with and repelled by her. She couldn't ignore the fact that Jeannine was Ken's wife, but at the same time she could barely conceal her suspicion that Jeannine was partly responsible for his death. Again and again, Celestine insisted that Ken and Frank should never have been sent to France, and refused to consider the suggestion that they had chosen to go. And it was all Jeannine's fault. Perhaps with an eye to her own past, she was convinced that, with Jeannine's pregnancy, Ken had been trapped into marriage. If she hadn't ensnared him, he would have completed his degree and returned to Canada. But now, it was Jeannine who felt trapped. Celestine constantly hovered around her and refused to introduce her to any of Ken's friends. Sometimes it was because the weather was too bad; other times, Celestine claimed to be feeling unwell. It wouldn't have been so bad if Jeannine had been able to spend more time with Alexander, whom she found to be delightful, but she was never permitted to be with Alexander unless Celestine too was there. Jeannine felt as if she was being slowly suffocated.

Finally, as summer came to Guelph, she was able to escape. She had been in touch with Jack Pickersgill, who had extended an open invitation to her to stay with his family in Ottawa. Jeannine found in the Pickersgill home the kind of welcoming environment that she had craved in Guelph. Together, they spent hours talking about Ken and Frank, and shared with each other everything they knew. They were the kind of conversations she could never have had in the Macalister home. She told Jack that Alexander had kept much of the truth from Celestine, in the belief that she couldn't cope with the truth. "She is not the kind to whom you can say very much," Jeannine wrote to Jack. She was even reluctant to share what she had learned in Ottawa with Alexander. As to Celestine's suggestion that Ken and Frank should never have gone to France, Jeannine told Jack that she thought it was the view of someone who had never experienced war first-hand. She tried to be patient with Celestine, who Jeannine suspected had been unhinged by the loss of her only son, but Ken's mother didn't seem to see that others had suffered loss as well. The war, after all, had taken Jeannine's husband and daughter, as well as her father, and she wasn't interested in a lecture on grief from Celestine. "Life has been easy to her," she wrote to Jack, "and that makes everything harder now."[9]

But *should* Ken and Frank have been sent to France? In hindsight, it's easy to say that they were parachuted into an impossible situation. They probably shouldn't have been sent to the Sologne at that particular time, when the situation on the ground was more dangerous than anyone in F Section was willing to believe. But in the early summer of 1943, nothing was so clear. Both men had come through training with flying colours, and had been praised for their keen sense of security. Perhaps their language skills were not all they should have been, but with the exception of a handful of agents, few anglophones in F Section spoke flawless French. It's hard to argue with Vera Atkins's conclusion, that Ken and Frank were the best candidates for a job that simply had to be done.

Of course, casualties were inevitable. Colin Gubbins had once told Maurice Buckmaster that F Section should be willing to sustain heavy casualties because France was the most important country strategically in the entire western theatre of operations. In fact, The Firm expected to lose half of the agents it sent to occupied Europe, so everyone leaving Tempsford was told that the odds of surviving were no better than fifty-fifty. But those casualties must be put in perspective. The generation of men who ran SOE—Gubbins, Buckmaster, Bodington—had fought in the First World War, when an infantry battalion might lose 90 per cent of its strength in a few hours. In early 1942, the average crew in Bomber Command had a one-in-ten chance of completing thirty operations. Put in these terms, F Section's loss rate for agents, about one in four, was actually fairly good.

Over the course of the war, 118 agents lost their lives on F Section operations; during the same period, the RAF squadrons that flew them and their supplies to France lost over 200 airmen, and casualties on flights serving other country sections were just as heavy. All things considered, the odds of Ken and Frank surviving their mission were probably better than the odds faced by one of the airmen who transported them.

•

Most of the world that Ken Macalister and Frank Pickersgill knew, the good and the bad, is now gone. Mrs. Lewis's dairy on Walton Street is now a high-end yarn shop; the humble flat where Ken and Frank spent so many happy days with Alison Grant, Kay Moore, and Mary Mundle would now command something in the neighbourhood of one million pounds. When the Special Operations Executive was closed down in 1946, its buildings were returned to their former occupants and, in many cases, to obscurity. The Hotel Victoria, now known as Northumberland House, is still used by the British government, recently as a daycare for employees of the Ministry of Defence. The buildings in the Baker Street complex have been either pulled down or renovated; Berkeley Court, for example, has been converted into luxury apartments priced in the high six figures. Thame Park, where Ken did his wireless training, has become a popular location for shooting such films as *Saving Private Ryan* and *The Madness of King George*. All that is left of Tempsford airfield and Gibraltar Farm is a few remnants of runway and the now restored barn that was the last stop of agents before they left England. A plaque has been erected there to mark the departure point of so many agents who never returned. There is another plaque at Beaulieu, and at Romorantin, a memorial to the townspeople who were victims of the Nazi occupation. Included on the memorial are the names of three adopted residents of Romorantin, Yvonne Rudelatt, Ken Macalister, and Frank Pickersgill. At the University of Toronto, Ken and Frank have joined the long list of names on the Soldiers' Tower, where a garden has also been dedicated to their memory. Did they ever imagine, as they stopped to read the names on the tower during their student days, that they might one day be added to the list?

Jeannine Macalister never returned to Canada after her visit in 1946, and she never remarried—whatever Celestine Macalister thought of the match, Ken and Jeannine were deeply, passionately in love. She devoted her life to working with juvenile delinquents and the mentally ill, work that she found very difficult but morally rewarding. In some ways, she never stopped trying to do what her young lover, the man she knew for only a few short years, had done. "These activities and contributions are only a very small thing," she wrote, "compared to Ken's sacrifice."[10] Like Jeannine, Jack Pickersgill never really got over the loss. He went on to have a long career as one of Canada's most distinguished public servants, but Frank's shadow loomed over him for the rest of his life. He became obsessed with searching out information on Frank's life, and pursued even the thinnest lead that might tell him more about his experiences. Pushing him was brotherly love, but perhaps also a certain amount of guilt: should he have done more to get Frank a safe job with the Canadian government? But nothing Jeannine or Jack could have done would have stopped Ken and Frank from accepting their task and seeing it through to its tragic end. On that point, everyone who knew them agrees: they were absolutely certain of the value of their work and their ability to carry it out. In 1942, Ken had described the task of building a better world after the war as "a glorious mission." There may have been little glory in their final eighteen months, but the pair never wavered in their commitment to their mission.

Looking back on the short lives of Ken Macalister and Frank Pickersgill, it's hard not to imagine what might have been. In the estimation of his teachers, Ken was one of the finest minds of his generation, a brilliant man who outshone his fellow students both at the University of Toronto and at Oxford. Anyone who has read Frank Pickersgill's articles can't help but be impressed by their lucidity, their acumen, their humanity; there is in them evidence of a remarkable journalistic talent in the making. And they both left large circles of friends who were devoted to them. There is, in George

Penfold's correspondence with their classmates from Guelph Collegiate–Vocational Institute and in the letters from Frank's friends when Jack was preparing *The Making of a Secret Agent*, a deep and abiding love of the two men, a love that didn't fade thirty, forty, or even fifty years after they died. It's tempting to find an explanation for that devotion in the way Ken and Frank died, but that would be a mistake. It's not how they died but how they lived that accounts for their enormous impact on the people they knew.

So as we look back on their lives, we shouldn't dwell on what might have been, but should remember what was: Ken Macalister, the shy, diffident man whose sheer brilliance wrestled with what his conducting officer referred to as nerve storms; and Frank Pickersgill, the modern philosopher and gifted raconteur who was plagued by insecurities and self-doubt. Until 1943, both of them were searching for their place in the world and an outlet for their prodigious talents. Not until they joined SOE did they find what they were looking for: an opportunity to put their idealism and their love of France into practice. That their war against Nazism was a short one is irrelevant. Reading through everything that Ken and Frank wrote, from their adolescent years right up to the summer of 1943, one can see hints of a willingness to sacrifice everything for their ideals. They could never have foreseen the manner of their death, but they surely had some inkling of its meaning.

ACKNOWLEDGEMENTS

Without the help of Frank Pickersgill's family, this book could never have been written. Ruth (Pickersgill) McKane and Alan Pickersgill have been more helpful and supportive than I could have wished. They allowed me to consult their father Jack's papers, and we spent many delightful hours chatting about their family and the uncle they knew only through stories. I was also delighted to be able to get to know Margaret (Beattie) Pickersgill, Jack's wife and Frank's friend from the University of Manitoba, to learn more about their student days.

None of Ken Macalister's close relatives have survived, but I am grateful to his many school friends from Guelph Collegiate–Vocational Institute and the University of Toronto for sharing their memories of him. I would particularly like to thank George Hindley, who has vivid memories of Ken from high school and university and who has carefully kept the yearbooks and other materials from their time together at GCVI.

As always, I have relied on archivists and librarians in Canada and Britain to help me track down leads in obscure places: Elaine Alahendra (Foreign and Commonwealth Office), Jody Erlandson (Winnipeg School Division), Darcy Hiltz (Guelph Public Library), Catherine King (Rhodes House), Jodi MacDonald (Manitoba Education, Citizenship and Youth), Ann Martin (Arisaig Centre), Joanne Peters (Kelvin High School), Jane Rosen (Imperial War Museum), Gail Singer (Earl Grey School), Elaine Sirois (Library and Archives Canada), Lewis St. George Stubbs (University of Manitoba Archives), Jennifer Thorp (New College, Oxford), and Kathleen Wall (Guelph Museums). I am enormously grateful to two of the foremost historians of the Special Operations Executive, Michael Foot and David Stafford, who were willing to help with any questions that cropped up as I tried to grapple with The Firm's history and the rise and fall of Physician. I would also like to thank some of the Allied airmen who arrived at Buchenwald in August 1944, particularly Ed Carter-Edwards, John Harvie, and Stan Hetherington, for sharing their memories of that horrific place. Despite my best efforts, I have been unable to determine the copyright holder for Douglas LePan's *Macalister, or Dying in the Dark*.

My research assistants, Dorotea Gucciardo, Anne Millar, and Helmi Trotter, were tireless in tracking down leads (and rumours of leads); if they couldn't find something, I was convinced it couldn't be found. And my friends and colleagues—Colin Burgess, Father John Comiskey, J.L. Granatstein, Francine Mckenzie, Barbara and Orm Mitchell, Pierre Claude Reynard, Neville Thompson—were always available with assistance in their own areas of expertise. Also, I owe much to my sister and my brother-in-law, Valerie and Ralph Carpenter, for helping me to navigate the British civil service in my quest for information, for photographing all of the places that Ken and Frank knew sixty years ago, and for Ralph's encyclopedic knowledge of the city of London.

I am so grateful to Phyllis Bruce for believing that I was the person to write this book, and for her sensitive editing that got it into shape. Thanks also to copy editor Susan Folkins and managing editor Noelle Zitzer for their help in bringing it to press. And as always, Linda McKnight of Westwood Creative Artists has been there to make things happen and offer wise counsel at every step.

Finally, my deepest thanks go to Frank Pickersgill and Ken Macalister. When I was a teenager, I read Michael Foot's *SOE in France* and was curious about the two Canadians who ended up in Nazi-occupied Europe. It never occurred to me that I would become acquainted with them even from a distance, but the process has been a joy. They were men worth knowing.

THE DEMISE OF PHYSICIAN

The collapse of the Physician network remains one of the most controversial incidents in SOE's covert war. The magnitude of the disaster has made it intriguing to historians, journalists, memoirists, novelists, and, yes, conspiracy theorists. Because so much about it is unknown (and unknowable), the temptation to fill in the gaps with inferences and deduction has been, for many writers, impossible to resist. Many new accounts, instead of clarifying things, seem only to muddy the waters further.

The problem lies in discovering the truth about an organization whose activities were clothed in secrecy. So much of what went on with SOE, both in the field and in England, was never recorded—what's the point of operating in secret, if everything is going to be committed to paper? The purging of The Firm's archives, either accidentally or intentionally, has merely made things more difficult for the historian. There are, of course, the testimonies of dozens of people, on both sides, who were involved in the network's life and death, but how much weight can be placed on that evidence? SOE, after all, spent a good deal of time teaching its operatives how to lie, to dissemble, to weave a plausible tale from half-truths and invention. Fabrication was to become second nature for a successful agent and such skills, once learned, were not soon forgotten. As F Section learned in the summer of 1943, it was very difficult to sort out the honest testimony from the fabricated and the self-serving; it has not become any easier in the intervening years.

The questions that F Section tried to answer at the time still preoccupy historians. What went wrong that brought down Physician and the circuits connected to it? Who was to blame, and was it malfeasance or carelessness? Anyone who has looked at SOE's documents must be impressed at how much energy F Section put into the search for the truth; it is unfortunate that so little of substance came from its investigations.

F Section's conclusion at the time was that everything could be traced to a few individuals who turned, although its leaders were reluctant to admit that any of the fault rested in Baker Street. When Maurice Southgate repeated after the war the SD's claim that it had mountains of information about SOE's inner workings, he was dismissed as mad. His "swallowing of the Gestapo allegations is further proof of the completely exhausted frame of mind he naturally was in," noted the officer who debriefed him.[1] Of course, his allegations were entirely true, but F Section's refusal to consider the possibility led it to look for the rot in other places. But who were the bad eggs? The detective work was complicated by the fact that some of the agents didn't like each other very much, and mutual animosities were often vented in debriefings. SOE personal files are full of backstabbing and unfounded allegations that F Section had to sort through and weigh. France Antelme admitted in his debriefing that he didn't like Armel Guerne, but at least he had the decency to emphasize to his superiors that, despite his personal feelings, he couldn't find any hard evidence against him.

The culpability of a few people—Roger Bardet, Maurice Benoist, Pierre Cartaud, Renée Garry—was beyond question, but only a few lives were lost because of their collaboration. Others were in a position to do much greater damage. The SD's usual story, that there was a German mole in Baker Street, must be dismissed as a fairy tale. In my view, Gilbert Norman was the weak link and most of what followed can be traced back to his willingness to open up to Josef Kieffer. At the same time, I accept that, from his perspective and facing the evidence that was in front of him, Norman probably believed sincerely that cooperation was the lesser of evils.

I found no compelling evidence that Francis Suttill played an active role in the destruction of Physician, and a good deal to suggest that he was uninvolved and perhaps even unaware of what was going on. Others, however, are not so sure. It is here that some writers have moved from evidence to conjecture to conspiracy. One lays the blame for everything on Suttill's rashness and SOE's callousness. While he was in London in the spring of 1943, goes the story, Suttill angrily confronted his superiors about their failure to launch a cross-Channel invasion. To hurry them along, he made a threat: if the Allies didn't invade France within a few months, he would call out the resistance. This would force the Allies either to invade, or to watch idly while the Germans destroyed the entire French underground movement. The British agreed to Suttill's ultimatum, and promised that the invasion would be mounted by 1 July 1943; then, they betrayed him to the SD to prevent him from carrying out his threat.[2] This scenario is so patently implausible as to require no further comment.

Another theory holds that Physician was sacrificed as part of the Allies' strategic deception plan, either to draw German attention away from the Allied invasion of Sicily or to build the false belief that an invasion of France was coming in the late summer of 1943. The Allied goal, supposedly, was to convince the Germans that a cross-Channel invasion would be mounted in September 1943; if they could be fooled, they might well ignore the real invasion when it was launched at a later date. Accordingly, Physician was beefed up with huge shipments of arms in the spring of 1943 (which would suggest to the Germans that the resistance was being made ready to become operational) and Suttill himself was told, by none other than Winston Churchill, that the invasion was coming that summer. Then, Physician was betrayed in the hopes that, under torture, Suttill would reveal this most important of secrets.[3] Again, it is an interesting story, but one without a shred of corroborating evidence.

Robert Marshall has argued that Henri Déricourt was planted by MI6, the British military intelligence service. Citing evidence that Déricourt, Nicholas Bodington, and Karl Boemelburg, the head of the Paris SD and the highest-ranking SD officer in France, had known each other before the war, perhaps in the summer of 1938, he believes that MI6 gave Déricourt to F Section as an operative, while his real task was to barter SOE personnel for the only German code that the British hadn't broken, the code used by the Gestapo and the SD. This argument, however, is based largely on much later (and certainly self-serving) accounts from participants, and is far from convincing. No more satisfactory is the argument that Déricourt was working for the KGB and betrayed Physician on the orders of his masters in Moscow.

In the final analysis, as Michael Foot has pointed out, the simplest explanation is the most convincing: that Physician was brought down by a combination of betrayal and blunders. That Déricourt allowed the SD to read and copy the circuit's mail seems to me to be beyond dispute, and his defence—that he informed the SD of incoming and outgoing flight arrangements only on the condition that none of the agents would be arrested on the spot—is manifestly disingenuous; the fact that they weren't arrested until days or weeks later in no way lessens Déricourt's guilt. And there were others who were responsible for lesser betrayals—they all played a part in the debacle.

But the collapse would never have been as serious or as complete without some major blunders. Had Physician's inner circle observed basic security precautions, had there been more wireless operators so a few people didn't have to handle so much traffic, had Physician not taken on so many contaminated résistants from Autogiro and Carte—any of these measures would have contained or even prevented the worst of the damage. But Buckmaster's staff must be held accountable for the biggest blunder: the repeated failure to observe the security system of bluff and true checks. Marcel Rousset and Maurice Southgate were, in my view, completely justified in their outrage that F Section persistently ignored the security measures it drilled into wireless operators. But that is carelessness or incompetence, not conspiracy. To find the reasons behind the disaster in human weakness rather than in a carefully engineered, high-level plot may not be terribly satisfying in our conspiracy-addicted culture, but it is much more convincing.

Notes

In citations of works in the notes, short titles have generally been used. Works frequently cited have been identified by the following abbreviations:

DEA Records Library and Archives Canada: Department of External Affairs Records

FHDPP Private collection: F.H.D. Pickersgill Papers

Ford George H. Ford, ed., *The Making of a Secret Agent: Letters of 1934–1943 Written by Frank Pickersgill* (Toronto: McClelland & Stewart, 1978)

Foot M.R.D. Foot, *SOE in France: An Account of the Work of the British Special Operations Executive, 1940–1944* (London: HMSO, 1966)

JWPP Private collection: J.W. Pickersgill Papers

LAC Library and Archives Canada

RHMP Rhodes House, Oxford: J.K. Macalister Papers

TNA The National Archives (U.K.)

PROLOGUE: APRIL 1945

1. Alfred D. Chandler and Stephen Ambrose, eds., *The Papers of Dwight David Eisenhower*, vol. 4 (Baltimore: Johns Hopkins University Press, 1970), 2679.
2. LAC: Georges P. Vanier Papers, MG32 A2, vol. 17, f. 34, text of Buchenwald broadcast.

CHAPTER 1: TWO BOYS

1. J.W. Pickersgill, *Seeing Canada Whole: A Memoir* (Markham: Fitzhenry and Whiteside, 1994), 43.
2. RHMP, personal statement for the Rhodes Committee, 6 November 1936.
3. "G.C.V.I. Literary Society," *Acta Nostra* [Guelph Collegiate–Vocational Institute], 1929, 48.
4. J.K. Macalister, "Senior Rugby," *Acta Nostra*, 1931, 83.
5. Thomas Fisher Rare Book Library, University of Toronto: Douglas LePan papers, box 54, f. Guelph, interviews with Charles Crenna and Hazel Burrows.

CHAPTER 2: UNIVERSITY

1. Arthur R.M. Lower, *My First Seventy-Five Years* (Toronto: University of Toronto Press, 1967), 160–62.
2. JWPP, George Ford to Jack Pickersgill, 13 May 1945.
3. Ford, 23; JWPP, Ford to Jack Pickersgill, 13 May 1945.
4. JWPP, Elsa Lehman to her mother, 9 January 1962; Duncan to Jack Pickersgill, 3 July 1947.
5. Ford, 51, 55.
6. FHDPP, FHDP to George Ford, 8 February 1937.
7. RHMP, personal statement for the Rhodes Committee, 6 November 1936.
8. FHDPP, FHDP to Ford, 2 December 1936.
9. RHMP, Malcolm Wallace, Principal, University College, to the Ontario Rhodes Committee, 26 October 1936.
10. *The First Fifty Years of the Rhodes Trust and the Rhodes Scholarships, 1903–1953* (Oxford: Basil Blackwell, 1955), 3–4.
11. RHMP, references from Prof. W.P.M. Kennedy (11 November 1936), Prof. N.A. Mackenzie (17 November 1936), H.F. Gadsby (16 November 1936), Prof. Charles Cochrane (17 November 1936), and E.C. Young (11 November 1936).

12. RHMP, personal statement for the Rhodes Committee; essay "Canada's Part in International Affairs," submitted to the Rhodes Committee [1936]; J.K. Macalister, "A Transition Viewed" (Prize Senior Essay), in *Acta Nostra*, 1932, 36.

CHAPTER 3: SEARCHING FOR A PATH

1. Virgil Hancher, quoted in F.H. Lawson, *The Oxford Law School, 1850–1965* (Oxford: Clarendon Press, 1968), 241.
2. RHMP, undated report, Rhodes House [1938].
3. Ford, 33.
4. JWPP, Brock King to Jack Pickersgill, 5 May 1945.
5. Ford, 79.
6. FHDPP, FHDP to Jack Pickersgill, 16 July 1938.
7. JWPP, Jean Varille to Jack Pickersgill, 15 October 194; FHDPP, FHDP to Jack Pickersgill, 15 April 1939.
8. FHDPP, FHDP to Sara and Jack Pickersgill, 30 July 1938.
9. Ibid., FHDP to Helen Magill, 26 September 1938.
10. Ibid., FHDP to W.F. Butcher, 17 February 1939; FHDP to Jack Pickersgill, 12 August 1939.
11. Ibid., FHDP to Jack Pickersgill, 11 January 1939; FHDP to Butcher, 6 August 1938.
12. Ibid., FHDP to Margaret (Beattie) Pickersgill, 12 August 1939; FHDP to Jack Pickersgill, 15 April 1939.
13. Ibid., FHDP to George Ford, 27 July 1939.

CHAPTER 4: THE DARKNESS DESCENDS

1. FHDPP, Frank Pickersgill, "War of Nerves," written Paris, 20 February 1940; JWPP, Madeleine Probert to Jack Pickersgill, 10 June 1948.
2. FHDPP, FHDP to Jack Pickersgill, 28 September 1939.
3. Ibid., 21 February 1940; 28 September 1939.
4. Ibid., 29 May 1940.
5. Ibid., 9 September 1939; 31 October 1939; 4 September 1939.

6. FHDPP, FHDP to Sara Pickersgill, 23 December 1939; FHDP to Jack Pickersgill, 27 May 1940.

7. Vanier Papers, MG32 A2, vol. 12, f. 12–23A2, report on the Canadian Legation, Paris, 20 August 1940.

8. JWPP, FHDP to Brock King, 9 June 1940.

9. Vanier Papers, MG32 A2, vol. 12, f. 12–23A2, report on the Canadian Legation, Paris, 20 August 1940.

10. Ibid., Édouard Fiset to J.L. Delisle, 28 September 1945.

11. Georges Savaria, *Hors de portée: Un récit d'exode, de captivité et d'évasion* (Mandeville, PQ: Le Citoyen Éditeur, 1980), 104.

12. RHMP, JKM to Allen, 22 September 1939.

13. Ibid., 14 October 1939.

14. Ibid., 24 November 1939.

15. New College, Oxford: J.K. Macalister Papers, confidential report by David Boult, 11 June 1940.

16. RHMP, JKM to Allen, 2 July 1940.

17. Ibid., 9 July 1940.

18. RHMP, Allen to Lord Elton, 12 July 1940; minutes of Trustees meeting, 29 July 1940.

Chapter 5: In Uniform

1. RHMP, JKM to C.K. Allen, 31 August 1940.

2. Ibid., Allen to Lord Elton, 24 August 1945.

3. Ibid., Allen to E.C. Young, 20 September 1940.

4. Ibid., Young to Allen, undated [October 1940].

5. Ibid., JKM to Allen, 13 October 1940.

6. Ibid., Allen to Young, 15 October 1940.

7. Humphrey Searle, *Quadrille with a Raven* (New York: Riverrun Press, 1985), *http://www.musicweb-international.com/searle/titlepg.htm* (accessed 28 March 2008).

8. Noel Annan, *Changing Enemies: The Defeat and Regeneration of Germany* (London: HarperCollins, 1995), 32.

9. RHMP, Walton Ferris, U.S. Embassy, London, to Allen, 1 November 1940.

10. Ibid., JKM to Allen, 9 November 1940; JKM to Dorothy Allen, 9 November 1940.

11. Ibid., Evans to Allen, 19 February 1946.

12. Ibid., Allen to Young, 19 December 1940.

13. Ibid., George Ignatieff to Allen, 9 April 1941; JKM to Allen, 4 April 1941.

14. Ibid., JKM to Allen, 22 June 1942.

15. Ibid., JKM to Allen, September 1941.

16. FHDPP, FHDP to family, 1 October 1942; FHDP to Jack Pickersgill, 30 October 1942.

17. DEA Records, J.V. Allard, Canadian Legation, Washington, to Secretary of State for External Affairs, 14 October 1942.

18. FHDPP, FHDP to Jack Pickersgill, 12 October 1942; JWPP, Elsa Lehman to her mother, 9 January 1962.

19. Ford, 197.

20. Ibid., 234; FHDPP, FHDP to Jack Pickersgill, December 1942.

21. FHDPP, Frank Pickersgill, "Thoughts," n.d. [November/December 1942]; DEA Records, High Commission to Secretary of State for External Affairs, 27 and 31 October 1942.

22. Ford, 198–99.

23. JWPP, Gordon Wright to Jack Pickersgill, 24 December 1970; Brock King to Jack Pickersgill, 5 May 1945.

24. LAC: Mackenzie King Papers, microfilm reel C6809, Norman Robertson to King, n.d., 281336.

25. King Papers, microfilm reel C6809, Secretary of State for External Affairs to High Commission, London, 31 October 42, 281331; Vincent Massey to Secretary of State for External Affairs, 31 October 1942, 281335.

26. FHDPP, FP to Jack Pickersgill, 12 October 1942.

27. TNA: FHDP personal file, HS9 1186/2, personnel form A2, 26 November 1942.

28. Ford, 220.

29. FHDPP, FHDP to Jack Pickersgill, 30 November 1942; FHDP to Tom and Margaret Pickersgill, 1 December 1942.

30. FHDP personal file, declaration, 1 February 1943.

CHAPTER 6: THE FIRM

1. Foot, 1–2.

2. David Stafford, *Britain and European Resistance, 1940–1945: A Survey of the Special Operations Executive* (Toronto: University of Toronto Press, 1980), 23; Foot, 6–7.

3. E.H. Cookridge, *Inside SOE: The Story of Special Operations in Western Europe, 1940–45* (London: Arthur Barker, 1966), 5.

4. Foot, 8; W.J.M. Mackenzie, *The Secret History of SOE: The Special Operations Executive, 1940–1945* (London: St. Ermin's Press, 2000 [1948]), appendix A.

5. Stafford, *Britain and European Resistance,* 220.

6. "The Distant Future," Joint Planning Staff review of future strategy, 14 June 1941, in Stafford, *Britain and European Resistance,* 235.

7. "Special Operations Executive," Joint Planning Staff report, 9 August 1941, in Stafford, *Britain and European Resistance,* 241, 244.

8. Mackenzie, *The Secret History of SOE,* 339.

9. Stafford, *Britain and European Resistance,* 37; Cookridge, *Inside SOE,* 19.

10. Foot, 10.

11. Peter Wilkinson and Joan Bright Astley, *Gubbins and SOE* (London: Leo Cooper, 1993), 99–100.

12. Sarah Helm, *A Life in Secrets: The Story of Vera Atkins and the Lost Agents of SOE* (London: Little Brown, 2005).

13. Foot, 50.

14. Foot, 311; Sydney Hudson, *Undercover Operator: Wartime Experiences with SOE in France and the Far East* (Barnsley: Leo Cooper, 2003), xi.

15. Quoted in Foot, 51.

16. Savaria, *Hors de portée,* 193.

Chapter 7: Secret Agent School

1. FHDP personal file, training assessments from STS 5, 11 December and 18 December 1942.
2. FHDP personal file, training assessments from STS 5, 3 December 1942.
3. FHDPP, FHDP to Jack Pickersgill, 30 November 1942; Ford, 194.
4. Christopher Murphy, *Security and Special Operations: SOE and MI5 during the Second World War* (Houndmills: Palgrave Macmillan, 2006), 5–6.
5. TNA: G.B. McBain personal file HS 9/954/6, report from STS 7, 18 September 1943.
6. Murphy, *Security and Special Operations*, 7.
7. TNA: JKM personal file, HS9 954/2, memo by Maj. Kennedy, ISRB, 12 January 1942.
8. George Langelaan, *Knights of the Floating Silk* (London: Hutchinson, 1959), 43.
9. Ford, 236–37.
10. Russell Miller, *Behind the Lines: The Oral History of Special Operations in World War II* (New York: St. Martin's Press, 2002), 12; Douglas Botting, *Gavin Maxwell: The Life of the Man Who Wrote "Ring of Bright Water"* (London: HarperCollins, 1993), 56; Langelaan, *Knights of the Floating Silk*, 47.
11. FHDP personal file, report 15 January 1943; report 23 January 1943.
12. JKM personal file, report 26 January 1943.
13. FHDP personal file, report 8 February 1943; Ford, 236.
14. FHDP personal file, report on signals training, n.d.; JKM personal file, report 12 February 1943.
15. *SOE Syllabus: Lessons in Ungentlemanly Warfare, World War II* (Richmond: The National Archives, 2004), 47.
16. TNA: Gilbert Norman personal file, HS9 110/5, cover story, n.d.
17. Ford, 238–39.
18. Francis Cammaerts, quoted in Rita Kramer, *Flames in the Field: The Story of Four SOE Agents in Occupied France* (London: Michael Joseph, 1995), 240.

19. TNA: Andrée Borrel personal file, HS9 183, operational order, 22 September 1942.
20. *SOE Syllabus*, 38.
21. JKM personal file, report May 1943.

CHAPTER 8: PROSPER

1. TNA: Henri Frager personal file, HS9 536/1, debriefing notes, 22–26 October 1943.
2. Elizabeth Nicholas, *Death Be Not Proud* (London: Cresset Press, 1958), 175.
3. Stella King, *"Jacqueline": Pioneer Heroine of the Resistance* (London: Arms and Armour Press, 1989), 129.
4. Charles Wighton, *Pin-Stripe Saboteur: The Story of "Robin," British Agent and French Resistance Leader* (London: Odhams Press, 1959), 104.
5. Cookridge, *Inside SOE*, 203, 205.
6. TNA: Yvonne Rudelatt personal file, HS9 1289/7, report from STS 31, 21 June 1942; Pierre Culioli personal file, HS9 379/8, report by Suttill, 18 May 1943.
7. JWPP, Kay Moore to Jack Pickersgill, 25 February 1959; Kay Moore to Sarah Pickersgill, 11 April 1943; Alison Grant to Jack Pickersgill, undated [September/October 1944].
8. Ford, 242.
9. JWPP, Saul Rae to Jack Pickersgill, 9 May 1943; Kay (Moore) Gimpel to Jack Pickersgill, 25 February 1959.

CHAPTER 9: THE COLLAPSE

1. Benjamin Cowburn, *No Cloak, No Dagger* (London: The Adventure Club, 1960), 149; quoted in Kramer, *Flames in the Field*, 95.
2. Foot, 310.
3. Ibid., 290.
4. King, *"Jacqueline,"* 309.
5. Ibid., 307–8.
6. Foot, 284.

Chapter 10: The Radio Game

1. *Samedi Soir* (Paris: 1 May 1947), 4.

2. Foot, 317.

3. TNA: Norman personal file, notes by Atkins, 1945; Culioli personal file, debriefing notes, 1945.

4. Joe Saward, *The Grand Prix Saboteurs: The Extraordinary Untold Story of the Grand Prix Drivers Who Became British Secret Agents in World War II* (London: Morienval Press, 2006), 183.

5. Jacques Bureau, *Un Soldat Menteur* (Paris: Robert Laffont, 1992), 163; Kramer, *Flames in the Field*, 293.

6. Culioli personal file, debriefing of Suttill, May 1943.

7. Jean Overton Fuller, *Déricourt: The Chequered Spy* (Salisbury, UK: Michael Russell, 1989), 47.

8. Norman personal file, Antelme's debriefing report, 7 August 1943.

9. Ibid., 7 August 1943.

10. Norman personal file, Antelme's debriefing report, 7 August 1943.

11. Beryl E. Scott, *Mission Improbable: A Salute to the RAF Women of SOE in Wartime France* (Sparkford, UK: Patrick Stephens, 1991), 60.

12. JWPP, Alison Grant to Jack Pickersgill, 22 November 1943; War Office to Jack Pickersgill, 14 December 1943.

13. Ibid., Kay (Moore) Gimpel to Jack Pickersgill, 25 February 1959; War Office to Jack Pickersgill, 23 May 1944.

14. TNA: Roméo Sabourin personal file, HS9 1296/4, reports 27 August 1943, 30 December 1943.

15. JWPP, Kay (Moore) Gimpel to Jack Pickersgill, 25 February 1959.

16. Leo Marks, *Between Silk and Cyanide: The Story of SOE's Code War* (London: HarperCollins, 1998), 522; Helm, *A Life in Secrets*, 47, 57.

Chapter 11: Nacht und Nebel

1. TNA: Maurice Southgate personal file, HS9 1395/3, debriefing report, 1945.

2. Ibid., Harry Peulevé personal file, HS9 1178/6, debriefing report, 1945.

Chapter 12: Remembering

1. JWPP, telegram from Vanier, 20 April 1945.
2. FHDP personal file, memo from War Office, April 1945; Pickersgill, *Seeing Canada Whole*, 259.
3. RHMP, Alexander Macalister to Allen, 21 August 1945.
4. Ibid., Allen to the Warden of New College, 24 August 1945; Allen to Morrell, Peel and Gamlen, Oxford, 28 January 1946.
5. JWPP: Christopher Burney to War Office, 1 July 1945; RHMP, Burney to Allen, 18 August 1945.
6. Norman personal file, letter from Vera Atkins, 22 June 1945.
7. JWPP, Kay Moore to Sara Pickersgill, 4 October 1944.
8. Ibid., Jean Pouillon to Jack Pickersgill, 4 November 1945.
9. Ibid., Jeannine Macalister to Jack Pickersgill, 14 June 1946; 16 July 1946.
10. Fisher Rare Book Library, University of Toronto: Douglas LePan Papers, Jeannine Macalister to George Penfold, 22 December 1977.

Appendix: The Demise of Physician

1. Southgate personal file, debriefing notes, 1945.
2. Fuller, *Déricourt*, 96.
3. Jones, *A Quiet Courage*, 133.

A Note on Sources

As soon as I began working on this book, it became clear that I was facing two problems in terms of sources: Frank Pickersgill has a large extended family and an embarrassment of riches in terms of the documentary record; Ken Macalister, on the other hand, has no surviving relatives and almost none of his personal papers have survived.

The best sources of information on Frank are his personal papers, which were retained by Jack Pickersgill, and Jack's own personal papers. Both of these collections remain with the Pickersgill family. The two published versions of Frank's letters are invaluable sources, and I was fascinated to see what had been deleted and what subtle changes had been made to the letters for publication. There are also references to Frank in Jack's political and ministerial papers and in the records of the Department of External Affairs, held at Library and Archives Canada. Other useful sources in Ottawa were the records of the Maison des étudiants canadiens à Paris, and the personal papers of Georges P. Vanier.

There are scattered references to the Macalister family in the Guelph Museum, the Guelph Public Library, and the Wellington County Archives, but the largest collections of Ken's papers are in New College and Rhodes House in Oxford. Also invaluable are the personal papers of Douglas LePan, which include all of the research materials he collected when writing *Macalister, or Dying in the Dark*.

Even though 85 per cent of SOE's archival record has been lost, the remainder is an excellent source. The planning and operational documents are useful but I relied more on the personal files, especially those of the following agents: France Antelme, Alfred Balachowski, Andrée Borrel, Pierre Culioli, Ange Defendini, Henri Frager, Armel Guerne, J.K. Macalister, Gilbert Norman, F.H.D. Pickersgill, Adolphe Rabinovitch, Yvonne Rudelatt, Roméo Sabourin, and Francis Suttill.

There are many published accounts that bear on the lives of Ken and Frank, from their childhood to their deaths in Buchenwald concentration camp. The following list includes some of the most useful and reliable works.

General

Ford, George, ed. *The Making of a Secret Agent: Letters of 1934–1943 Written by Frank Pickersgill.* Toronto: McClelland & Stewart, 1978.

LePan, Douglas. *Macalister, or Dying in the Dark: A Fiction Based on What Is Known of His Life and Fate.* Kingston, ON: Quarry Press, 1995.

Pickersgill, J.W. *Seeing Canada Whole: A Memoir.* Markham: Fitzhenry and Whiteside, 1994.

Childhood and Education

Bedford, A.G. *The University of Winnipeg: A History of the Founding Colleges.* Toronto: University of Toronto Press, 1976.

Bissell, Claude. *Halfway Up Parnassus: A Personal Account of the University of Toronto, 1932–1971.* Toronto: University of Toronto Press, 1974.

Bumsted, J.M. *The University of Manitoba: An Illustrated History.* Winnipeg: University of Manitoba Press, 2001.

Duckworth, Henry E. *One Version of the Facts: My Life in the Ivory Tower.* Winnipeg: University of Manitoba Press, 2000.

Elwand, Geoffrey. "The Mercury Rising. James Innis: The 'Honesty of Purpose and Sound Judgement' of a Victorian Journalist." MA thesis, University of Guelph, 1997.

Friedland, Martin L. *The University of Toronto: A History.* Toronto: University of Toronto Press, 2002.

Johnson, Leo A. *History of Guelph, 1827–1927.* Guelph: Guelph Historical Society, 1977.

Kuz, Tony J. *Winnipeg 1874–1974: Progress and Prospects.* Winnipeg: Manitoba Department of Industry and Commerce, 1974.

Lower, Arthur R.M. *My First Seventy-Five Years.* Toronto: Macmillan, 1967.

Marchand, Philip. *Marshall McLuhan: The Medium and the Messenger.* Toronto: Random House, 1989.

Mitchell, Barbara and Ormond. *W.O.: The Life of W.O. Mitchell. The Beginnings to "Who Has Seen the Wind," 1914–1947.* Toronto: McClelland & Stewart, 1999.

Morton, W.L. *One University: A History of the University of Manitoba.* Toronto: McClelland & Stewart, 1957.

Rutherdale, Robert. *Hometown Horizons: Local Responses to Canada's Great War.* Vancouver: UBC Press, 2004.

Shutt, Greta May. *The High Schools of Guelph, Being the Story of the Wellington District Grammar School, Guelph Grammar School, Guelph High School, and Guelph Collegiate Institutes.* Toronto: University of Toronto Press, 1961.

Sirluck, Ernest. *First Generation: An Autobiography.* Toronto: University of Toronto Press, 1996.

Taming a Wilderness: A History of Ashern and District. Ashern, MB: Ashern Historical Society, 1976.

Urquhart, Hugh M. *The History of the 16th Battalion.* Toronto: Macmillan, 1932.

TRAVELS TO EUROPE

Allen, Dorothy. *Sunlight and Shadow: An Autobiography.* London: Oxford University Press, 1960.

The First Fifty Years of the Rhodes Trust and the Rhodes Scholarships, 1903–1953. Oxford: Basil Blackwell, 1955.

Kestling, Robert W. "Blacks under the Swastika: A Research Note." *Journal of Negro History* 83/1 (winter 1998): 84–99.

Lawson, F.H. *The Oxford Law School, 1850–1965.* Oxford: Clarendon Press, 1968.

Mason, W. Wynne. *Prisoners of War.* Wellington, NZ: War History Branch, Department of Internal Affairs, 1954.

Mookerjee, Girija. *This Europe.* Calcutta: Saraswaty, 1950.

Myers, Bessie. *Captured: My Experiences as an Ambulance Driver and as a Prisoner of the Nazis.* London: George G. Harrap, 1941.

Peschanski, Denis. *Le France des Camps: L'internement, 1938–1946.* Paris: Gallimard, 2002.

Pickersgill, Frank. "The French Press and War Aims." *University of Toronto Quarterly,* vol. 9, no. 3 (April 1940), 262–69.

Reed Anderson, Paulette. *Rewriting the Footnotes: Berlin and the African Diaspora.* Berlin: Commission for Foreigners' Affairs, 2000.

Savaria, Georges. *Hors de portée: Un récit d'éxode, de captivité et d'évasion.* Mandeville, PQ: Le Citoyen Éditeur, 1980.

Sigot, Jacques. *Ces Barbelés Oubliés par l'Histoire: Un camp pour les Tsiganes . . . et les autres, Montreuil-Bellay, 1940–1945.* Châteauneuf-les-Martigues, France: Éditions Wallada, 1994.

ENLISTMENT, TRAINING, AND THE FIRM

Annan, Noel. *Changing Enemies: The Defeat and Regeneration of Germany.* London: HarperCollins, 1995.

Beevor, J.G. *SOE: Recollections and Reflections, 1940–1945.* London: Bodley Head, 1981.

Botting, Douglas. *Gavin Maxwell: The Life of the Man Who Wrote "Ring of Bright Water."* London: HarperCollins, 1993.

Buckmaster, Maurice J. *Specially Employed: The Story of British Aid to French Patriots of the Resistance.* London: Batchworth Press, 1952.

———. *They Fought Alone: The Story of British Agents in France.* London: Popular Book Club, 1958.

Cookridge, E.H. *Inside SOE: The Story of Special Operations in Western Europe, 1940–45.* London: Arthur Barker, 1966.

Cunningham, Cyril. *Beaulieu: The Finishing School for Secret Agents, 1941–1945.* London: Leo Cooper, 1998.

Foot, M.R.D. *SOE in France: An Account of the Work of the British Special Operations Executive, 1940–1944.* London: HMSO, 1966.

———. *SOE: An Outline History of the Special Operations Executive, 1940–1946.* London: BBC, 1984.

Harrison, David. *Special Operations Executive: Para-Military Training in Scotland during World War 2.* Arisaig, U.K.: The Land and Sea Centre, 2001.

Helm, Sarah. *A Life in Secrets: The Story of Vera Atkins and the Lost Agents of SOE.* London: Little Brown, 2005.

Hinsley, F.H. *British Intelligence in the Second World War,* five vols. London: HMSO, 1979–90.

Mackenzie, W.J.M. *The Secret History of SOE: The Special Operations Executive, 1940–1945.* London: St. Ermin's Press, 2000 [1948].

MacLaren, Roy. *Canadians behind Enemy Lines, 1939–1945.* Vancouver: UBC Press, 2004 [1981].

Marks, Leo. *Between Silk and Cyanide: The Story of SOE's Code War.* London: HarperCollins, 1998.

Murphy, Christopher. *Security and Special Operations: SOE and MI5 during the Second World War.* Houndmills: Palgrave Macmillan, 2006.

Ruby, Marcel. *F Section SOE: The Story of the Buckmaster Network.* London: Leo Cooper, 1988.

Searle, Humphrey. *Quadrille with a Raven.* New York: Riverrun Press, 1985. *http://www.musicweb-international.com/searle/titlepg.htm* (accessed 28 March 2008).

SOE Syllabus: Lessons in Ungentlemanly Warfare, World War II. Richmond: The National Archives, 2004.

Stafford, David. *Britain and European Resistance, 1940–1945: A Survey of the Special Operations Executive.* Toronto: University of Toronto Press, 1980.

Stevenson, William. *A Man Called Intrepid: The Secret War.* London: Macmillan, 1976.

Wilkinson, Peter, and Joan Bright Astley. *Gubbins and SOE.* London: Leo Cooper, 1993.

In the Field

Basu, Shrabani. *Spy Princess: The Life of Noor Inayat Khan.* Stroud: Sutton Publishing, 2006.

Binney, Marcus. *The Women Who Lived for Danger: The Women Agents of SOE in the Second World War.* London: Coronet Books, 2002.

Bureau, Jacques. *Un Soldat Menteur.* Paris: Robert Laffont, 1992.

Churchill, Peter. *The Spirit in the Cage.* London: Hodder & Stoughton, 1954.

———. *Duel of Wits.* Morley, UK: Elmfield Press, 1974.

Clark, Freddie. *Agents by Moonlight: The Secret History of RAF Tempsford during World War II.* Stroud: Tempus, 1999.

Colm, Ian, ed. *Colonel Henri's Story: The War Memoirs of Hugo Bleicher, Former German Secret Agent.* London: William Kimber, 1954.

Cowburn, Benjamin. *No Cloak, No Dagger.* London: The Adventure Club, 1960.

Fuller, Jean Overton. *Déricourt: The Chequered Spy.* Salisbury, UK: Michael Russell, 1989.

———. *Double Webs: Light on the Secret Agents' War in France.* London: Putnam's, 1958.

———. *The German Penetration of SOE, 1941–1944.* London: William Kimber, 1975.

———. *The Starr Affair.* London: Victor Gollancz, 1954.

Giskes, H.J. *London Calling North Pole.* London: William Kimber, 1953.

Goldsmith, John. *Accidental Agent.* London: Leo Cooper, 1971.

Guillaume, Paul. *La Sologne aux temps de l'héroïsme et de la trahison.* Orléans: Imprimerie Nouvelle, 1950.

Heslop, Richard. *Xavier: The Famous British Agent's Dramatic Account of His Work in the French Resistance.* London: Rupert Hart-Davis, 1970.

Hudson, Sydney. *Undercover Operator: Wartime Experiences with SOE in France and the Far East.* Barnsley: Leo Cooper, 2003.

Johnson, Kate, ed. *The Special Operations Executive: Sound Archive Oral History Recordings.* London: Imperial War Museum, n.d.

Jones, Liane. *A Quiet Courage.* London: Bantam Press, 1990.

King, Stella. *"Jacqueline": Pioneer Heroine of the Resistance.* London: Arms and Armour Press, 1989.

Kramer, Rita. *Flames in the Field: The Story of Four SOE Agents in Occupied France.* London: Michael Joseph, 1995.

Lalande, Pierre. *Special Agent: The Wartime Memoirs of Guido Zembsch-Schreve.* Translated by John Brownjohn. London: Leo Cooper, 1996.

Langelaan, George. *Knights of the Floating Silk.* London: Hutchinson, 1959.

Marshall, Robert. *All the King's Men: The Truth behind SOE's Greatest Wartime Disaster.* London: Collins, 1988.

Merrick, K.A. *Flights of the Forgotten: Special Duties Operations in World War Two.* London: Arms and Armour Press, 1989.

Miller, Russell. *Behind the Lines: The Oral History of Special Operations in World War II.* New York: St. Martin's Press, 2002.

Nicholas, Elizabeth. *Death Be Not Proud.* London: Cresset Press, 1958.

Noguères, Henri. *Histoire de la Résistance en France, de 1940–1945,* five vols. Paris: R. Laffont, 1967.

Paturau, J. Maurice. *Agents secrets mauriciens en France.* Mauritius: Broche, 1995.

Poirier, Jacques. *The Giraffe Has a Long Neck . . .* London: Leo Cooper, 1995.

Saward, Joe. *The Grand Prix Saboteurs: The Extraordinary Untold Story of the Grand Prix Drivers Who Became British Secret Agents in World War II.* London: Morienval Press, 2006.

Scott, Beryl E. *Mission Improbable: A Salute to the RAF Women of SOE in Wartime France.* Sparkford, UK: Patrick Stephens, 1991.

Vader, John. *The Prosper Double-Cross.* Goonengerry, NSW: Sunrise Press, 1977.

Verity, Hugh. *We Landed by Moonlight: Secret RAF Landings in France, 1940–1944.* Revised edition. Manchester: Crécy Publishing, 1998 [1978].

Vomécourt, Philippe de. *Who Lived to See the Day: France in Arms, 1940–1945.* London: Hutchinson, 1961.

Wighton, Charles. *Pin-Stripe Saboteur: The Story of "Robin," British Agent and French Resistance Leader.* London: Odhams Press, 1959.

CAPTIVITY

Antelme, Robert. *L'espèce humaine: récit*. Paris: Gallimard, 1957.

Bard, Michael G. *Forgotten Victims: The Abandonment of Americans in Hitler's Camps*. Boulder, CO: Westview Press, 1994.

Buchenwald Camp: The Report of a Parliamentary Delegation. London: HMSO, 1945.

Burgess, Colin. *Destination Buchenwald*. Kenthurst: Kangaroo Press, 1995.

Burney, Christopher. *The Dungeon Democracy*. New York: Duell, Sloan and Pearce, 1946.

Calet, Henri. *Les Murs de Fresnes*. Paris: Viviane Hamy, 1993 [1946].

Childers, Thomas. *In the Shadows of War: An American Pilot's Odyssey through Occupied France and the Camps of Nazi Germany*. New York: Henry Holt, 2002.

Harvie, John D. *Missing in Action: An RCAF Navigator's Story*. Montreal: McGill-Queen's University Press, 1995.

Kinnis, Arthur G., and Stanley Booker. *168 Jump into Hell: A True Story of Betrayed Allied Airmen*. Privately published, 1999.

Marshall, Bruce. *The White Rabbit*. London: Evans Brothers, 1952.

Porter, Mackenzie. "The Last Days of Frank Pickersgill." *Maclean's*, 2 December 1961, 43–48.

Rousset, David. *The Other Kingdom*. New York: Fertig, 1982.

Speight, Robert. *Vanier: Soldier, Diplomat, and Governor General*. Toronto: Collins, 1970.

INDEX

Note: Although I have refrained from using agents' code names in the text, the relevant aliases are included in the index to assist readers who are familiar with the literature on F Section.